9-4-02
Mom & Dad —
Hope you enjoy
this one!
Love —
R. Barri & H. Lorraine

MURDER, AT THE END
OF THE DAY AND NIGHT

MURDER, AT THE END OF THE DAY AND NIGHT

A Study of Criminal Homicide Offenders, Victims, and Circumstances

By

R. BARRI FLOWERS

Charles C Thomas
PUBLISHER • LTD.
SPRINGFIELD • ILLINOIS • U.S.A.

Published and Distributed Throughout the World by

CHARLES C THOMAS • PUBLISHER, LTD.
2600 South First Street
Springfield, Illinois 62794-9265

©2002 by CHARLES C THOMAS • PUBLISHER, LTD.

ISBN 0-398-07307-4 (hard)
ISBN 0-398-07308-2 (paper)

Library of Congress Catalog Card Number: 2002020011

Printed in the United States of America
TH-R-3

Library of Congress Cataloging-in-Publication Data

Flowers, Ronald B.
    Murder, at the end of the day and night : a study of criminal homicide offenders, victims, and circumstances / by R. Barri Flowers
        p. cm.
Includes bibliographical references and index.
ISBN 0-398-07307-4 (hbk.) -- ISBN 0-398-07308-2 (paper)
    1. Murder--United States. I. Title.

HV6529 .F574 2002
364.15'23'0973--dc21

                                            2002020011

Dedicated to victims of the terrorist attack on the United States on September 11, 2001, as well as the victims of anthrax biological terrorism to follow.

• • •

And to the memory of Sharon Tate, Marilyn Sheppard, Elizabeth Short, and Nicole Brown Simpson.

PREFACE

Murder is the most serious crime in society for victims, offenders, and the general public. The number of murders in the United States has been on the decline as fewer people, particularly youth, are involved in lethal gun violence, the leading cause of criminal homicide. This notwithstanding, tens of thousands of people are involved in murder offenses as victims and perpetrators every year in this country.

Certain types of homicides have become all too common, such as those involving intimates, family, juveniles, and youth gangs, as well as stranger homicides and drug- or alcohol-related homicides. However, in recent years, there has been a surge in school shootings, workplace homicides, hate violence, and deadly terrorists attacks in the United States. This has resulted in a greater focus on homicidal behavior, its antecedents, and ways to recognize the warning signs of at-risk victims and offenders, and preventative measures. It has also led to increased efforts by lawmakers to create and pass tough crime legislation, and improved federal, state, and local law enforcement response to murder and other violent crimes.

MURDER, AT THE END OF THE DAY AND NIGHT: A Study of Criminal Homicide Offenders, Victims, and Circumstances offers a comprehensive exploration of the crime of murder in American society. The book breaks new ground in homicide studies in examining issues generally ignored or neglected among researchers such as workplace homicides, bias-related homicides, and terrorist perpetrated homicides. Particular attention is also given to school killings, intimate killings, intrafamilial homicides, gang homicides, sexual killers, serial murderers, mass murder, suicide, and theories on murder and violence.

The book is written as a textbook and for assigned reading for both undergraduate and graduate students in the following disciplines: criminal justice, criminology, law, police studies, corrections, violence in society, terrorism, firearms and violence, hate crimes, domestic violence, gender and crime, gender studies, racial and ethnic studies, African American studies, Hispanic studies, urban studies, substance abuse, alcohol and drugs, child abuse and neglect, juvenile delinquency, school violence, youth gangs, sociology, social science, psychology, and related disciplines.

Additionally, the timely and detailed material is appropriate for professionals in law, law enforcement, government, corrections, delinquency, family violence, intimate partner violence, substance abuse, social services, child welfare, education, race relations, medicine, psychology, sociology, psychiatry, and other occupations with an interest in homicide and its impact on individuals and society. Researchers and fellow criminologists and social scientists should also benefit from the wealth of information, findings, and references on murder and violent crime afforded them within this text.

I would like to offer thanks to Charles C Thomas for recognizing the importance of undertaking this project in contributing to the body of work in the study of murder, murderers, and victims, as well as correlates and theories of homicidal and violent behavior.

Finally, my task would not be complete if I did not offer my profound gratitude to my wife of more than twenty years for her tireless devotion to me and my writings, and the professionalism to which she has used her own secretarial skills superbly to transform my often complicated and unkempt manuscripts into polished works of art. Thank you, H. Loraine (Sleeping Beautiful).

R.B.F.

INTRODUCTION

In the aftermath of the September 11, 2001 terrorist hijackings of four air-liners that resulted in the deaths of thousands of people and brought down the twin towers of the World Trade Center and seriously damaged the Pentagon, the dynamics of murder in the United States has been given new attention in criminological and sociological studies.

However, while such instances of mass murder are horrifying and deserve exploration, in reality, these types of killings (including recent deadly school shootings and workplace homicides) represent only a fraction of overall homicides in this country. Far more common are intimate partner homicides, intrafamilial murders, youth homicides, sexual homicides, single victim-single offender homicides, and those influenced by drug and alcohol abuse and related offending. As such, it is important to keep a proper perspective in the study of homicidal behavior, while at the same time, seeking to understand the differences, similarities, and patterns of criminal homicide.

MURDER, AT THE END OF THE DAY AND NIGHT is a multifaceted probe of murder offenses, offenders, victims, and characteristics of homicide in American society. Within this context, the focus will be on examining the nature and causes of murder, the relationship between firearms and lethal violence, the criminal justice system and homicide offenders, different types of murders and murderers, antecedents and correlates to homicidal and violent behavior, and a theoretical basis for murder.

The book is divided into six parts. Part I examines the dynamics of murder including its nature; guns, substance abuse, and murder; and murder offending and the criminal justice system. Part II explores domestic murder such as intimate homicide, infanticide, parricide, and other family involved homicides.

Part III discusses interpersonal and societal murder crimes including workplace homicides, bias-motivated homicides, and terrorism and murder. Part IV focuses on youth and murder including youth gangs and homicide and school killings.

Part V examines particular categories of killers including sexual killers, serial killers, mass murderers, and self-killers. Part VI explores theories on murder.

Tables and figures accompany the text throughout the book to illustrate major points. A complete index is also provided for simple access to information and material found in the text.

CONTENTS

PART I: THE DYNAMICS OF MURDER

PART II: DOMESTIC MURDER

PART III: INTERPERSONAL AND SOCIETAL MURDER

PART IV: YOUTH AND MURDER

TABLES

FIGURES

MURDER, AT THE END
OF THE DAY AND NIGHT

Part I

THE DYNAMICS OF MURDER

Chapter 1

THE NATURE OF MURDER

Murder is considered the most serious and violent criminal offense in society. Tens of thousands of people are murdered in the United States annually. The crime of murder is most often perpetrated by offenders using firearms, but can also occur through numerous other methods such as fists, hands, knives, poison, bombs, bats, and suffocation. Murder victims and offenders come from all walks of life, but certain groups and individuals are at higher risk for involvement than others, such as family members, intimates, youth, gang members, work associates, minorities, and those residing in high crime areas. Recent years have seen a decline in the homicide rate, due in part to tougher gun control laws, a drop in youth gun violence, and a general decrease in overall crimes, particularly violent crime. However, a number of recent school shootings, mass killings, and deadly terrorist attacks illustrate the continual threat and concern with homicidal behavior.

WHAT IS MURDER?

In general, murder refers to the criminal or unlawful taking of a life. However, the term is often used interchangeably with homicide, which is defined as the killing of a person by another. Additionally, there are a number of types and subtypes of each.

The term *murder* originated sometime before the twelfth century in part from "Middle English *murther* . . . Old English *morthor* [and] . . . Middle English *murdre*," to mean "the crime of unlawfully killing a person especially with malice aforethought."[1] *The World Book Encyclopedia* defines murder as "when one person intentionally kills another without legal justification or excuse."[2] Murder and nonnegligent manslaughter are combined in the Uniform Crime Reporting Program administered by the Federal Bureau of

5

Investigation (FBI) to refer to "the willful (nonnegligent) killing of one human being by another."[3]

The term *manslaughter* originated in the fourteenth century, and is defined as "the unlawful killing of a human being without express or implied malice."[4] *Voluntary manslaughter* is "a killing that takes place in the heat of anger and is not premeditated or committed with malice."[5] *Involuntary manslaughter* is the killing of another due to a person's negligence or "manslaughter resulting from the failure to perform a legal duty expressly requested to safeguard human life, from the commission of an unlawful act not constituting a felony, or from the commission of a lawful act in a negligent or improper manner."[6]

Within the broad category of murder is *first-degree murder*, defined as a killing that is "willful, deliberate and premeditated," and *second-degree murder*, a killing defined as "malicious and/or reckless without premeditation or necessarily with intent."[7]

The term *homicide* originated sometime in the fourteenth century from the Latin *homicida*, *homo human being*, and *idd-cide*.[8] Homicide is defined as a person who kills another or "the killing of one human being by another."[9]

There are a number of types of homicide. *Justifiable homicide* is "a killing that has legal justification," such as by a police officer in the course of duty, one that occurs in self-defense, and the killing of an individual by a private citizen in stopping a felony in progress.[10] *Excusable homicide* refers to a completely accidental or unintentional killing without blame or fault on the part of the killer, per se, though still classified as a homicide. *Vehicular homicide* is the killing of a person by another during the operation of a motor vehicle, through criminal negligence or while driving under the influence of alcohol or drugs.

Murder and nonnegligent manslaughter fall within the definition of homicide. Other subtypes of homicide refer to specific kinds of murders or killings, and include:

- *Familicide* is the murder of most or all of a person's family or close relatives.
- *Fratricide* is the killing of one's brother.
- *Infanticide* is the killing of an infant, usually by a parent.
- *Matricide* is the killing of one's mother.
- *Multicide* is the killing of two or more people.
- *Parricide* is the murder of one's father or mother.
- *Patricide* is the murder of one's father.
- *Sororicide* is the murder of one's sister.
- *Suicide* is the killing of oneself.
- *Uxoricide* is the murder by a man of his wife.[11]

Based on a study of homicide in Chicago from the 1960s to 1990s, Carolyn Block and Antigone Christakos argued that rather than one type of event, homicide is in fact the result of a series of events. According to the researchers, Homicide Syndromes "categorize homicides according to the offender's primary motive or goal at the immediate time of the incident. Each Homicide Syndrome corresponds to a nonlethal sibling offense, and these lethal and nonlethal events are linked because they occupy the same position on an expressive versus instrumental continuum."[12]

In *expressive violence*, the offender's main goal "is violence itself," with other motives for the criminal behavior being of a secondary nature; whereas, in *instrumental violence*, the primary goal is "not to hurt, injure or kill, but to acquire money or property."[13] Block and Christakos maintain that virtually all homicides "aside from gangland hits or contract murders correspond to a sibling offense–murder incidents in which a fatal outcome did not occur."[14] Examples of expressive fatal violence include those involving a domestic dispute, child abuse, and stranger attacks. Instrumental fatal violence may be a robbery, street gang violence, or a rape in which the sexual assault was the primary motive.

TRENDS IN HOMICIDES

The number of homicides in the United States has dropped significantly in recent years. The U.S. Department of Justice reported that in 1998 the nation's murder rate had fallen to its lowest level in three decades. The decline was most evident in cities with over a million inhabitants, with the murder rate going from 35.5 per 100,000 in 1991 to less than half at 16.1 per 100,000 in 1998.[15]

This represents a reversal of trends recorded in the late 1980s that showed a sharp rise in homicides in the United States. Both the increase and drop in the murder rate are seen as indicative of changing levels of gun violence involving juveniles and young adults. In spite of this positive sign, experts point out that the levels of firearms-related homicides by young people were still much higher than in the early 1980s.

Intimate homicides declined during the 1990s, particularly those involving male victims. The number of black male victims of intimate murder fell 74 percent and the number of white male victims fell 44 percent in the mid 1990s. White female victims of intimate partner homicide showed low levels not seen since the 1970s, while black female victims of intimate murder fell 44 percent.[16]

After significant increases in rates of homicide offending and victimization among black male youths during the late 1980s and early 1990s, recent years have seen a drop in both murders and victimization within this group.[17]

Other notable homicide trends and findings include:

- Males are more than nine times as likely to commit murder as females.
- Males are more likely to be victims of male and female murderers than females.
- Blacks are seven times as likely as whites to commit murders.
- Blacks are six times as likely to be victims of homicide as whites.
- Homicide is primarily an intraracial crime.
- Infanticide is primarily committed by parents.
- Elderly victims have the highest percentage of murders taking place during the commission of a felony.
- Few murders involve multiple perpetrators.
- Even less homicides involve multiple victims.
- Arguments tend to be the most frequent circumstance leading to murder.[18]

In 1999, the murder rate of 5.7 per 100,000 inhabitants was the lowest in the United States since 1966, and a 39 percent drop from 1990.19 As shown in Figure 1.1, the overall volume of murders nationwide declined in 1999, dropping nearly 9 percent from 1998, while lowering 28 percent from 1995, and decreasing by almost 34 percent from 1990. The number of murders declined in all four regions of the country between 1998 and 1999, with the drop greatest in the South at 11 percent, followed by the West at 8 percent, and declines of 7 percent in the Midwest and 5 percent in the Northeast.[20]

Figure 1.1
Ten Year Murder Trends, 1990-1999

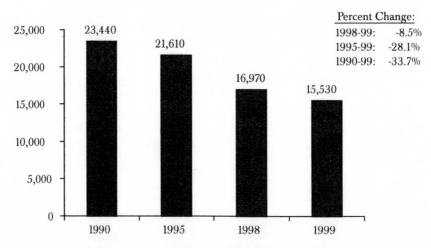

Source: Derived from U.S. Department of Justice, Federal Bureau of Investigation, *Crime in the United States: Uniform Crime Reports 1999* (Washington: Government Printing Office, 2000), p. 64.

Preliminary figures for 2000 indicate that the number of murders committed in the United States continued to drop from 1999. According to the FBI, overall murder declined 1.1 percent in 2000.[21] By region, the West showed the greatest drop in murders at 3.9 percent, followed by a 2.3 percent decline in the Midwest. However, an increase in murders was recorded in the Northeast, rising 1.3 percent, and the South, where murders rose nearly 1 percent between 1999 and 2000.

THE DYNAMICS OF MURDER

According to the Department of Justice, there were an estimated 15,533 victims of murder in the United States in 1999.[22]

More than three-quarters of the murder victims were male. An estimated 14,112 persons committed murder during the year, of which 90 percent were male, when gender was reported.

Regionally, the South recorded the most number of murders, constituting 43 percent of all murders, followed by the West and Midwest, each accounting for 22 percent of murders, and the Northeast, which had 14 percent of the murders.

Tables 1.1 and 1.2 reflect official supplemental murder offender and victim data for 1999. Males constituted nearly 65 percent of total murder offenders, while females accounted for just over 7 percent. Nearly three in ten murder offenders' sex was unknown. Almost 36 percent of the murderers were black, with just over 32 percent white, and around 2 percent other races. Race was unknown for nearly three in ten murder offenders. Killers were more than nine times as likely to be over eighteen years of age as under age eighteen. Around one in four murderers were under the age of twenty-two.

Table 1.1
MURDER OFFENDERS, BY AGE, SEX, AND RACE, 1999

Age	Total	Sex			Race			
		Male	*Female*	*Unknown*	*White*	*Black*	*Other*	*Unknown*
Total	14,112	9,140	1,046	3,926	4,684	5,038	307	4,083
Percent distribution[a]	100.0	64.8	7.4	27.8	33.2	35.7	2.2	28.9
Under 18[b]	941	843	98	–	411	479	43	8
Under 22[b]	3,384	3,119	264	1	1,404	1,849	106	25
18 and over[b]	8,332	7,406	918	8	4,034	3,992	249	57

[a] Because of rounding, the percentages may not add to total.

[b] Does not include unknown ages.

Source: Adapted from U.S. Department of Justice, Federal Bureau of Investigation, *Crime in the United States: Uniform Crime Reports 1999* (Washington: Government Printing Office, 2000), p. 16.

Table 1.2

MURDER VICTIMS, BY AGE, SEX, AND RACE, 1999

Age	Total	Sex			Race			
		Male	*Female*	*Unknown*	*White*	*Black*	*Other*	*Unknown*
Total	12,658	9,558	3,085	15	6,310	5,855	369	124
Percent distribution[a]	100.0	75.5	24.4	.1	49.8	46.3	2.9	1.0
Under 18[b]	1,449	953	496	–	736	629	67	17
Under 22[b]	3,322	2,551	771	–	1,520	1,663	111	28
18 and over[b]	10,997	8,464	2,528	5	5,465	5,152	300	80

[a] Because of rounding, the percentages may not add to total.
[b] Does not include unknown ages.

Source: Adapted from U.S. Department of Justice, Federal Bureau of Investigation, *Crime in the United States: Uniform Crime Reports 1999* (Washington: Government Printing Office, 2000), p. 16.

Among murder victims, over 75 percent were male, with females constituting just over 24 percent of victims. Nearly 50 percent of murder victims were white, while black victims were overrepresented, accounting for more than 46 percent of the total. Around 3 percent of murder victims were of other races, and 1 percent were of an unknown race.

Almost 87 percent of all victims of murder were over the age of seventeen. Nearly eight persons age eighteen and older were murdered for every one person age seventeen and under during the year. More than one in four murder victims were under the age of twenty-two.

CIRCUMSTANCES OF MURDER

The majority of murders committed in the United States in 1999 were nonfelony homicides as the result of firearms, as shown in Table 1.3. Of 12,658 murders for which supplemental information was provided by law enforcement agencies, 6,678 victims were killed by other than felony-type circumstances, representing nearly 53 percent of all murder victims. These included such circumstances as a romantic triangle, brawls due to alcohol or narcotics influence, juvenile gang killings, and other arguments.

There were 2,137 murders of a felony type, constituting almost 17 percent of total murders that involved such circumstances as rape, robbery, burglary, arson, narcotics law violations, and sex offenses. Around three in ten murders had circumstances that were unknown.

Table 1.3

MURDER CIRCUMSTANCES, BY OFFENSE AND FIREARMS, 1999

Circumstances	Total murder victims	Total firearms	Hand-guns	rifles	Shot-guns	Other guns or types not stated
Total[a]	12,658	8,259	6,498	387	503	871
Felony type total:	2,137	1,453	1,216	59	60	118
Rape	46	2	2	–	–	–
Robbery	1,010	738	627	24	18	69
Burglary	79	35	23	7	2	3
Larceny-theft	14	6	4	–	–	2
Motor vehicle theft	13	10	5	2	2	1
Arson	63	1	–	1	–	–
Prostitution & commercialized vice	7	4	–	–	–	4
Other sex offenses	19	2	1	–	–	1
Narcotic drug laws	564	482	423	17	21	21
Gambling	17	16	12	–	–	4
Other - not specified	305	157	119	8	17	13
Suspected felony type	64	55	48	1	1	5
Other than felony type total:	6,678	4,220	3,321	252	331	316
Romantic triangle	133	100	77	6	12	5
Child killed by babysitter	32	–	–	–	–	–
Brawl due to influence of alcohol	187	89	67	5	12	5
Brawl due to influence of narcotics	111	84	73	1	7	3
Argument over money or property	211	145	109	7	11	18
Other arguments	3,391	2,071	1,669	127	155	120
Gangland killings	116	102	87	2	2	11
Juvenile gang killings	579	539	471	24	16	28
Institutional killings	11	1	1	–	–	–
Sniper attack	4	4	4	–	–	–
Other - not specified	1,903	1,085	763	80	116	126
Unknown	3,779	2,531	1,913	75	111	432

[a]Total murder victims for whom supplemental homicide data were received.

Source: Adapted from U.S. Department of Justice, Federal Bureau of Investigation, *Crime in the United States: Uniform Crime Reports 1999* (Washington: Government Printing Office, 2000), p. 21.

Firearms killed nearly two-thirds of murder victims in 1999. Of these, around 79 percent were the victims of handguns. A number of studies support the strong relationship between lethal violence and firearms, particularly handguns.[23] About 68 percent of the felony-type murders and 63 percent of the nonfelony murders were perpetrated with firearms.

Table 1.4 describes the type of weapons used on murder victims from 1997 to 1999. While the number of victims and weapons used against them declined each year, firearms were by far still responsible for most murder victimizations. Handguns were the most likely weapon used to kill victims, followed by knives or cutting instruments, personal weapons such as fists, blunt objects, and other types of firearms such as shotguns and rifles. (See also Chapter 2.)

Table 1.4
MURDER VICTIMS, BY TYPES OF WEAPONS USED, 1997-1999

Weapons	1997	1998	1999
Total	15,837	14,276	12,658
Total firearms	10,729	9,257	8,259
Handguns	8,441	7,430	6,498
Rifles	638	548	387
Shotguns	643	633	503
Other guns	35	16	90
Firearms, not stated	972	630	781
Knives or cutting instruments	2,055	1,899	1,667
Blunt objects (clubs, hammers, etc.)	724	755	736
Personal weapons (hands, fists, feet, etc.)[a]	1,010	964	855
Poison	6	6	11
Explosives	8	10	–
Fire	140	132	125
Narcotics	37	35	23
Drowning	34	28	26
Strangulation	224	213	190
Asphyxiation	88	101	103
Other weapons or weapons not stated	782	876	663

[a] Pushed is included in personal weapons.

Source: Adapted from U.S. Department of Justice, Federal Bureau of Investigation, *Crime in the United States: Uniform Crime Reports 1999* (Washington: Government Printing Office, 2000), p. 18.

CHARACTERIZING THE MURDER OFFENDER-VICTIM RELATIONSHIP

More than four in ten murders committed in the United States in 1999 involved an unknown relationship between the victim and offender (see Figure 1.2). Over one-third of the murder victims knew their offender or offenders apart from family members, such as boyfriend or girlfriend, acquaintance, friend, or coworker. Nearly 14 percent of murders were intrafamilial in nature, whereas around 12 percent involved strangers to the victims.

Table 1.5 shows the murder victim-offender relationship for single victim-offender homicides, by age, in 1999. The vast majority of murder offenders and victims were age eighteen and over. Eighty-six percent of known killers

Figure 1.2

Murder Victim-Offender Relationship, 1999

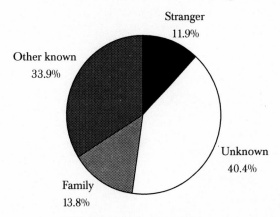

Source: Derived from U.S. Department of Justice, Federal Bureau of Investigation, *Crime in the United States: Uniform Crime Reports 1999* (Washington: Government Printing Office, 2000), p. 20.

and 87 percent of known murder victims were adults. Juveniles were much more likely to be victims of murder than perpetrators, with 776 known victims under the age of eighteen, compared to 460 known offenders younger than eighteen.

The relationship between victims and offenders in single victim-single offender homicides by sex and race in 1999 can be seen in Table 1.6. In nearly nine out of ten such murders where gender was known, both victim and murderer were male; while almost nine in ten murders of females were committed by males. Female killers of males and females constituted only around one in every ten killers.

Table 1.5

VICTIM/OFFENDER RELATIONSHIP, BY AGE, 1999

Single Victim/Single Offender

Age	Total	Age of offender		
		Male	*Female*	*Unknown*
Total	6,434	460	5,532	442
Under 18	776	148	596	32
18 and over	5,579	310	4,870	399
Unknown	79	2	66	11

Source: U.S. Department of Justice, Federal Bureau of Investigation, *Crime in the United States: Uniform Crime Reports 1999* (Washington: Government Printing Office, 2000), p. 17.

With respect to race and murder, the victim and offender relationship is largely intraracial. More than 93 percent of black homicide victims were murdered by black offenders in 1999; while nearly 84 percent of white homicide victims were killed by white perpetrators. Around 70 percent of victims of other races were slain by offenders of other races.

Table 1.6

VICTIM/OFFENDER RELATIONSHIP, BY SEX AND RACE 1999

Single Victim/Single Offender

Race of victim	Total	Sex of Offender			Race of Offender			
		Male	*Female*	*Unknown*	*White*	*Black*	*Other*	*Unknown*
White victims	3,336	2,939	343	54	2,779	452	51	54
Black victims	2,869	2,510	328	31	154	2,674	10	31
Other race victims	181	156	22	3	34	17	127	3
Unknown race	48	26	4	18	17	12	1	18

Sex of victim	Total	Sex of Offender			Race of Offender			
		Male	*Female*	*Unknown*	*White*	*Black*	*Other*	*Unknown*
Male victims	3,336	2,939	343	54	2,779	452	51	54
Female victims	2,869	2,510	328	31	154	2,674	10	31
Unknown sex	48	26	4	18	17	12	1	18

Source: Adapted from U.S. Department of Justice, Federal Bureau of Investigation, *Crime in the United States: Uniform Crime Reports 1999* (Washington: Government Printing Office, 2000), p. 17.

The disproportionate involvement of blacks as murder offenders and victims has been noted and examined by a number of researchers,[24] relating it to such variables as the high rate of crime in inner cities, access and arming with illegal weapons, youth gangs, drug dealing, and even discrimination within the criminal justice system in arrests and incarceration.[25]

Although ethnicity is often excluded from official data on murder, persons of Hispanic origin have been found to be disproportionately likely to be murder offenders and victims—linking this to culture, drug offending, youth gangs, territorial disputes, and gun possession and accessibility.[26]

THE RISK OF MURDER VICTIMIZATION

What are the risks over a lifetime of becoming a murder victim? Data for 1997 on the lifetime victimization rate of murder based on the Uniform Crime Reports' Supplemental Homicide Report, the National Center for Health Statistics' United States Life Tables, and United States population estimates from the U.S. Bureau of the Census can be seen in Table 1.7.

Table 1.7
LIFETIME VICTIMIZATION RATE OF MURDER (5 YEAR)*

Age	Total	Male	Female	White	White Male	White Female	Black	Black Male	Black Female	Other	Other Male	Other Female
0	240	155	553	410	280	794	68	40	199	407	288	709
5	248	158	595	426	288	848	69	41	213	424	296	764
10	250	159	603	429	289	859	70	41	216	429	298	787
15	252	160	614	433	291	874	70	41	219	436	302	799
20	291	186	674	488	330	957	81	48	239	523	370	909
25	381	250	789	600	413	1,106	110	66	282	623	457	992
30	487	328	921	730	513	1,263	145	89	337	742	568	1,095
35	620	422	1,133	895	632	1,520	191	117	427	853	678	1,184
40	786	536	1,418	1,092	769	1,843	251	154	558	1,014	823	1,373
45	998	684	1,751	1,336	951	2,177	332	202	741	1,169	931	1,647
50	1,287	889	2,177	1,670	1,197	2,646	440	268	959	1,524	1,315	1,964
55	1,610	1,125	2,610	2,079	1,513	3,150	554	313	1,158	1,805	1,572	2,345
60	2,033	1,434	3,162	2,610	1,927	3,782	679	411	1,397	2,242	2,079	2,782
65	2,556	1,857	3,661	3,138	2,410	4,175	898	538	1,801	2,846	3,235	3,064
70	3,117	2,335	4,157	3,734	3,025	4,522	1,106	631	2,335	3,118	3,755	3,461
75	3,918	3,043	4,836	4,639	3,874	5,322	1,362	800	2,436	3,829	6,595	3,938
80	4,653	3,603	5,567	5,333	4,380	6,068	1,697	993	2,756	5,814	N/A	5,511

*Table shows only 80 years of age because the low number of U.S. citizens and murders occurring in age groups over the age of 80 may improperly inflate odd ratios and murder rates and may not reflect the true nature of murder in these groups.

*Based on 1997 murder rates, which may not remain constant over time.

*There were no reported murders for Other males aged 80 and older in 1997.

Source: U.S. Department of Justice, Federal Bureau of Investigation, *Crime in the United States: Uniform Crime Reports 1999* (Washington: Government Printing Office, 2000), p. 281.

Over the course of a lifetime males are much more likely to be murdered than females; while blacks have a far greater chance than whites or other races to become murder victims; with black males being more likely to be murdered than any other group when combining race and sex.

In 1997, one out of 240 persons per 100,000 in the U.S. population would become a murder victim. The probability of a male being murdered was one in 155, or more than three times that of a female, at one in 553. Blacks had a victimization rate of one out of sixty-eight, which meant they were around six times as likely to be murdered as whites, at one in 410, or persons of other races, at one in 407.

Black males had a likelihood of one in forty of being murdered over a life span, with black females second most likely at one in 199. Compared to other groups, when broken down by race and sex, black males were seven times more likely to be victims of murder than white males or other males and had nearly a twenty times greater probability to be murdered than white females, who had the lowest victimization rate at one in 794.

The risk of murder victimization decreased with age for all groups. Although blacks continued to be more likely to be murdered at any age than persons of other races at age thirty, the black murder rate decreased more than 100 percent from at birth. Males age thirty were about half as likely and females age thirty were one-third less likely to be murder victims as at age fifteen.

As indicated earlier, murder rates have dropped in recent years, reducing the likelihood of victimization for most people in every age, racial, and gender group.

MURDER AND THE LAW

Murder is primarily controlled in society through laws prohibiting it and serious consequences for those perpetrating the act of murder. Murder is a felony crime or criminal homicide in every state, with penalties for offenders usually ranging from long prison terms to capital punishment, depending on the degree of murder, nature of the crime, and the state where it was committed.

A representative murder statute is Michigan's Criminal Code on first and second degree murder, which reads:

> A person who commits any of the following is guilty of *first degree* murder and shall be punished by imprisonment for life: (1) murder perpetrated by means of poison, lying in wait, or any other willful, deliberate, and premeditated killing; (2) murder committed in the perpetration of, or attempt to perpetrate, arson, criminal sexual conduct in the first or third degree, child abuse in the first degree, a major controlled substance offense, robbery, breaking and entering of a dwelling, larceny of any kind, extortion, or kidnapping; (3) a murder of a peace officer or a corrections officer committed while the [person] is lawfully engaged in the performance of any of his or her duties as a peace officer or corrections officer, with knowledge that the [person] is . . . engaged in the performance of his or her duty.[27]

> All other kinds of murder shall be murder of the *second degree,* and shall be punished by imprisonment in the state prison for life, or any term of years, in the discretion of the court trying the same.[28]

Furthermore, the Michigan Criminal Code on manslaughter states that: "Any person who shall commit the crime of *manslaughter* shall be guilty of a felony punishable by imprisonment in the state prison, not more than fifteen years or by fine of not more than $7,500, or both, at the discretion of the court."[29]

On the federal level, the crime of murder and other violent offenses, particularly those committed when using lethal weapons, recently led to the most sweeping crime bill in United States history. The Violent Crime Control and Law Enforcement Act (Federal Crime Bill) was signed into law in 1994.[30] The Act provided for 100,000 new police officers to fight violent crime, almost $10 billion for prison construction, more than $16 billion for crime prevention programs, and $2.6 billion for new federal law enforcement personnel. Penalties were also stiffened for many types of offenses including federal crimes, violent crimes, gang-involved crimes, sex offenses, and white collar crimes.

Highlights of the Act's provision include the following:

- The ban of manufacturing nineteen military assault weapons and weapons with certain combat features.
- Expands the death penalty to include about sixty offenses, such as homicides associated with terrorism, the murder of a federal law officer, carjackings and drive-by shootings resulting in death, and large scale drug trafficking operations.
- New and stiffer penalties for gang crimes of violence and drug trafficking.
- Strengthened federal licensing requirements for dealers of firearms.
- Prohibiting the sale to or possession of firearms by individuals with domestic violence restraining orders against them.
- Requirement of sexually violent criminals to register with state law enforcement agencies.
- Doubling the penalties for repeat sex criminals convicted of federal sex crimes.
- A mandatory sentence of life in prison with no possibility of parole for federal offenders with three or more convictions for serious violent felonies or drug trafficking offenses.
- The authorization of prosecuting in adult criminal court persons thirteen years of age and older charged with certain types of serious violent crimes.
- The creation of new crimes or increasing penalties for such offenses as the use of semiautomatic weapons, interstate trafficking of firearms, hate crimes, drive-by shootings, sex crimes, crimes against the elderly, and interstate domestic violence.

Additionally, recent federal laws enacted to respond to criminal homicide and other violent crimes include hate crime statutes and antiterrorism legislation (see Chapters 9 and 10).

NOTES

1. YourDictionary.com, http://yourdictionary.com/.
2. World Book Encyclopedia, http://search.cssvc.worldbook.compuserve.com/wbol/wbsearch/na/se/co?st1=murder.
3. U.S. Department of Justice, Federal Bureau of Investigation, *Crime in the United States: Uniform Crime Reports 1999* (Washington: Government Printing Office, 2000), p. 13.
4. YourDictionary.com.
5. David Lester, *Serial Killers: The Insatiable Passion* (Philadelphia: Charles Press, 1995), p. 10.
6. YourDictionary.com.
7. Lester, *Serial Killers*, p. 10. *See also* Maureen Harrison and Steve Gilbert, *The Murder Reference: Everything You Never Wanted to Know About Murder in America* (San Diego: Excellent Books, 1996), pp. 34, 48, 57-58, 72.
8. YourDictionary.com.
9. *Ibid.*
10. Charles F. Welford, "Homicide," *World Book Online Americas Edition*, http://www.cssvc.worldbook.compuserve.com/wbol/wbpage/na/ar/co/260800, November 25, 2001.
11. See R. Barri Flowers and H. Loraine Flowers, *Murders in the United States: Crimes, Killers and Victims of the Twentieth Century* (Jefferson: McFarland, 2001); Charles P. Ewing, *Fatal Families: The Dynamics of Intrafamilial Homicide* (Thousand Oaks: Sage, 1997).
12. Carolyn R. Block and Antigone Christakos, "Chicago Homicide From the Sixties to the Nineties: Major Trends in Lethal Violence," in U.S. Department of Justice, *Trends, Risks, and Interventions in Lethal Violence: Proceedings of the Third Annual Spring Symposium of the Homicide Research Working Group* (Washington: National Institute of Justice, 1995), p. 28.
13. *Ibid. See also* Leonard Berkowitz, "Some Varieties of Human Aggression: Criminal Violence as Coercion, Rule-Following, Impression Management and Impulsive Behavior," in Anne Campbell and John J. Gibbs, eds., *Violent Transactions: The Limits of Personality* (Oxford: Basil Blackwell, 1986), pp. 87-103.
14. Block and Christakos, "Chicago Homicide From the Sixties to the Nineties," p. 29.
15. U.S. Department of Justice, Bureau of Justice Statistics Crime Data Brief, *Homicide Trends in the United States: 1998 Update* (Washington: Office of Justice Programs, 2000), p. 1.
16. *Ibid.*, p. 2.
17. *Ibid.*
18. *Ibid.*, pp. 1-3.
19. *Crime in the United States*, p. 14.
20. *Ibid.*
21. Uniform Crime Reports preliminary data for 2000, http://www.fbi.gov.
22. *Crime in the United States*, p. 14.

23. See, for example, Philip J. Cook and Mark H. Moore, "Guns, Gun Control, and Homicide," in M. Dwayne Smith and Margaret A. Zahn, eds., *Studying and Preventing Homicide: Issues and Challenges* (Thousand Oaks: Sage, 1999), pp. 246-71; G. Kleck, *Point Blank: Guns and Violence in America* (New York: Aldine de Gruyter, 1991); J. D. Wright, J. F. Sheley, and M. D. Smith, "Kids, Guns, and Killing Fields," Society 30, 1 (1992): 84-89.

24. See, for example, R. Barri Flowers, *Minorities and Criminality* (Westport: Greenwood, 1988), pp. 83-94; Edward Green, "Race, Social Status, and Criminal Arrest," *American Sociological Review 35* (1970): 476-90; Darnell F. Hawkins, "African Americans and Homicide," in M. Dwayne Smith and Margaret A. Zahn, eds., *Studying and Preventing Homicide: Issues and Challenges* (Thousand Oaks: Sage, 1999), pp. 143-56; H. M. Rose and P. D. McClain, Race, Place, and Risk: Black Homicide in Urban America (Albany: State University of New York Press, 1990).

25. Flowers, *Minorities and Criminality*, pp. 83-94, 121-22; Hawkins, "African Americans and Homicide," pp. 143-56; K. Harries, *Serious Violence: Patterns of Homicide and Assault in America* (Springfield: Charles C Thomas, 1990).

26. Flowers, *Minorities and Criminality*, pp. 95-104; J. W. Moore, *Homeboys: Gangs, Drugs and Prison in the Barrios of Los Angeles* (Philadelphia: Temple University Press, 1978), pp. 100-6; Leo M. Romero and Luis G. Stelzner, "Hispanics and the Criminal Justice System," in Pastora Cafferty and William C. McCready, eds., *Hispanics in the United States: A New Social Agenda* (New Brunswick: Transaction Books, 1985); Ramiro Martinez, Jr., "Latinos and Lethal Violence: The Impact of Poverty and Inequality," *Social Problems 43* (1996): 131-46; Ramiro Martinez, Jr., and Matthew T. Lee, "Latinos and Homicide," in M. Dwayne Smith and Margaret A. Zahn, eds., *Studying and Preventing Homicide: Issues and Challenges* (Thousand Oaks: Sage, 1999), pp. 159-72.

27. Michigan Criminal Code 750.316. *See also* Harrison and Gilbert, *The Murder Reference*, pp. 65-66.

28. Michigan Criminal Code 750.317.

29. Harrison and Gilbert, *The Murder Reference*, pp. 65-66; Michigan Criminal Code 750.321/.329.

30. P. L. 103-322 (1994).

Chapter 2

FIREARMS, SUBSTANCE ABUSE, AND MURDER

The most common correlates of murder are use of firearms and the influence of drugs or alcohol in the perpetrator's commission of the crime. Around two in every three murders in the United States were committed with firearms. Handguns are the weapons of choice for most murderers. Homicides involving guns are especially associated with intimate murders, gang homicides, drug-related murders, mass murders, youth homicides, and school killings. Recent gun control legislation has helped reduce firearm-related lethal violence in society, however weapons possession and use continue to have the strongest cause and effect relationship to murder.

Much of the research on homicide shows a strong association between deadly violence and substance abuse, as well as drug and alcohol use and other violent offenses, and serious drug offenses such as drug dealing. Prisoner data reveals that nearly half the violent inmates had used drugs in the month prior to committing the crimes, while more than one in five violent prisoners had been under the influence of alcohol when perpetrating the offense. Many incarcerated violent offenders admit to using drugs and alcohol while committing the violent crime.

Arrest trends indicate that fewer persons are being arrested for murder and weapons offenses, as well as some alcohol-related crimes. However, drug abuse violations have shown a sharp rise, while liquor law violations have risen slightly–suggesting that the tripartite relationship between murder, firearms, and substance abuse is unclear, with the negative connotations nevertheless potentially lethal.

FIREARMS AND MURDER

Firearms are closely related to murder, according to experts. Guns are believed to be responsible for tens of thousands of murders and at least three times as many nonfatal injuries sustained by victims, while being used to threaten hundreds of thousands of others each year.[1] The Federal Bureau of Investigation (FBI) estimated firearms were used in almost two out of every three of the 15,533 murders committed in the United States in 1999.[2] In the National Crime Victimization Survey, it was reported that in 2000, there were 533,470 victims of such serious violent crimes as aggravated assault, rape, and robbery, where the perpetrator(s) possessed a firearm.[3] A weapon of some sort is present in more than one in every four crimes of violence.[4]

Handguns are used to commit murder more than any other type of weapon. As shown in Figure 2.1, in 1999, 51 percent of all murders involved the use of a handgun, while 14 percent were perpetrated with other firearms. Thirteen percent of homicides were committed with knives, 6 percent with blunt objects, and 16 percent were as a result of other weapons. Among firearms-related homicides, types of firearms not stated were second most likely to handguns to be used by offenders, followed by shotguns, rifles, and other guns.[5]

Figure 2.1
Murders in the United States, by Type of Weapon Used, 1999

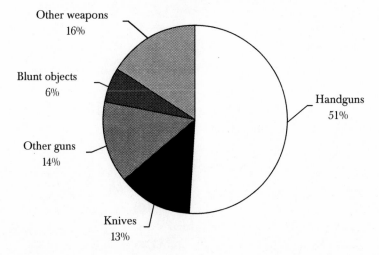

Source: Derived from U.S. Department of Justice, Federal Bureau of Investigation, *Crime in the United States: Uniform Crime Reports 1999* (Washington: Government Printing Office, 2000), p. 18.

Table 2.1

MURDER CIRCUMSTANCES INVOLVING FIREARMS, BY OFFENSE, 1999

Circumstances	Total murder victims	Total firearms	Handguns
Total[a]	12,658	8,259	6,498
Felony type total:	2,137	1,453	1,216
Rape	46	2	2
Robbery	1,010	738	627
Burglary	79	35	23
Larceny-theft	14	6	4
Motor vehicle theft	13	10	5
Arson	63	1	–
Prostitution & commercialized vice	7	4	–
Other sex offenses	19	2	1
Narcotic drug laws	564	482	423
Gambling	17	16	12
Other - not specified	305	157	119
Suspected felony type	64	55	48
Other than felony type total:	6,678	4,220	3,321
Romantic triangle	133	100	77
Child killed by babysitter	32	–	–
Brawl due to influence of alcohol	187	89	67
Brawl due to influence of narcotics	111	84	73
Argument over money or property	211	145	109
Other arguments	3,391	2,071	1,669
Gangland killings	116	102	87
Juvenile gang killings	579	539	471
Institutional killings	11	1	1
Sniper attack	4	4	4
Other - not specified	1,903	1,085	763
Unknown	3,779	2,531	1,913

[a] Total murder victims for whom supplemental homicide data were received.

Source: Adapted from U.S. Department of Justice, Federal Bureau of Investigation, *Crime in the United States: Uniform Crime Reports 1999* (Washington: Government Printing Office, 2000), p. 21.

The circumstances of murder involving firearms in 1999 can be seen in Table 2.1. According to the data provided by law enforcement agencies for 12,658 murder victims, more than 65 percent were killed by firearms. Of this group, nearly 79 percent were victimized by handguns. Most murders committed with firearms were other than felony types, representing just over 51 percent of the homicides. These included murders involving romantic triangles, brawls due to alcohol or narcotics influence, other arguments, and juvenile gang killings. Nearly 18 percent of murders perpetrated with firearms were felony types such as those involving rape, robbery, burglary, and narcotics drug laws.

TRENDS IN FIREARM-RELATED INJURIES AND FATALITIES

Violent crimes involving firearms have declined in recent years. FBI figures indicate that between 1990 and 1999, arrests for murder and nonnegligent manslaughter decreased by more than 39 percent. During the same period, arrests for weapons violations dropped nearly 25 percent (see Figure 2.2). The interrelationship of homicides and weapons—particularly firearms—is believed to account for much of the rise and fall in the murder rate.

Figure 2.2
Ten Year Arrest Trends for Murder[a] and Weapons Offenses,[b] 1990-1999

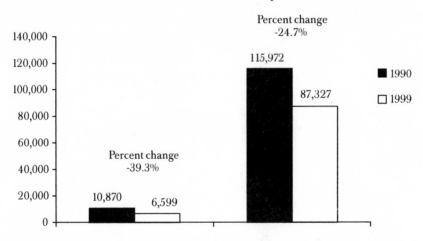

[a] Includes nonnegligent manslaughter.
[b] Includes carrying and possessing weapons.

Source: Derived from U.S. Department of Justice, Federal Bureau of Investigation, *Crime in the United States: Uniform Crime Reports 1999* (Washington: Government Printing Office, 2000), p. 216.

According to the Bureau of Justice Statistics (BJS), between 1993 and 1997, homicides perpetrated with a firearm dropped 27 percent, while the number of nonfatal gunshot injuries due to assaults decreased 39 percent (see Figure 2.3). About 30 percent of nonfatal violent crimes were perpetrated with a firearm, while 44 percent of all fatalities resulting from a firearm were homicides during the period.[6]

Victims of fatal and nonfatal gunshot injuries were predominantly male, constituting four of every five victims. Black males were disproportionately

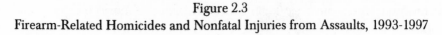

Figure 2.3
Firearm-Related Homicides and Nonfatal Injuries from Assaults, 1993-1997

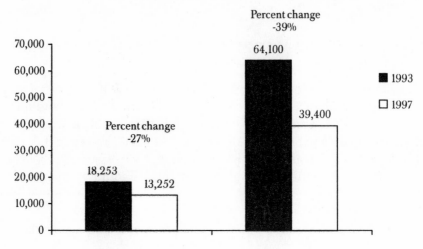

Source: Derived from U.S. Department of Justice, Statistics Selected Findings, *Firearm Injury and Death fromCrime, 1993-97* (Washington: Government Printing Office, 2000), p. 7.

likely to be victims of firearms-related fatal and nonfatal violence. Nearly half of all victims of lethal and nonfatal gunshot injuries were black males, with around one-fourth between the ages of fifteen and twenty-four.

Other trends in firearm-related violence over the span include:

• More than six in ten victims of nonfatal firearm-associated injuries receiving treatment in emergency departments came as the result of an assault.

• More than half the victims of nonfatal firearm-related injuries due to a crime were under the age of twenty-five.

• Murder victims of firearms tended to be older.

• Around two in ten victims of homicide and nonfatal injuries sustained from gunshot violence were Hispanic.[7]

• In 44 percent of firearms-related homicides, the murderer was known to the victim.

• In 12 percent of gunshot-related fatalities, the victim-offender was an intimate or relative.

• In 41 percent of homicides caused by gun violence, the relationship between killer and offender was not known.

• In 15 percent of homicides involving firearms, the murderer was a stranger.

• In 56 percent of nonfatal gunshot assaults, the relationship between victim and offender was not known.[8]

• Suicide attempts using firearms were more likely to result in fatalities than other types of gunshot injuries.[9]

GUN OWNERSHIP, AVAILABILITY, AND LETHALITY

The relationship between gun laws, gun ownership, availability, and lethality as a consequence is strongly supported in studies.[10] According to the National Opinion Research Center's General Social Survey, more than four in every ten households in the United States have one or more firearms.[11] Around three in ten persons of adult age claim gun ownership.[12] In a recent survey of private gun ownership, it was estimated that there were an average of 4.4 guns in households owning firearms.[13] It is estimated that there may be as many as 200 million guns currently in circulation.[14]

The handgun has proven particularly popular among gun owners and is used primarily in self-defense, suicide, or to commit a crime.[15] Approximately 30,000 people die from homicide, suicide, and accidental death due to gunfire each year in the United States.[16]

Firearms related homicide victims and offenders are greatly overrepresented among males, youth, and African Americans.[17] The latter group is particularly disproportionately involved in lethal gun violence and criminality involving handguns and more sophisticated firearms,[18] as are people of Hispanic origin or Latinos.[19]

Supply and demand is believed to be a key factor in gun violence and fatalities. Relatively easy access to both legal and illegal guns increases the risk that these guns will be used to kill. Arthur Kellerman and colleagues found that homicide was more likely to occur in the home when a firearm was present.[20] A high percentage of teenagers, students, and youth gang members have reported having easy access to guns and other weapons.[21] Studies show that criminals often circumvent the licensed gun dealers and legal requirements for gun ownership in favor of obtaining illegal guns from family, associates, theft, street connections, and other sources.[22] Furthermore, increased possession of legal guns in public by citizens and potential victims as a self-protective device in troubled times merely increases the risk for personal victimization and general gun violence in society, often with deadly results.[23]

ALCOHOL, DRUGS, AND MURDER

Alcohol and drug use have been commonly associated with violent crimes, particularly the crime of murder.[24] According to the Uniform Crime

Reports, in 1999, there were nearly 900 murders committed in the United States that were directly attributed to circumstances involving narcotic drug laws and brawls due to the influence of drugs or alcohol.[25] However, many criminologists believe there to be a much greater cause and effect correlation between alcohol, drugs, and murder.

In a study of criminal homicide, Marvin Wolfgang and R. B. Strohm found alcohol to be a factor in more than 60 percent of the cases.[26] Wolfgang further found that criminal homicides involving alcohol tended to be the most violent.[27] A study by Harwin Voss and John Hepburn reached similar conclusions. They found alcohol was a factor in over half the 370 cases examined.[28] Herbert Block and Gilbert Geis linked alcohol to homicide, aggravated assault, and sexual crimes;[29] whereas R. N. Parker and L. Rebhun focused on the relationship between alcohol, selective disinhibition, and homicide.[30]

Other research has associated drug use with homicide and other violent crimes.[31] The National Institute of Justice recently found that more than half the persons arrested in Washington, D.C. and New York City for violent crimes had been using one or more illicit drugs when the crime was perpetrated.[32] Another study found that anywhere from one-half to three-quarters of violent crime arrestees in twelve large cities tested positive for illegal drug use.[33]

Such drugs as cocaine, crack cocaine, and marijuana and their use have been related to homicide offenders in studies by B. Spunt and colleagues,[34] and P. Goldstein and associates.[35] Researchers have found that offenders and victims in drug-involved homicides were far more likely than those in homicides not related to drugs to be known to law enforcement as drug users or traffickers in drugs.[36] Drug use has been shown in a number of studies to have a positive correlation to drug dealing and violent crime, including murder.[37]

In a study of murder cases in the seventy-five largest counties in the country, illegal drugs related to use, buying, dealing, and manufacturing were found to be involved in 16 percent of the murders and 18 percent of the defendants.[38] Violence associated with drug use and illegal drug networks has been referred to as "systemic" or the "traditionally aggressive patterns of interaction within the system of drug distribution and use."[39]

Arrest trends indicate that arrests for drug abuse offenses are on the rise, while alcohol-related offenses are declining overall. As seen in Table 2.2, from 1990 to 1999, total arrests for drug abuse violations increased more than 36 percent. Among arrests for alcohol-related crimes, driving under the influence arrests dropped nearly 27 percent, with arrests for drunkenness falling almost 32 percent. Only arrests for liquor law violations rose, at nearly 2 percent over the period.

Table 2.2

TEN-YEAR ARREST TRENDS FOR DRUG ABUSE VIOLATIONS
AND ALCOHOL-RELATED OFFENSES, 1990-1999

Offense	*1990*	*1999*	*Percent Change*
Drug abuse violations	589,944	805,024	+36.5%
Driving under the influence	1,021,753	749,454	-26.7%
Liquor laws	350,108	355,761	+1.6%
Drunkenness	554,867	378,234	+31.8%

Source: Adapted from U.S. Department of Justice, Federal Bureau of Investigation, *Crime in the United States: Uniform Crime Reports 1999* (Washington: Government Printing Office, 2000), p. 216.

In spite of the drop in homicide rates, the significant correlation between substance abuse and homicide or other violent crimes is clearly evident in self-report prisoner surveys. According to the Bureau of Justice Statistics (BJS), more than half of jail inmates convicted of violent crimes had been drinking alcohol before committing the crime.[40] Almost seven in ten persons convicted of manslaughter had used alcohol prior to the incident. More than four in ten violent prison inmates had used illegal drugs in the month preceding the offense, while nearly half of all male and female prisoners were under the influence of drugs or alcohol at the time of the crime.

Domestic Partner Homicide and Substance Abuse

Domestic homicides involving intimate partners has been strongly linked to substance abuse by the perpetrator and/or victim.[41] Abusive and homicidal male partners have been especially associated with alcohol and drug abuse,[42] including use of psychoactive drugs and a combination of alcohol and drug use.[43]

Studies on intimates, drugs, and homicide have found that battered women who murdered their batterers were more likely than abused women who did not kill their partners to use alcohol and other types of drugs.[44] Furthermore, male homicide victims of battered women have been shown to be almost twice as likely to have used alcohol on a daily basis than male partners of women nonkillers.[45]

Minorities, Substance Abuse, and Homicide

It appears that race and ethnicity does play a role with respect to substance abuse and homicide. A number of studies have found a disproportionate involvement of persons in minority racial and ethnic groups in alcohol- or drug-related homicides.[46] In particular, African Americans, Native Americans, and Hispanics tend to have a significantly higher rate of homicide offending associated with alcohol or drugs than do other groups.[47] Researchers have further shown a strong relationship between minorities, gang involvement, drug crimes, the inner city, and murder.[48] (See also Chapter 1.) However, some studies have found a lower rate of alcohol or drug involvement among some minority homicide offenders, such as African Americans.[49]

Juveniles, Substance Abuse, and Murder

A significant correlation has been shown to exist between juveniles who kill and substance abuse.[50] According to Kathleen Heide, the majority of the juveniles she evaluated who committed felony homicides used drugs and/or alcohol.[51] Other researchers have linked youth substance abuse to possession of firearms, bullying, gangs, and violent behavior, including murder.[52] Recent acts of school killings and juvenile parricide have predominantly involved substance abuse.[53] Drug and alcohol use by teenagers appears to predispose them to a number of violent behaviors such as murder and suicide.

NOTES

1. U.S. Department of Justice, Bureau of Justice Statistics Selected Findings, *Firearm Injury and Death From Crime, 1993-97* (Washington: Office of Justice Programs, 2000), pp. 1-7; Philip J. Cook and Mark H. Moore, "Guns, Gun Control, and Homicide," in M. Dwayne Smith and Margaret A. Zahn, eds., *Studying and Preventing Homicide: Issues and Challenges* (Thousand Oaks: Sage, 1999), pp. 246-50.
2. U.S. Department of Justice, Federal Bureau of Investigation, *Crime in the United States: Uniform Crime Reports 1999* (Washington: Government Printing Office, 2000), pp. 14-19.
3. U.S. Department of Justice, National Crime Victimization Survey, 2000, http://www.ojp.usdoj.gov.bjs/.
4. Cited in Bureau of Justice Statistics, http://www.ojp.usdoj.gov/ bjs/cvict_c.htm.
5. *Crime in the United States*, p. 18.
6. *Firearm Injury and Death From Crime, 1993-97*, p. 1.
7. *Ibid.*, p. 4.
8. *Ibid.*, p. 5.
9. V. Beaman, J. L. Annest, J. A. Mercy, M. Kresnow, and D. A. Pollock, "Lethality of Firearm-Related Injuries in the United States Population," *Annals of Emergency Medicine 35* (2000): 258-66.
10. See, for example, R. S. Jung and L. A. Jason, "Firearm Violence and the Effects of Gun Control Legislation," *American Journal of Community Psychology 16* (1988):

515-24; P. J. Cook, "The Effect of Gun Availability on Violent Crime Patterns," *Annals of the American Academy of Political and Social Sciences 455* (1981): 63-79; S. H. Decker, S. Pennell, and A. Caldwell, *Illegal Firearms: Access and Use by Arrestees* (Washington: National Institute of Justice, 1997).

11. Cited in Cook and Moore, "Guns, Gun Control, and Homicide," p. 247.

12. *Ibid.*

13. P. J. Cook and J. Ludwig, *Guns in America: Results of a Comprehensive National Survey on Firearms Ownership and Use* (Washington: Police Foundation, 1996).

14. *Ibid.*

15. Cook and Moore, "Guns, Gun Control, and Homicide," p. 248; *Firearm Injury and Death From Crime, 1993-97*, pp. 1-5.

16. Cook and Moore, "Guns, Gun Control, and Homicide," p. 248.

17. *Ibid.*, p. 249; A. Blumstein, "Youth Violence, Guns, and the Illicit-Drug Industry," *Journal of Criminal Law and Criminology 86* (1995): 10-36; K. M. Heide, "Why Kids Keep Killing: The Correlates, Causes, and Challenges of Juvenile Homicide," *Stanford Law and Policy Review 71* (1996): 43-49; H. M. Rose and P. D. McClain, *Race, Place, and Risk: Black Homicide in Urban America* (Albany: State University of New York Press, 1990).

18. *Firearm Injury and Death from Crime, 1993-97*, p. 2; *Crime in the United States*, pp. 14-16; Darnell F. Hawkins, "Explaining the Black Homicide Rate," *Journal of Interpersonal Violence 5* (1990): 151-63; R. Barri Flowers, *Minorities and Criminality* (Westport: Greenwood, 1988).

19. Flowers, *Minorities and Criminality*, pp. 95-104; R. W. Beasley and G. Antunes, "The Etiology of Urban Crime: An Ecological Analysis," *Criminology 22* (1974): 531-50; C. R. Block, "Race/Ethnicity and Patterns of Chicago Homicide, 1965-1981," *Crime and Delinquency 31* (1985): 104-16; Ramiro Martinez, "Latinos and Lethal Violence: The Impact of Poverty and Inequality," *Social Problems 43* (1996): 131-46.

20. A. L. Kellerman, F. P. Rivara, N. B. Rushforth, J. G. Banton, D. T. Reay, J. T. Francisco, A. B. Locci, J. P. Prodzinski, B. B. Hackman, and G. Somes, "Gun Ownership as a Risk Factor for Homicide in the Home," *New England Journal of Medicine 329* (1993): 1084-91.

21. Blumstein, "Youth Violence, Guns, and the Illicit-Drug Industry," pp. 10-36; J. F. Sheley and J. D. Wright, *In The Line of Fire: Youth, Guns, and Violence in America* (New York: Aldine de Gruyter, 1995); R. Barri Flowers, *Kids Who Commit Adult Crimes: A Study of Serious Juvenile Criminality and Delinquency* (Binghampton: Haworth, 2002).

22. Cook and Moore, "Guns, Gun Control, and Homicide," p. 256; Decker, Pennell, and Caldwell, *Illegal Firearms*; M. D. Smith, "Sources of Firearm Acquisition Among a Sample of Inner city Youths: Research Results and Policy Implications," *Journal of Criminal Justice 24* (1996): 361-67.

23. Cook and Moore, "Guns, Gun Control, and Homicide," pp. 256-65; D. McDowall, C. Loftin, and B. Wiersema, "Easing Concealed Firearms Laws: Effects on Homicide in Three States," *Journal of Criminal Law and Criminology 86* (1995): 193-206; F. E. Zimring and G. Hawkins, *Crime is Not the Problem: Lethal Violence in America* (New York: Oxford University Press, 1997).

24. See, for example, W. Wieczorek, J. Welte, and E. Abel, "Alcohol, Drugs, and Murder: A Study of Convicted Homicide Offenders," *Journal of Criminal Justice 18* (1990): 217-27; Kathleen Auerhahn and Robert N. Parker, "Drugs, Alcohol, and Homicide," in M. Dwayne Smith and Margaret A. Zahn, eds., *Studying and Preventing Homicide: Issues and Challenges* (Thousand Oaks: Sage, 1999), pp. 97-114; P. Lindquist, "Homicides Committed by Abusers of Alcohol and Illicit Drugs," *British Journal of Addiction 86* (1991): 321-26.

25. *Crime in the United States,* p. 19.

26. Marvin E. Wolfgang and R. B. Strohm, "The Relationship Between Alcohol and Criminal Homicide," *Quarterly Journal of Studies on Alcoholism 17* (1956): 411-26.

27. Marvin E. Wolfgang, *Patterns in Criminal Homicide* (Philadelphia: University of Pennsylvania Press, 1958).

28. Harwin L. Voss and John R. Hepburn, "Patterns in Criminal Homicide in Chicago," *Journal of Criminal Law, Criminology, and Political Science 59* (1968): 499-508.

29. Herbert A. Block and Gilbert Geis, *Man, Crime, and Society* (New York: Random House, 1962).

30. R. N. Parker and L. Rebhun, *Alcohol and Homicide: A Deadly Combination of Two American Traditions* (Albany: State University of New York Press, 1995).

31. R. Barri Flowers, *Drugs, Alcohol and Criminality in American Society* (Jefferson: McFarland, 1999), pp. 40-43, 148-50.

32. Cited in *Ibid.,* p. 42.

33. *Ibid.*

34. B. Spunt, H. Brownstein, P. Goldstein, M. Fendrich, and H. J. Liberty, "Drug Use by Homicide Offenders," *Journal of Psychoactive Drugs 27* (1995): 125-34.

35. P. Goldstein, H. H. Brownstein, P. J. Ryan, and P. A. Bellucci, "Crack and Homicide in New York City, 1988: A Conceptually Based Event Analysis," *Contemporary Drug Problems 16* (1989): 651-87.

36. H. H. Brownstein, H. Baxi, P. Goldstein, and P. Ryan, "The Relationship of Drugs, Drug Trafficking, and Drug Traffickers to Homicide," *Journal of Crime and Justice 15* (1992): 25-44.

37. Flowers, *Drugs, Alcohol, and Criminality in American Society,* pp. 42-43, 148-50.

38. U.S. Department of Justice, Bureau of Justice Statistics, *Murder in Large Urban Counties, 1988* (Washington: Government Printing Office, 1993), p. 5.

39. U.S. Department of Justice, Bureau of Justice Statistics, *Drugs, Crime, and the Justice System* (Washington: Government Printing Office, 1992), p. 5.

40. Flowers, *Drugs, Alcohol, and Criminality in American Society,* pp. 40-42, 170-72; U.S. Department of Justice, Bureau of Justice Statistics, *Survey of State Prison Inmates,* 1991 (Washington: Government Printing Office, 1993), p. 23.

41. R. Barri Flowers, *Domestic Crimes, Family Violence, and Child Abuse: A Study of Contemporary American Society* (Jefferson: McFarland, 2000), pp. 61-64; J. C. Campbell, *Assessing Dangerousness: Violence by Sexual Offenders, Batterers, and Child Abusers* (Thousand Oaks: Sage, 1995); N. C. Jurik and R. Winn, "Gender and Homicide: A Comparison of Men and Women Who Kill," *Violence and Victims 5,* 4 (1990): 227-42; Glenda K. Kantor and Murray A. Straus, "Substance Abuse as a Precipitant of Wife Abuse Victimization," *American Journal of Drug and Alcohol Abuse 15* (1989): 173-89.

42. Glenda K. Kantor and Jana L. Jasinski, "Dynamics and Risk Factors in Partner Violence," in Jana L. Jasinski and Linda M. Williams, eds., *Partner Violence: A Comprehensive Review of 20 Years of Research* (Thousand Oaks: Sage, 1998), pp. 20-23; Richard J. Gelles, *The Violent Home: A Study of Physical Aggression Between Husbands and Wives* (Thousand Oaks: Sage, 1972); J. Fagan, *Set and Setting Revisited: Influences of Alcohol and Illicit Drugs on the Social Context of Violent Events* (Rockville: National Institution on Alcohol Abuse and Alcoholism Research, 1993), pp. 161-91.

43. J. Fagan, "Intoxication and Aggression," in M. Tonry and J. Q. Wilson, eds., *Drugs and Crime* (Chicago: University of Chicago Press, 1990), pp. 241-320; P. J. Goldstein, P. A. Bellucci, B. J. Spunt, and T. Miller, *Frequency of Cocaine Use and Violence: A Comparison Between Women and Men* (New York: Narcotic and Drug Research, 1989).

44. W. R. Blount, I. J. Silverman, C. S. Sellers, and R. A. Seese, "Alcohol and Drug Use Among Abused Women Who Kill, Abused Women Who Don't, and Their Abusers," *Journal of Drug Issues 24* (1994): 165-77.

45. *Ibid. See also* J. W. Welte and E. L. Abel, "Homicide: Drinking by the Victim," *Journal of Studies on Alcohol 50* (1989): 197-201.

46. Flowers, *Minorities and Criminality*, pp. 83-130; D. Huizinga, R. Loeber, and T. P. Thornberry, *Urban Delinquency and Substance Abuse* (Washington: Office of Justice Programs, 1994); G. LaFree, "Race and Crime Trends in the United States, 1946-1990," in D. F. Hawkins, ed., *Ethnicity, Race and Crime: Perspectives Across Time and Place* (Albany: State University of New York Press, 1995), pp. 169-93.

47. Flowers, *Minorities and Criminality*, pp. 39-55, 83-130; R. T. Schaefer, *Racial and Ethnic Groups*, 5th ed. (New York: Harper Collins, 1993); M. B. Harris, "Aggression, Gender, and Ethnicity," *Aggression and Violent Behavior 1*, 2 (1996): 123-46; A. Valdez, "Persistent Poverty, Crime, and Drugs: U.S.-Mexican Border Region," in J. Moore and R. Pinderhughes, eds., *In the Barrios: Latinos and the Underclass Debate* (New York: Russell Sage, 1993), pp. 195-210; R. Bachman, *Death and Violence on the Reservation: Homicide, Family Violence, and Suicide in American Indian Populations* (Westport: Auburn House, 1992).

48. J. Fagan, "The Social Organization of Drug Use and Drug Dealing Among Urban Gangs," *Criminology 27* (1989): 633-69; P. J. Meehan and P. W. O'Carroll, "Gangs, Drugs, and Homicide in Los Angeles," *American Journal of Disease Control 146* (1992): 683-87; H. J. Brumm and D. O. Cloninger, "The Drug War and the Homicide Rate: A Direct Correlation?" *Cato Journal 14* (1995): 509-17; J. Kasarda, "Inner-City Concentrated Poverty and Neighborhood Distress: 1970-1990," *Housing Policy Debate 4*, 3 (1993): 253-302.

49. See, for example, Wieczorek, Welte, and Abel, "Alcohol, Drugs, and Murder," pp. 217-27.

50. Blumstein, "Youth Violence, Guns, and the Illicit-Drug Industry," pp. 10-36; M. Fendrich, M. E. Mackesy-Amiti, P. Goldstein, B. Spunt, and H. Brownstein, "Substance Involvement Among Juvenile Murderers: Comparisons with Older Offenders Based on Interviews with Prison Inmates," *International Journal of the Addictions 30* (1995): 1363-82.

51. Kathleen M. Heide, "Youth Homicide," in M. Dwayne Smith and Margaret A. Zahn, eds., *Studying and Preventing Homicide: Issues and Challenges* (Thousand Oaks: Sage, 1999), p. 188.

52. Flowers, *Kids Who Commit Adult Crimes;* Heide, "Youth Homicide," p. 188; D. W. Osgood, *Drugs, Alcohol, and Violence* (Boulder: University of Colorado, Institute of Behavioral Science, 1995); R. M. Lerner, *America's Youth in Crisis* (Thousand Oaks: Sage, 1994).

53. Flowers, *Kids Who Commit Adult Crimes;* R. Barri Flowers and H. Loraine Flowers, *Murders in the United States: Crimes, Killers, and Victims of the Twentieth Century* (Jefferson: McFarland, 2001), pp. 147-52, 183-87.

Chapter 3

MURDER AND THE CRIMINAL JUSTICE SYSTEM

Violent crimes have been on the decline in recent years in the United States, with murder and nonnegligent manslaughter, in particular, showing the greatest reduction. This is attributed to a combination of factors including a decrease in gun violence by young people, law enforcement crackdowns on violent crime, and new laws imposing stiffer penalties and longer periods of incarceration for violent offenders. As a result, fewer people are being arrested for murder and going through the criminal justice process. However, the felonious killing of law enforcement has been on the rise, causing concern among those responsible for bringing violent and homicidal offenders to justice. Moreover, thousands of homicides continue to be committed each year in this country, affecting individuals from every walk of life. Blacks and Hispanics tend to be disproportionately involved in arrests and incarceration for murder, but whites and offenders from other racial and ethnic groups are represented as well in homicide offender statistics. The crime of murder remains the top priority of law enforcement on the whole and convicted murderers represent the most serious offenders among the nation's inmate population, including virtually all death row inmates.

ARRESTS AND MURDER

Official arrest data is collected through the Federal Bureau of Investigation's Uniform Crime Reporting (UCR) Program, which is a "nationwide cooperative statistical effort of over 17,000 city, county, and state law enforcement agencies voluntarily reporting data on crimes brought to their attention."[1] According to the UCR, in 1999 there were an estimated 14,790 arrests for murder and nonnegligent manslaughter in the United

States, defined as "the willful (nonnegligent) killing of one human being by another. The classification of this offense . . . is based solely on police investigation as opposed to the determination of a court, medical examiner, coroner, jury, or other judicial body."[2] The figure excludes "deaths caused by negligence, suicide, or accident; justifiable homicides; and attempts to murder or assaults to murder, which are scored as aggravated assaults."[3]

Murder Clearances

A crime is cleared or solved by a law enforcement agency "when at least one person is arrested, charged with the commission of an offense, and turned over to the court for prosecution. . . . Just as the arrest of one individual may clear multiple crimes, the arrest of many persons may clear only one offense. Furthermore, clearances recorded for a specific year . . . may include offenses that occurred in previous years."[4] Exceptional clearances may occur when circumstances prevent formally charging an offender, such as the person's death due to suicide or justifiable homicide, or inability to extradite the offender.

In 1999, 69 percent of murders in the United States were cleared by law enforcement agencies, giving it the highest clearance rate among Crime Index offenses, consisting of the eight most serious and violent crimes recorded. The rate of clearance for murder tended to be lowest in cities and highest in rural counties (see Figure 3.1). Seventy-five percent of murders in rural counties were cleared, with clearances of 74 percent of suburban counties, and 67 percent in cities.

Figure 3.1
Clearance Rates for Murder, by Population, 1999

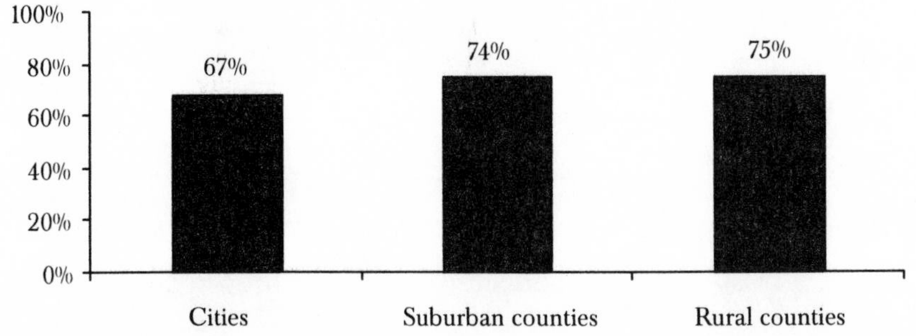

Source: Derived from U.S. Department of Justice, Federal Bureau of Investigation, *Crime in the United States: Uniform Crime Reports 1999* (Washington: Government Printing Office, 2000), p. 23.

As shown in Figure 3.2, of the geographical regions in the country, the clearance rate for murders was highest in 1999 among Northeastern states at 78 percent, followed by Southern states at 71 percent, and Midwestern and Western states, which both had a clearance rate of 63 percent.

Figure 3.2
Clearance Rates for Murder, by Geographic Region, 1999

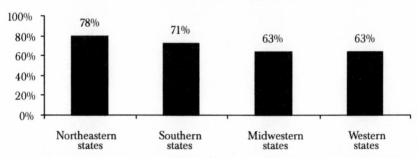

Source: Derived from U.S. Department of Justice, Federal Bureau of Investigation, *Crime in the United States: Uniform Crime Reports 1999* (Washington: Government Printing Office, 2000), p. 23.

Murder clearances predominantly link homicides to adult offenders. In 1999, 94 percent of the murders cleared across the United States involved persons age eighteen and over. Proportionately, the rate of juvenile involvement in murder clearances was lower than for any other Crime Index offense.

Age and Arrestees for Murder

The vast majority of persons arrested for murder and nonnegligent manslaughter are age eighteen and older (see Figure 3.3). Ninety-one percent of the arrestees in the United States in 1999 were of adult age, with 9 percent juvenile. More than half the persons arrested for murder and nonnegligent manslaughter were under the age of twenty-five, with nearly 42 percent between eighteen and twenty-four years of age. The highest number of arrestees of any age group was eighteen and nineteen. Among juveniles, almost 75 percent of arrestees were ages sixteen and seventeen.[5]

Sex and Arrestees for Murder

Murder is largely a male crime. In 1999, males constituted nearly 89 percent of the persons arrested for murder and nonnegligent manslaughter in

Figure 3.3
Persons Arrested for Murder and Nonnegligent Manslaughter, by Age, 1999

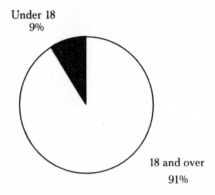

Source: Derived from U.S. Department of Justice, Federal Bureau of Investigation, *Crime in the United States: Uniform Crime Reports 1999* (Washington: Government Printing Office, 2000), p. 222.

the United States with females representing just over 11 percent of the arrestees (see Figure 3.4). With respect to sex and age, a proportionately higher number of adult females than adult males were arrested for murder and nonnegligent manslaughter, with nearly 94 percent of female arrestees age eighteen and older compared to around 91 percent of male arrestees.

Figure 3.4
Persons Arrested for Murder and Nonnegligent Manslaughter, by Sex, 1999

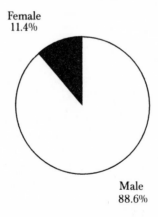

Source: Derived from U.S. Department of Justice, Federal Bureau of Investigation, *Crime in the United States: Uniform Crime Reports 1999* (Washington: Government Printing Office, 2000), p. 229.

Race and Arrestees for Murder

Blacks are overrepresented in homicide arrests relative to their population figures. In 1999, blacks constituted more than half of all persons arrested in the United States for murder and nonnegligent manslaughter (see Figure 3.5). Just over 52 percent of the arrestees were black, with nearly 46 percent white, 1 percent American Indian or Alaska Native, and slightly more than 1 percent Asian or Pacific Islanders.

Figure 3.5
Persons Arrested for Murder and Nonnegligent Manslaughter, by Race, 1999

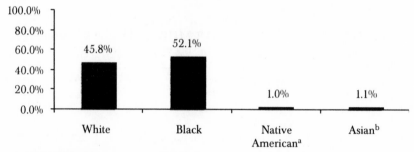

a Includes American Indians or Alaskan Natives.
b Includes Pacific Islanders.

Source: Derived from U.S. Department of Justice, Federal Bureau of Investigation, *Crime in the United States: Uniform Crime Reports 1999* (Washington: Government Printing Office, 2000), p. 231.

A smaller proportion of juvenile arrestees for murder were black, while the proportion of persons from other races was slightly higher. Blacks accounted for 49 percent of those under the age of eighteen arrested for murder and nonnegligent manslaughter, with whites comprising 47 percent of the arrestees, and other racial minorities making up 4 percent of the total.[6]

Young blacks, in particular, face the highest risk for involvement in homicidal behavior as arrestees, offenders, and victims.[7] Various studies have supported this conclusion, relating it to such correlates as a higher concentration of blacks in high crime rate inner cities, possession of illegal weapons, youth gangs, and drug dealing.[8]

Although the UCR does not record ethnic differences among arrestees, many studies have found that Hispanics have a disproportionately high rate of involvement in homicides as arrestees and offenders.[9] Hispanic murder offenders tend to have some of the same characteristics of African American murder offenders with regard to inner-city dynamics and gang and drug involvement;[10] though some cultural differences exist in the commission and nature of homicides.[11]

Geographic Region and Arrests for Murder

The rate of arrests for murder nationally is lower than that of any other Crime Index offense. As shown in Table 3.1, in 1999 the rate of arrests for murder and nonnegligent manslaughter in the United States was 5.7 per 100,000 inhabitants, compared to an overall Crime Index arrest rate of 880.0 and violent crime arrests rate of 244.5 per 100,000 persons.

Geographically, the highest recorded rate of arrests for murder and non-negligent manslaughter in 1999 was in the Midwest at 8.7 per 100,000 inhabitants, followed by the South at 6.1, and West at 4.8, with the lowest rate in the Northeast at 3.3 per 100,000 inhabitants.

Table 3.1

NUMBER AND RATE OF ARRESTS FOR MURDER AND NONNEGLIGENT MANSLAUGHTER, BY GEOGRAPHIC REGION, 1999

Offense charged	United States total (8,546 agencies; population 171,831,00)	Northeast (2,078 agencies; population 32,633,000)	Midwest (1,856 agencies; population 32,405,000)	South (3,004 agencies; population 51,697,00)	West (1,608 agencies; population 55,096,000)
TOTAL	9,136,294	1,378,177	1,798,752	3,119,227	2,840,138
Rate[a]	5,317.0	4,223.3	5,550.8	6,033.8	5,154.9
Murder and nonnegligent manslaughter	9,727	1,080	2,817	3,158	2,672
Rate	5.7	3.3	8.7	6.1	4.8
Violent crime[b]	420,156	70,132	68,666	112,551	168,807
Rate	244.5	214.9	211.9	217.7	306.4
Crime Index total[c]	1,512,073	238,520	277,577	461,518	534,458
Rate	880.0	730.9	856.6	892.8	970.0

[a] Rate is for number of arrests per 100,000 inhabitants.

[b] Violent crimes are offenses of murder, forcible rape, robbery, and aggravated assault.

[c] Includes arson.

Source: Adapted from U.S. Department of Justice, Federal Bureau of Investigation, *Crime in the United States: Uniform Crime Reports 1999* (Washington: Government Printing Office, 2000), p. 23.

Arrest Trends for Murder

UCR data indicates that fewer persons are being arrested for murder. Ten-year arrest trends show that between 1990 and 1999, total arrests for murder and nonnegligent manslaughter in the United States dropped by more than

Figure 3.6
Ten-Year Arrest Trends for Murder and Nonnegligent Manslaughter, 1990-1999

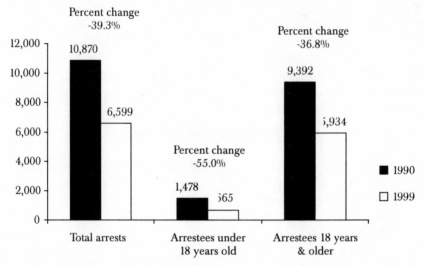

Source: Derived from U.S. Department of Justice, Federal Bureau of Investigation, *Crime in the United States: Uniform Crime Reports 1999* (Washington: Government Printing Office, 2000), p. 217.

Figure 3.7
Ten-Year Arrest Trends for Murder and Nonnegligent Manslaughter, by Gender, 1990-1999

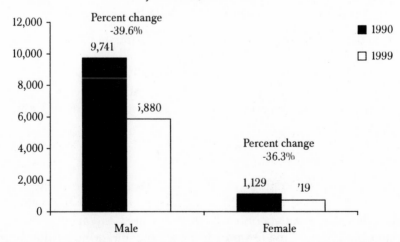

Source: Derived from U.S. Department of Justice, Federal Bureau of Investigation, *Crime in the United States: Uniform Crime Reports 1999* (Washington: Government Printing Office, 2000), p. 217.

39 percent (see Figure 3.6). The decline was even more dramatic among arrestees under the age of eighteen, decreasing by 55 percent.

Significant reductions in homicide arrests were also recorded by gender (see Figure 3.7). Between 1990 and 1999, male arrests for murder and non-negligent manslaughter fell by almost 40 percent, while female arrests dropped more than 36 percent.

Preliminary data for 2000 reveals that homicide arrests continued to be on the decline in most categories.[12]

Limitations of the Uniform Crime Reports

Though the UCR Program is currently the most important measurement of homicide and other serious and violent offenses, including arrest and offender characteristics, there are shortcomings that hamper the Program's effectiveness. The most important with respect to homicide data may be the "unknown relationship between the number of crimes actually committed, the number of those reported to the police, and the number of those so reported, actually recorded and reported by the police."[13]

Each year there are hundreds, perhaps thousands, of people reported (or not reported) missing in the United States and never heard from again. Many of these people could be the victims of foul play, but cannot be ascertained as such. In other instances where law enforcement may be aware of a homicide, more than three in ten such cases are never cleared or solved to appear in UCR arrest data.

Other common criticisms against the UCR Program include:

• Official data reflect only those crimes law enforcement agencies are aware of.
• Law enforcement agencies may be politically motivated or have other motives in underreporting or inflating arrest statistics.
• An overreliance on percent changes in the total volume of Crime Index offenses.
• An overlapping in defining what constitutes a crime—such as arrest, charge, conviction, and/or incarceration.[14]

Some of the shortcomings of the UCR Program are being addressed through its redesigned or new National Incidence-Based Reporting System (NIBRS) that "collects data on each single incident and arrest within twenty-two offense categories made up of forty-six specific crimes called Group A offenses."[15] Included amongst these offenses are the homicide offenses of murder and nonnegligent manslaughter, negligent manslaughter, and justifiable homicide.

According to the FBI, "The goals of NIBRS are to enhance the quantity, quality, and timeliness of crime data collected by law enforcement and to improve the methodology used for compiling, analyzing, auditing, and publishing the collected crime data."[16] As such, the NIBRS is believed to be able to "provide law enforcement with . . . more detailed, accurate, and meaningful data than produced by the traditional summary UCR Program."[17]

In spite of the promise of the NIBRS, in a study of its effects on UCR crime statistics with respect to homicide data, it was found that "when comparing data from the same year for the jurisdictions in this study. . .murder rates are the same," for Summary UCR and NIBRS.[18]

Currently there are nineteen state programs certified for participation in the NIBRS and fourteen other state programs seeking inclusion.

LAW ENFORCEMENT OFFICERS KILLED

As the front line in the war on violent crimes and homicide, the police are vulnerable when attempting to make arrests or investigating crimes. According to the FBI, in 2000 there were fifty-one law enforcement officers killed in the line of duty in the United States—nine more than the forty-three killed while on duty in 1999.[19]

Firearms were the weapon used most often in the killing of police officers, with thirty-three dying by handguns, ten from rifles, and four by shotgun death. Thirty officers died in spite of wearing body armor during the fatal encounter.

Regionally, the vast majority of police officers were killed in the South (see Figure 3.8). Thirty-two officers were killed in the line of duty in Southern states, followed by Midwestern states with thirteen, Western states with four, and two were homicide victims in the United States territory of Puerto Rico.

Figure 3.8
Law Enforcement Officers Killed While on Duty, by Geographic Region, 2000

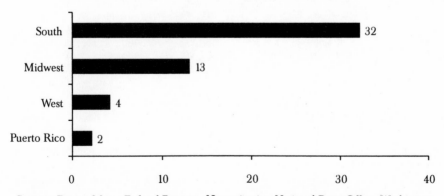

Source: Derived from Federal Bureau of Investigation National Press Office, Washington, May 15, 2001.

The fifty-one law enforcement officer homicides involved fifty different incidents; forty-eight of which were cleared by the arrest of one or more persons or through exceptional means.

MURDER AND PRISON INMATES

According to the Bureau of Justice Statistics, around 12 percent of state prison inmates and 2 percent of federal prison inmates in the United States were convicted of murder or nonnegligent manslaughter.[20] The vast majority of homicide offenders behind bars are male. Overall, males constitute more than nine in ten state and federal prisoners, and persons age eighteen and over represent more than 99 percent of all persons under state and federal correctional authority.[21]

The characteristics of state prison inmates convicted of murder can be seen in Table 3.2. In 1998, there were an estimated 134,600 sentenced prisoners under state jurisdiction for murder and nonnegligent manslaughter. Of these, 128,500–or nearly 96 percent–were male inmates, with less than 5 percent female inmates.

With respect to race, there were an estimated 67,100 blacks incarcerated for murder and nonnegligent manslaughter, compared to 42,400 whites. Blacks are overrepresented in prison figures, accounting for more than 50 percent of inmates convicted of violent crimes.[22]

Table 3.2

ESTIMATED NUMBER OF SENTENCED PRISONERS UNDER STATE JURISDICTION FOR HOMICIDE OFFENSES, BY GENDER, RACE, AND HISPANIC ORIGIN, 1998[a]

Offense	All	Male	Female	White	Black	Hispanic
Total	1,141,700	1,071,400	70,300	380,400	531,100	194,000
Violent offenses[b]	545,200	525,100	20,100	180,300	257,700	87,600
Murder[c]	134,600	128,500	6,100	42,400	67,100	21,500
Manslaughter	17,600	15,800	1,800	6,200	7,100	3,400

[a] Data are for inmates with a sentence of more than one year under the jurisdiction of State correctional authorities.

[b] Includes rape, other sexual assault, robbery, assault, and other violent offenses.

[c] Includes nonnegligent manslaughter.

Source: Adapted from U.S. Department of Justice, Bureau of Justice Statistics Bulletin, *Prisoners in 1999* (Washington: Office of Justice Programs, 2000), p. 10.

Hispanics are also disproportionately represented as prison inmates and violent offenders. In 1998, there were approximately 21,500 state prisoners of Hispanic origin incarcerated for murder and nonnegligent manslaughter.

Nearly 18,000 inmates were imprisoned in state facilities for manslaughter in 1998, defined as "the unlawful killing of one human being by another without express or implied intent to do injury."[23]

Among sentenced federal prisoners in 1998, there were 1,344 inmates convicted of homicide offenses. This represented a 9 percent increase from 1990 (see Figure 3.9). However, between 1995 and 1999, the number of sentenced inmates in federal prisons for murder, nonnegligent manslaughter, and negligent manslaughter grew by more than 39 percent.

Figure 3.9
Sentenced Federal Prisoners Convicted of Homicide[a], 1990-1999

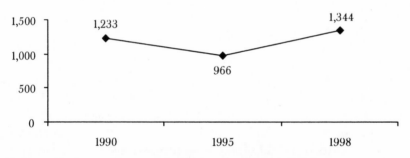

[a]Includes murder, nonnegligent manslaughter, and negligent manslaughter

Source: Derived from U.S. Department of Justice, Federal Bureau of Investigation, *Prisoners in 1999* (Washington: Government Printing Office, 2000), p. 23.

Overall, the number of state prisoners held for violent offenses has risen sharply in recent years. Between 1990 and 1998, violent sentenced prisoners increased by 229,300, representing 51 percent of the total growth in state prison inmates (see Table 3.3). With regard to race and ethnicity, black and Hispanic inmates had the highest rate of growth among violent offenders over the period, rising 52 and 56 percent, respectively, while the number of violent white prisoners grew 45 percent. The percentage of sentenced prisoners convicted of violent crimes in total and by race and ethnicity far exceeded that of prisoners convicted of all other offenses.

Surveys of inmates show that a high percentage of homicide offenders were victims of abuse, or abused drugs or alcohol prior to being admitted to state prison.[24] Studies on homicide have found that killers often have histories of child physical or sexual abuse and substance abuse, both seen as antecedents to homicidal behavior.[25]

Table 3.3

TOTAL GROWTH OF SENTENCED PRISONERS UNDER STATE
JURISDICTION, BY OFFENSE, RACE, AND HISPANIC ORIGIN, 1990-1998

	Total		White		Black		Hispanic	
	Increase, 1990-98	*% of Total*	*Increase, 1990-98*	*% of Total*	*Increase, 1990-98*	*% of Total*	*Increase, 1990-98*	*% of Total*
Total	452,100	100%	137,000	100%	216,400	100%	78,700	102%
Violent	229,300	51%	62,700	45%	111,600	52%	43,900	56%
Property	67,900	15%	29,000	21%	26,800	12%	9,800	12%
Drug	87,100	19%	16,700	12%	55,000	25%	13,000	18%
Public-order	68,100	15%	29,500	21%	22,800	11%	11,800	15%

Source: Adapted from U.S. Department of Justice, Bureau of Justice Statistics Bulletin, *Prisoners in 1999* (Washington: Office of Justice Programs, 2000), p. 10.

CAPITAL PUNISHMENT

In 1999, there were 3,527 prisoners on death row for various murder offenses in the United States, according to the Justice Department.[26] Of these, 3,477 were men and fifty were women. The oldest inmate sentenced to death was eighty-four, the youngest eighteen. Ninety-eight inmates were executed during the year—all men. Of these, there were sixty-one whites, thirty-three blacks, two American Indians, and one Asian. Nine of the inmates put to death were classified as Hispanic. Ninety-six percent of death row inmates were executed by lethal injection.

Table 3.4 profiles the criminal history of prisoners under a sentence of death, by race and Hispanic origin in 1999. Nearly two-thirds of the 3,527 death row inmates had a prior felony conviction, while more than 8 percent had a prior homicide conviction. Almost seven in ten blacks had a previous felony conviction, with just over six in ten whites, and just under six in ten Hispanics. A roughly equal percentage of inmates by race had a prior murder conviction.

At the time of the capital offense, 40 percent of the inmates had a criminal justice status such as charges pending, probation, or parole. Six in ten death row inmates had no legal status at the time of the capital offense.

Between 1977 and 1999, a total of 6,365 persons were under a sentence of death in the United States (see Table 3.5). The vast majority were white or black. Among those executed over the period, nearly 11 percent were white, 8 percent black, almost 9 percent Hispanic, and nearly 11 percent belonging to other racial groups. More than 35 percent of persons on death row received dispositions other than being executed.

Table 3.4

CRIMINAL HISTORY PROFILE OF PRISONERS UNDER SENTENCE OF DEATH, BY RACE AND HISPANIC ORIGIN, 1999

Prisoners under sentence of death

	Number				Percent[a]			
	All[b]	White	Black	Hiapanic	All[b]	White	Black	Hispanic
U.S. total	3,527	1,651	1,500	325	100%	100%	100%	100%
Prior felony convictions								
Yes	2,085	949	939	172	64.1%	61.9%	68.3%	58.3%
No	1,166	584	436	123	35.9%	38.1%	31.7%	41.7%
Not reported	276							
Prior homicide convictions								
Yes	290	134	128	22	8.4%	8.3%	8.7%	6.9%
No	3,166	1,487	1,337	297	91.6%	91.7%	91.3%	93.1%
Not reported	71							
Legal status at time of capital offense								
Charges pending	228	127	90	11	7.4%	8.6%	6.9%	4.0%
Probation	311	134	144	27	10.0%	9.1%	11.1%	9.9%
Parole	554	229	250	65	17.9%	15.5%	19.2%	23.8%
Prison escapee	39	25	10	3	1.3%	1.7%	0.8%	1.1%
Incarcerated	86	36	44	5	2.8%	2.4%	3.4%	1.8%
Other status	21	11	8	1	0.7%	0.7%	0.6%	0.4%
None	1,860	916	755	161	60.0%	62.0%	58.0%	59.0%
Not reported	428							

[a] Percentages are based on those offenders for whom data were reported. Detail may not add to total because of rounding.
[b] Includes persons of other races.

Source: U.S. Department of Justice, Bureau of Justice Statistics Bulletin, *Capital Punishment 1999* (Washington: Office of Justice Programs, 2000), p. 10.

In preliminary data for 2000, there were 85 prisoners put to death in the United States, a 13 percent decline from the total in 1999. Of these, forty-eight were white, thirty-six black, and one was Native American. Two women were among those who were executed.

Table 3.5
PRISONERS UNDER SENTENCE OF DEATH WHO WERE EXECUTED OR
RECEIVED OTHER DISPOSITIONS, BY RACE AND HISPANIC ORIGIN,
1977-1999

Race/Hispanic origin[b]	Total under sentence of death, 1977-99[c]	Prisoners executed		Prisoners who received other dispositions	
		Number	Percent of total	Number	Percent of total
Total	6,365	598	9.4%	2,240	35.2%
White	3,141	334	10.6%	1,156	36.8%
Black	2,633	211	8.0%	922	35.0%
Hispanic	498	43	8.6%	130	26.1%
Other	93	10	10.8%	32	34.4%

[a] Includes persons removed from under a sentence of death because of statutes struck down on appeal, sentences or convictions vacated, commutations, or death other than by execution.

[b] White, black, and other categories exclude Hispanics.

[c] Includes persons sentenced to death prior to 1977 who were still under sentence of death on 12/31/99 (9), persons sentenced to death prior to 1977 whose death sentence was removed between 1977 and 12/31/99 (371), and persons sentenced to death between 1977 and 12/31/99 (5,985).

Source: U.S. Department of Justice, Bureau of Justice Statistics Bulletin, *Capital Punishment 1999* (Washington: Office of Justice Programs, 2000), p. 11.

JUVENILE KILLERS IN DETENTION

Although an increasing number of juvenile murderers are being tried as adults, less than 1 percent of persons in state and federal adult correctional facilities are seventeen years of age and younger.[28] Most juveniles convicted of murder are held in juvenile residential placement facilities. According to the Department of Justice's 1999 national report, *Juvenile Offenders and Victims*, as of October 29, 1997, there were approximately 2,000 juveniles in residential placement for criminal homicide.[29] This represented around 2 percent of the total population of juvenile inmates. Virtually all juvenile homicide offenders in residential placement are held in public facilities as opposed to private facilities.

Minorities are disproportionately likely to be in juvenile residential placement for murder. As shown in Figure 3.10, 44 percent of juveniles being held for criminal homicide in 1997 were black and 30 percent were classified as Hispanic. White juveniles made up 19 percent of those confined to residential placement facilities for criminal homicide, with Asians and American Indians accounting for 5 percent and 2 percent of the total, respectively.

Figure 3.10
Juveniles in Residential Placement on October 29, 1997, for
Criminal Homicide, by Race and Ethnicity

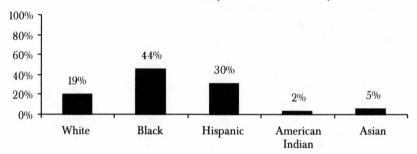

Source: Derived from U.S. Department of Justice, Federal Bureau of Investigation, *Juvenile Offenders and Victims: 1999 National Report* (Washington: Government Printing Office, 1999), p. 195.

NOTES

1. U.S. Department of Justice, Federal Bureau of Investigation, *Crime in the United States: Uniform Crime Reports 1999* (Washington: Government Printing Office, 2000), p. 1.
2. *Ibid.*, pp. 13, 212.
3. *Ibid.*, p. 13.
4. *Ibid.*, p. 201.
5. *Ibid.*, p. 224.
6. *Ibid.*, p. 231.
7. R. Barri Flowers, *Minorities and Criminality* (Westport: Greenwood, 1988), pp. 83-88, 131-39; L. A. Fingerhut and J. C. Kleinman, "International and Interstate Comparisons of Homicide Among Young Males," *Journal of the American Medical Association 263* (1990): 292-95; W. Bonger, *Race and Crime* (New York: Columbia University Press, 1943); H. M. Rose and P. D. McClain, *Race, Place, and Risk: Black Homicide in Urban America* (Albany: State University of New York Press, 1990).
8. See, for example, Darnell F. Hawkins, "Explaining the Black Homicide Rate," *Journal of Interpersonal Violence 5* (1990): 151-63; Y. Shin, D. Jedlicka, and E. S. Lee, "Homicide Among Blacks," *Phylon 39* (1977): 399-406; A. Blumstein, "Youth Violence, Guns, and the Illicit-Drug Industry," *Journal of Criminal Law and Criminology 86* (1995): 10-36.
9. Flowers, *Minorities and Criminality*, pp. 95-104; Ramiro Martinez, Jr., and Matthew T. Lee, "Latinos and Homicide," in M. Dwayne Smith and Margaret A. Zahn, eds., *Studying and Preventing Homicide: Issues and Challenges* (Thousand Oaks: Sage, 1999), pp. 159-74; F. Bean and M. Tienda, *The Hispanic Population of the United States* (New York: Russell Sage, 1987).
10. Flowers, *Minorities and Criminality*, pp. 83-104, 131-38; Martinez, Jr., and Lee, "Latinos and Homicide," pp. 159-72; R. N. Parker, "Poverty, Subculture of Violence, and Type of Homicide," *Social Forces 67* (1989): 983-1007.

11. R. T. Shaefer, *Racial and Ethnic Groups*, 5th ed. (New York: Harper Collins, 1993); R. Martinez, "Homicide Among Miami's Ethnic Groups: Anglos, Blacks, and Latinos in the 1990s," *Homicide Studies 1* (1997): 17-34; R. D. Alba, J. R. Logan, and P. Bellair, "Living With Crime: The Implications of Racial/Ethnic Differences in Suburban Location," *Social Forces 73* (1994): 395-434.

12. Uniform Crime Reports preliminary figures for 2000, http://www.fbi.gov.

13. Charles H. Shireman and Frederic G. Reamer, *Rehabilitating Juvenile Justice* (New York: Columbia University Press, 1986), p. 20.

14. R. Barri Flowers, *Female Crime, Criminals and Cellmates: An Exploration of Female Criminality and Delinquency* (Jefferson: McFarland, 1995), p. 20; Edwin W. Sutherland and Donald R. Cressey, Criminology, 10th ed. (Philadelphia: J. B. Lippincott, 1978), p. 29.

15. FBI National Incidence-Based Reporting System, http://www.fbi.gov/ucr/faqs.htm.

16. FBI, http://www/fbi.gov/hq/cjisd/ucr.htm.

17. FBI National Incidence-Based Reporting System.

18. U.S. Department of Justice, Bureau of Justice Statistics Special Report, *Effects of NIBRS on Crime Statistics* (Washington: Office of Justice Programs, 2000), p. 1.

19. FBI National Press Office, 2001, http://www.fbi.gov.

20. U.S. Department of Justice, Bureau of Justice Statistics, *Correctional Populations in the United States*, 1997 (Washington: Department of Justice, 2000).

21. *Ibid.*

22. U.S. Department of Justice, Bureau of Justice Statistics Bulletin, *Prisoners in 1999* (Washington: Office of Justice Programs, 2000), p. 10.

23. *American Heritage Dictionary* (New York: Dell, 1994), p. 506.

24. U.S. Department of Justice, Bureau of Justice Statistics, *Prior Abuse Reported by Inmates and Probationers* (Washington: Office of Justice Programs, 1999), p. 3; R. Barri Flowers, *Drugs, Alcohol and Criminality in American Society* (Jefferson: McFarland, 1999), pp. 171-73.

25. Flowers, *Drugs, Alcohol and Criminality in American Society*, pp. 163-73; R. Barri Flowers, *Domestic Crimes, Family Violence and Child Abuse: A Study of Contemporary American Society* (Jefferson: McFarland, 2000), pp. 197-202, 217.

26. U.S. Department of Justice, Bureau of Justice Statistics Bulletin, *Capital Punishment 1999* (Washington: Office of Justice Programs, 2000), p. 1.

27. *Ibid.*, p. 12.

28. *Correctional Populations in the United States, 1997.*

29. U.S. Department of Justice, *Juvenile Offenders and Victims: 1999 National Report* (Washington: Office of Juvenile Justice and Delinquency Prevention, 1999), p. 188.

Part II

DOMESTIC MURDER

Chapter 4

INTIMATE HOMICIDE

Domestic homicides are most likely to involve intimates. Each year in the United States, thousands of people are killed by husbands, wives, ex-spouses, boyfriends, girlfriends, and other ex-intimates. These homicides are typically a symptom of overall violence between intimates and often correlate with substance abuse, possession of firearms, sexual jealousy, separation, and related factors. Women are especially likely to be victims of intimate homicide, usually after a pattern of spousal or domestic violence. On the other hand, women are most likely to kill male intimates in self-defense from male violence or the threat of violence. Intimate homicides have been on the decline in recent years, but still possess a serious threat among intimates and are often reflective of other intrafamilial violent and homicidal behavior.

THE EXTENT OF INTIMATE PARTNER HOMICIDE

How significant is the problem of homicide involving intimates? According to the U.S. Department of Justice, there were 1,642 persons murdered by an intimate–defined as a current or former spouse, or boyfriend or girlfriend–in the United States in 1999.[1] Intimate partner murders represented 11 percent of all homicides.

Women are far more likely to be victims of intimate homicide than men (see Figure 4.1). In 1999, 74 percent of those murdered by an intimate partner were female, compared to 26 percent male. Females in every age category were more likely to be victims of intimate partner homicide than males. Both female and male victims age thirty-five to forty-five were murdered at higher rates than intimates slain in other age categories. In all, homicides involving an intimate constituted 32 percent of the females murdered and 4 percent of the males murdered.[2]

Figure 4.1

Victims of Intimate Partner Homicides, by Gender, 1999

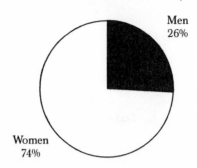

Source: Derived from U.S. Department of Justice, Bureau of Justice Statistics, 2001, http://www.ojp.usdoj.gov/bjs/abstract/pva99.htm.

Women are more likely to be murdered by a male intimate than any other type of killer.[3] Studies show that more than twice as many women are murdered by an intimate partner as a stranger.[4] Seven in ten female victims of homicide were killed by a husband, ex-husband, boyfriend, or ex-boyfriend.[5] Separated or divorced women are especially at risk for being murdered by an ex-intimate. In one study, approximately half the intimate homicides of women were committed after the victim separated from the male murderer.[6] Another study found that one in four women slain by intimate partners were killed while trying to separate.[7]

In spite of the general one-sided nature of intimate partner homicides, both men and women have shown themselves to be capable of committing intimate murder, as the following cases indicate:

- On March 10, 1980, 56-year-old Jean Harris shot and killed her lover, Herman Tarnower, in his home in Purchase, New York. The murder of the author of *The Scarsdale Diet* book came following a fourteen-year tumultuous relationship between the two. Harris was convicted and sentenced to fifteen years to life in prison. In January 1993, she was released after the governor commuted her sentence.

- In the 1980s, Betty Lou Beets murdered two husbands and attempted to murder a third in Texas. The Black Widow murderess was motivated by monetary gain in collecting on life insurance and a pension. Beets was charged with capitol murder in the shooting deaths of Doyle Barker and James Beets, found guilty, and sentenced to death. She was executed in February 2000.

- On March 4, 1985, 76-year-old Roswell Gilbert shot to death his 73-year-old wife, Emily, in the couple's condominium in Ft. Lauderdale, Florida. The victim suffered from Alzheimer's disease. Gilbert, a retired engineer, was found guilty of first-degree murder and sentenced to life in prison with no chance for parole. On August 2, 1990, the 81-year-old intimate killer was granted clemency by Florida's governor and released from prison.

- On October 23, 1989, 30-year-old Charles Stuart, shot to death his pregnant wife, Carol, in their car in Boston, Massachusetts. The couple's infant child, delivered by cesarean section, died seventeen days later. Stuart, who was having an affair, stood to gain financially by collecting on his wife's life insurance. In January 1990, he committed suicide as authorities closed in on him.
- On January 16, 1997, Scott Falater stabbed his wife, Yarmila, to death at the couple's home in Phoenix, Arizona. The 42-year-old engineer had a history of sleepwalking and was under tremendous work stress when he

Table 4.1

INTIMATE PARTNER HOMICIDE, BY GENDER, 1976-1999

	Number of victims of intimate partner homicide	
Year	*Male*	*Female*
1976	1,357	1,600
1977	1,294	1,437
1978	1,202	1,482
1979	1,262	1,506
1980	1,221	1,549
1981	1,278	1,572
1982	1,141	1,481
1983	1,113	1,462
1984	989	1,442
1985	957	1,546
1986	985	1,586
1987	933	1,494
1988	854	1,582
1989	903	1,415
1990	859	1,501
1991	779	1,518
1992	722	1,455
1993	708	1,581
1994	692	1,405
1995	547	1,321
1996	515	1,324
1997	451	1,217
1998	512	1,317
1999	424	1,218

Source: Derived from U.S. Department of Justice, Bureau of Justice Statistics Special Report, *Intimate Partner Violence* (Washington: Office of Justice Programs, 2000), p. 10; FBI Supplementary Homicide Reports, 1976-1999, http://www.ojp.usdoj.gov/bjs/homicide/intimates.htm#intimates.

killed his wife. A jury found him guilty of first-degree murder and sentenced him to life in prison with no chance of parole.
• On May 28, 1998, 40-year-old Brynn Hartman shot to death her 49-year-old actor husband, Phil Hartman, before killing herself in their home in Encino, California. Brynn Hartman, a one-time model, had a history of substance abuse, temper tantrums, and jealousy.[8]

Trends in Intimate Partner Homicides

Homicide long-term trends indicate a decrease in the number of intimate-related murders. According to the Federal Bureau of Investigation's Supplementary Homicide Reports, there were an estimated 57,000 women and men killed by an intimate partner in the United States between 1976 and 1999 (see Table 4.1). As shown in Figure 4.2, the number of males murdered by an intimate fell by nearly 69 percent from 1976 to 1999, while females killed by an intimate dropped nearly 24 percent over the period. However, from 1997 to 1999, the number of females murdered by an intimate partner has remained stable, with the number of male victims of intimate homicide decreasing only 6 percent over the period.

Figure 4.2
Victims of Intimate Partner Homicides, by Gender, 1999

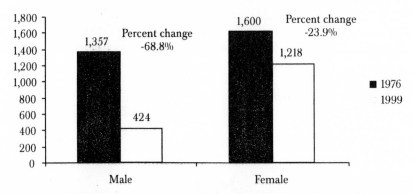

Source: Derived from U.S. Department of Justice, Bureau of Justice Statistics Special Report, Intimate Partner Violence (Washington: Office of Justice Programs, 2000), p.10; FBI Supplementary Homicide Reports, 1976-1999, http://www.ojp.usdoj.gov/bjs/homicide/intimates.htm#intimates.

Since 1976, approximately 30 percent of all female homicide victims were killed by an intimate partner, compared to 6 percent of total male homicide victims being murdered by an intimate.[9] In a study of gender-specific differences in homicide rates between 1976 and 1987, involving victims and offenders age sixteen and older, A. L. Kellermann and J. A. Mercy found that more than twice the number of women were shot and killed by their spouses or other intimate partners than were slain by strangers with firearms, knives, or by other methods.[10]

Most victims of intimate partner homicide are killed by a husband or wife (see Figures 4.3 and 4.4). Between 1976 and 1996, more than six in ten female and male murder victims were killed by a spouse, while around one-third were slain by a nonmarital intimate such as a boyfriend or girlfriend. Only 5 percent of female victims and 4 percent of male victims of intimate homicide were murdered by an ex-spouse.

Figure 4.3

Female Intimate Partner Homicide Victims, by Type of Relationship to Killer, 1976-1996

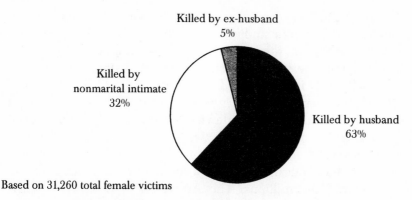

Based on 31,260 total female victims

Source: Derived from U.S. Department of Justice, Bureau of Justice Statistics Factbook, *Violence by Intimates* (Washington: Office of Justice Programs, 1998), p.6.

Figure 4.4

Male Intimate Partner Homicide Victims, by Type of Relationship to Killer, 1976-1996

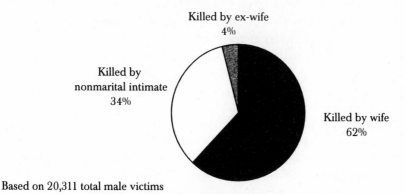

Based on 20,311 total male victims

Source: Derived from U.S. Department of Justice, Bureau of Justice Statistics Factbook, *Violence by Intimates* (Washington: Office of Justice Programs, 1998), p.6.

With respect to race and gender, most victims of domestic homicide have shown a decline in victimization. According to the Bureau of Justice Statistics (BJS) Special Report, *Intimate Partner Violence*, between 1976 and 1998, the number of black female victims of partner homicide fell by 45 percent, black male victims by 74 percent, and white male victims by 44 percent. Only the homicide victimization of white females by intimates has not declined considerably since 1976. In fact, between 1997 and 1998, the number of white female victims of intimate partner homicide rose 15 percent.[11]

THE DYNAMICS OF DOMESTIC VIOLENCE

The strong relationship between domestic violence and intimate homicide has been clearly documented in studies.[12] According to the National Crime Victimization Survey (NCVS), there were around one million crimes of violence perpetrated against persons by husbands, wives, former spouses, and boyfriends and girlfriends in the United States in 1998.[13] Of these, nearly 900,000–or roughly 85 percent–of the intimate partner victimizations were against women. Around four in ten female victims of domestic violence lived in households with children younger than twelve years of age; and half the victims sustained physical injuries as a result of the intimate partner violence.

Other researchers have put the number of intimate partners involved in domestic violence into the millions. The American Medical Association reported that four million spouses are beaten in the United States every year;[14] while the Family Violence Prevention Fund estimated that 3.9 million women married or living with someone were victims of intimate violence annually.[15]

Some studies show that males are also being battered, if not to the same degree and duration as females. Robert Langley and Richard Levy estimated that twelve million men have been physically abused by their spouses at some time during their marriage.[16] Suzanne Steinmetz estimated that 280,000 men are battered by their partners every year in this country.[17] Another study estimated that two million husbands and 1.8 million wives have been victims of severe marital violence.[18] Murray Straus approximated that 65 percent of all married couples were involved in spousal abuse, of which 25 percent were of a serious nature.[19]

Gender studies in domestic violence indicate that the typical pattern of abuse has the male as the aggressor and the female as the victim. According to the NCVS, the rate of female victimization in intimate violence was five times greater than the rate of male victimization.[20] Police reports of complaints of intimate violence perpetrated by males outnumber reports of domestic violence committed by females about twelve to one.[21] Richard Gelles found that 47 percent of the husbands sampled had ever battered a spouse, compared to 32 percent of wives.[22]

Studies show that in intimate homicides, men are significantly less likely than women to have been physically assaulted by the victim before committing the murder.[23] However, men are far more likely than women to kill an intimate somewhere other than a shared residence, as well as commit multiple murders in the process of killing a female intimate and take their own lives after perpetrating the intimate partner homicide.[24]

Researchers have further found the following characteristics and nature of intimate violence:

- One-third of women and men have been witnesses to an act of domestic violence.
- Three in ten women admitted to a hospital emergency department sustained injuries identified as due to battering.
- Four in ten severely injured battered women in hospital emergency departments required prior medical treatment due to intimate violence.
- Females age sixteen to twenty-four have the highest victimization rate of nonlethal intimate violence.
- Black women have a higher rate of victimization due to intimate violence than white women.
- Seven out of ten female victims of domestic violence were physically assaulted.
- Women in low-income households have a higher rate of nonlethal intimate violence than women in high-income households.
- Three-fourths of nonlethal intimate violence occurs at or near the victim's home.[25]

Intimate Violence Among Nonmarital and Estranged Couples

While much of the research on domestic violence has focused on married couples, studies show that the incidence of intimate violence among nonmarried or divorced intimates may be as high or higher, and is also a factor in intimate partner homicides. A disproportionate number of cohabiting couples have been found to be involved in intimate violence.[26] Kersti Yllo and Straus found that cohabiting couples reported more incidents of domestic violence than did married couples.[27]

According to the BJS, separated or divorced women are fourteen times more likely than married women to report having been battered by a spouse or ex-spouse.[28] Although separated or divorced women constitute only 10 percent of all women, they reported 75 percent of all violence between intimates.[29] Experts on intimate homicide have found that women who leave or threaten to leave their abusive spouse have a greater likelihood of being killed by their partner than women who stay in the marriage.[30]

Dating couples also face the risk of intimate violence and homicide. One study found that 60 percent of young women were currently in an abusive relationship.[31] Surveys reveal that about one in three females will be victimized by intimate violence before turning eighteen.[32] Dating violence has been shown to mirror marital violence in many respects. "Victims dating their batterers experience the same patterns of power and control as their counterparts in abusive marriages or cohabitators, and clearly dating violence can be just as lethal."[33]

WHY MEN MURDER INTIMATES

Men typically commit uxoricide or murder a nonmartial intimate in relation to such factors as a history of abusing the partner, arguments, sexual jealousy, separation or divorce, child custody issues, substance abuse, problems on the job, suicidal behavior, and mental illness.[34] Studies further show that homicidal men are at a significantly higher risk of murdering an intimate if such men were victims or witnesses to domestic violence during childhood;[35] have a history of involvement with the criminal justice stystem;[36] or had protective or restraining orders issues against them.[37]

Most experts agree that male loss of control over an intimate mate is one of the most important correlates of domestic homicide. According to Charles Ewing, "Batterers have an obsessive if not a pathological need to control the lives of the women with whom they share intimate relationships."[38] Ronald Holmes and Stephen Holmes have suggested that for many male perpetrators of intimate murder, killing may be viewed as "an act of control," in response to an inability to control a female mate's desire for independence or self-direction.[39]

Researchers have noted a correlation between uxoricidal men and their victim wives and abandonment, separation, rejection, and divorce. In G. W. Barnard and colleagues' study of spouse homicide, nearly 60 percent of the male offenders were separated from their wives when murdering them.[40] Similarly, more than half of the women murdered by intimates in J. Campbell's study were estranged from their spouses at the time of the homicide.[41] Angela Browne and associates found in their study of intimate partner homicides that the risk for women to become victims of spouse murder after a separation or divorce could last for years.[42]

Many men kill their intimates as a result of intense rage or an act of revenge. Such men are more likely to be especially brutal in intimate partner homicides. Studies have found a high percentage of overkill or violent murders (involving multiple types of acts perpetrated against or injuries sustained by the victim) among male perpetrated intimate killings.[43]

In exploring the differences between male and female intimate partner homicides, Rebecca Dobash and colleagues note that:

> men often kill wives after lengthy period of prolonged physical violence. . .the roles in such cases are seldom if ever reversed. . . . Men commonly hunt down and kill wives who have left them; women hardly ever behave similarly. Men kill wives as part of planned murder-suicides; analogous acts by women are almost unheard of. Men kill in response to revelations of wife infidelity; women almost never respond similarly. . . . A large proportion of the spouse-killing perpetrated by wives, but almost none . . . perpetrated by husbands, are acts of self-defense.[44]

WHY WOMEN MURDER INTIMATES

Most women who kill their intimate male partners do so in self-defense or to protect others from harm. Studies show that women perpetrators of spouse murder tend to more often kill as a self-defense mechanism when being battered, threatened as such, or feel that they or their children face the serious risk of bodily harm or death.[45]

The correlation between the battering of women and lethal violence perpetrated by or against their abusive mates has been clearly documented in the literature.[46] According to the book, *Domestic Crimes, Family Violence and Child Abuse*, a woman is battered by their husband every nine seconds in the United States; while one in five abused women have reported being the victim of at least three assaults by a husband or ex-husband within the past six months.[47] It has been estimated that up to two million women are the victims of severe intimate partner violence every year in this country.[48] Diana Russell reported that more than two out of every ten women who had ever been married were the victims of domestic spousal violence during some time in their lives.[49]

Research has shown that intimate violence accounts for roughly one-fifth of all violent crimes against women.[50] As many as seven in ten female homicide victims are killed by a spouse, ex-spouse, or boyfriend.[51] About two-thirds of the victims are battered women.[52]

For many women, within this dangerous, violent, and potentially deadly atmosphere, striking back with lethal force may seem the only option for survival. A study of female perpetrated spouse killings in Kansas City found that in 90 percent of the cases, the police had responded to domestic disturbance calls at least once in the two years prior to the homicide; and in half the cases the police had gone to the house of the offender-victim on at least five occasions.[53] In a study of thirty female state prisoners in California who had murdered their husbands, 28 percent were identified as victims of wife battering.[54]

A psychosocial study of homicidal women by J. Totman found that key factors in intimate partner homicides committed by women were male intimate physical aggression and the perception that there were no other viable choices to escape the abusive environment.[55] A similar finding was made by Browne in the study of why battered women kill their mates.[56]

According to Lenore Walker, "most women who killed their batterers have little memory of any cognitive processes other than an intense focus on their own survival."[57] Eilssa Benedek described the typical pattern of a battered woman driven to murder her male intimate partner:

> Such a woman often comes from a home where she has observed and experienced . . . violence and sees. . .as a norm in social interaction and as a solution for conflict. Marriage is frequently seen as an escape route, but her choice of husband is not intelligently determined. Thus, the potential offender often chooses a mate with a high penchant for violence. She has been beaten repeatedly and brutally for a period of years by a spouse or lover who may be drunk, sober, tired, depressed, elated, mentally ill, or just angry. Lacking educational and financial resources, she describes a feeling of being trapped. This feeling increases proportionately with the number of young children she has. . . . The battered wife has turned to social agencies, police, prosecutors, friends, ministers, and family, but they have not offered meaningful support or advice. . . . Abused women who have murdered their spouses reveal that they feel that homicide was the only alternative left to them.[58]

Although most female killers of intimates reflect the battered women's syndrome as the primary motivation, there are some women who kill their mates for other reasons, such as financial motives. History is replete with examples of women, known as Black Widows, who kill a mate or successive mates in order to collect insurance payments or other financial or material gain.[59] In fact, the evidence suggests that historically more females may have killed intimates for profit than males.[60]

Women have also been known to murder husbands or lovers due to jealousy, control issues, adultery one way or the other, substance abuse, stress, and mental illness.[61] Some studies suggest that biological factors such as depression and premenstrual syndrome may play a role in partner homicide and other crimes of violence committed by women.[62]

NOTES

1. U.S. Department of Justice, Bureau of Justice Statistics, 2001, http://www.ojp. usdoj.gov/bjs/abstract/pva99.htm.
2. *Ibid.*
3. A. Browne and K. R. Williams, "Exploring the Effect of Resource Availability and the Likelihood of Female-Perpetrated Homicides," *Law and Society Review 23* (1989): 75-94; A. L. Kellermann and J. A. Mercy, "Men, Women, and Murder: Gender-Specific Differences in Rates of Fatal Violence and Victimization," *Journal of Trauma 33* (1992): 1-5; M. A. Zahn, "Homicide in the Twentieth Century Trends, Types and Causes," in T. R. Gurr, ed., *Violence in America; Vol. 1. The History of Violence* (Thousand Oaks: Sage, 1989), pp. 216-34.
4. Kellermann and Mercy, "Men, Women, and Murder," pp. 1-5.
5. Jacquelyn Campbell, "Prediction of Homicide of and by Battered Women," in J. Campbell and J. Milner, eds., *Assessing Dangerousness: Potential for Further Violence of Sexual Offenders, Batterers, and Child Abusers* (Thousand Oaks: Sage: 1995).
6. U.S. Department of Justice, Bureau of Justice Statistics, *Female Victims of Violent Crime* (Washington: Office of Justice Programs, 1991), p. 5.
7. *Ibid.*; Linda Saltzman and James Mercy, "Assaults Between Intimates: The Range of Relationships Involved," in Anna Wilson, ed., *Homicide: The Victim/Offender Connection* (Cincinnati: Anderson, 1993).
8. R. Barri Flowers and H. Loraine Flowers, *Murders in the United States: Crimes, Killers and Victims of the Twentieth Century* (Jefferson: McFarland, 2001), pp. 77-78, 110, 118, 140.
9. Cited in R. Barri Flowers, *Domestic Crimes, Family Violence and Child Abuse: A Study of Contemporary American Society* (Jefferson: McFarland, 2000), p. 62.
10. Kellermann and Mercy, "Men, Women, and Murder," pp. 1-5.
11. U.S. Department of Justice, Bureau of Justice Statistics Special Report, *Intimate Partner Violence* (Washington: Office of Justice Programs, 2000), p. 3.
12. Flowers, *Domestic Crimes, Family Violence and Child Abuse,* pp. 17, 62-64; Campbell, "Prediction of Homicide of and by Battered Women;" Neil Websdale, *Understanding Domestic Homicide* (Boston: Northeastern University Press, 1999), pp. 19-23; Patricia W. Easteal, *Killing the Beloved: Homicide Between Adult Sexual Intimates* (Canberra: Australian Institute of Criminology, 1993).
13. *Intimate Partner Violence,* p. 1.
14. Cited in Flowers, *Domestic Crimes, Family Violence and Child Abuse,* p. 16.
15. The Commonwealth Fund, "First Comprehensive National Health Survey of American Women Finds Them at Significant Risk," news release, New York, July 14, 1993.
16. Robert Langley and Richard C. Levy, *Wife Beating: The Silent Crisis* (New York: Dutton, 1977).
17. Suzanne K. Steinmetz, "The Battered Husband Syndrome," *Victimology 2* (1978): 507.
18. Richard J. Gelles, "The Myth of Battered Husbands," *Ms* (October 1979): 65-66, 71-72.

19. Cited in Flowers, *Domestic Crimes, Family Violence and Child Abuse*, p. 30.
20. U.S. Department of Justice, Bureau of Justice Statistics Factbook, *Violence by Intimates* (Washington: Office of Justice Programs, 1998), p. 3.
21. R. Barri Flowers, *Demographics and Criminality: The Characteristics of Crime in America* (Westport: Greenwood, 1989), p. 154.
22. Richard J. Gelles, *The Violent Home: A Study of Physical Aggression Between Husbands and Wives* (Thousand Oaks: Sage, 1972), pp. 50-52.
23. Angela Browne, Kirk R. Williams, and Donald G. Dutton, "Homicide Between Intimate Partners," in M. Dwayne Smith and Margaret A. Zahn, eds., *Studying and Preventing Homicide: Issues and Challenges* (Thousand Oaks, Sage, 1999), p. 68.
24. *Ibid.*; P. M. Marzuk, K. Tardiff, and C. S. Hirsh, "The Epidemiology of Murder-Suicide," *Journal of the American Medical Association* 267 (1992): 3179-83.
25. Flowers, *Domestic Crimes, Family Violence and Child Abuse*, pp. 17-18, 45.
26. Bonnie E. Carlson, "Battered Women and Their Assailants," *Social Work 22*, 6 (1977): 456; J. J. Gayford, "Wife Battering: A Preliminary Survey of 100 Cases," *British Medical Journal 1* (1975): 194-97.
27. Kersti Yllo and Murray A. Straus, "Interpersonal Violence Among Married and Cohabitating Couples," paper presented at the annual meeting of the National Council on Family Relationships, Philadelphia, 1978.
28. *Female Victims of Violent Crime*, p. 5.
29. *Ibid.*
30. Campbell, "Prediction of Homicide of and by Battered Women."
31. Rebecca Bettin, Young Women's Resource Center, testimony at Iowa House of Representatives Public Hearing on Dating Violence, March 31, 1992.
32. S. Kuehl, "Legal Remedies for Teen Dating Violence," in Barbara Levy, ed., *Dating Violence: Young Women in Danger* (Seattle: Seal Press, 1998), p. 73.
33. Flowers, *Domestic Crimes, Family Violence and Child Abuse*, p. 78.
34. *Ibid.*, pp. 82-91; Websdale, *Understanding Domestic Homicide*, p. 19; Margo I. Wilson and Martin Daly, "Spousal Homicide Risk and Estrangement," *Violence and Victims 8*, 1 (1993): 3-16; Jacques Buteau, Alain Lesage, and Margaret Kiely, "Homicide Followed by Suicide: A Quebec Case series, 1988-1990," *Canadian Journal of Psychiatry 38* (1993): 552-56.
35. J. Fagan, D. Stewart, and K. Hanson, "Violent Men or Violent Husbands: Background Factors and Situational Correlates of Domestic and Extra-Domestic Violence," in D. Finkelhor, R. Gelles, G. Hotaling, and M. Straus, eds., *The Dark Side of Families* (Thousand Oaks: Sage, 1983); D. S. Kalmuss, "The Intergenerational Transmission of Marital Aggression," *Journal of Marriage and the Family 46* (1984): 16-19.
36. Angela Browne, *When Battered Women Kill* (New York: Free Press, 1987).
37. Websdale, *Understanding Domestic Homicide*, p. 19.
38. Charles P. Ewing, *Fatal Families: The Dynamics of Intrafamilial Homicide* (Thousand Oaks: Sage, 1997), p. 22.
39. Ronald M. Holmes and Stephen T. Holmes, *Murder in America* (Thousand Oaks: Sage, 1994), p. 27.
40. G. W. Barnard, M. Vera, and G. Newman, "'Till Death Do Us Part?' A Study of Spouse Murder," *Bulletin of the American Academy of Psychiatry and Law 10* (1982): 271-80.

41. J. Campbell, "'If I Can't Have You, No One Can': Power and Control in Homicide of Female Partners," in J. Radford and D. E. Russell, eds., *Femicide: The Politics of Woman Killing* (New York: Twayne, 1992), pp. 99-113.

42. Browne, Williams, and Dutton, "Homicide Between Intimate Partners," p. 71.

43. *Ibid.*, pp. 72-73; Campbell, "'If I Can't Have You, No One Can,'" pp. 99-113; M. A. Straus, "Domestic Violence and Homicide Antecedents," *Bulletin of the New York Academy of Medicine 62* (1976): 446-65.

44. Rebecca E. Dobash, Russell Dobash, Margo Wilson, and Martin Daly, "The Myth of Sexual Symmetry in Marital Violence," *Social Problems 39*, 1 (1992): 81.

45. Ewing, *Fatal Families*, pp. 26-36; Websdale, *Understanding Domestic Homicide*, pp. 19-21; R. Barri Flowers, *Female Crime, Criminals and Cellmates: An Exploration of Female Criminality and Delinquency* (Jefferson: McFarland, 1995), pp. 86-89.

46. Flowers, *Domestic Crimes, Family Violence and Child Abuse*, pp. 25-26, 61-64; Flowers, *Female Crime, Criminals and Cellmates*, pp. 86-89; Browne, Williams, and Dutton, "Homicide Between Intimate Partners," pp. 55-78.

47. Flowers, *Domestic Crimes, Family Violence and Child Abuse*, p. 15.

48. *Ibid.*

49. Diana E. Russell, *Rape in Marriage* (New York: Macmillan, 1982).

50. Flowers, *Domestic Crimes, Family Violence and Child Abuse*, p. 18.

51. *Ibid.*, p. 62; Campbell, "Prediction of Homicide of and by Battered Women."

52. Flowers, *Domestic Crimes, Family Violence and Child Abuse*, p. 62; *Violence by Intimates*, pp. 5-6.

53. Cited in Flowers, *Female Crime, Criminals and Cellmates*, p. 86.

54. *Ibid.*

55. J. Totman, *The Murderesses: A Psychosocial Study of Criminal Homicide* (San Francisco: R & E Associates, 1978).

56. Browne, *When Battered Women Kill.*

57. Lenore E. Walker, *The Battered Woman Syndrome* (New York: Springer, 1984), p. 40.

58. Elissa P. Benedek, "Women and Homicide," in Bruce L. Danto, John Bruhns, and Austin H. Kutscher, eds., *The Human Side of Homicide* (New York: Columbia University Press, 1982), p. 155.

59. Flowers and Flowers, *Murders in the United States*, pp. 109-16.

60. *Ibid.*

61. *Ibid.*, pp. 123-40; Websdale, *Understanding Domestic Homicide*, p. 20; Kenneth Polk and David Ransom, "The Role of Gender in Intimate Homicide," *Australian and New Zealand Journal of Criminology 24* (1991): 20.

62. Flowers, *Female Crime, Criminals and Cellmates*, pp. 88-89; Julie Horney, "Menstrual Cycles and Criminal Responsibility," *Law and Human Behavior 2*, 1 (1978): 25-36; Saleem Shah and Loren Roth, "Biological and Psychological Factors in Criminality," in Daniel Glaser, ed., *Handbook of Criminology* (Chicago: Rand McNally, 1974), p. 145.

Chapter 5

INFANTICIDE

Every year hundreds of infants are victims of intrafamilial homicide in the United States. Young mothers are predominantly responsible for these deaths, which typically involves suffocating, drowning, dumping in garbage, and poisoning. Experts on infanticide attribute this form of homicide to various causes including mental illness, depression, jealousy, child abuse and/or neglect, unwanted children, financial problems, and a history of violent behavior. Recent high profile cases of mothers murdering their children has placed greater focus on this disturbing problem as a reflection of the overall issue of violence in the family.

INFANTICIDE HISTORICALLY

Infanticide—or the killing of infants, usually by parents, family, or with the consent of the community—is believed to be the single greatest cause of child deaths in history, with the possible exception of the bubonic plague.[1] The practice of infanticide has taken place in virtually every nation since the beginning of recorded time, resulting in the murder of untold numbers of children.

The literature is filled with references of infanticide. The Old Testament describes the killing of countless children in Jericho by Joshua and his nomadic warriors;[2] while the New Testament tells of the "slaughter of the innocents," from which Jesus was saved.[3] King Nimrod killed every first born in his kingdom after being told by his astrologer that a boy would be born in Mesopotamia who would declare war upon the king.[4] An estimated 70,000 children were slain.

Young children were burned at the stake during the reign of Queen Mary;[5] and "in rural areas of Ireland 'changeling babies' were sometimes roasted alive over fires, even in the twentieth century."[6] The killing of female infants was once such a common practice that in many societies the male population was four to five times greater than the female population.[7]

Up until the nineteenth century, dead or abandoned infants were almost commonplace in the United States. Historically, infanticide has been characterized by the "silent acceptance or active participation by elements in the society in which it flourished."[8] Its existence has been attributed to individual and collective acts of faith, proof of worthiness, religious appeasement, in response to prophecies of doom, Darwinian survival, Malthusian population control, illegitimate births, and medical reasons.

WOMEN AND INFANTICIDE

Infanticide is defined today as the killing of an infant, usually shortly after birth. This form of homicide is almost always perpetrated by women. Infanticide has traditionally been viewed as a sex-specific offense, which "actually excludes the members of one sex by legal definition."[9] Under the English legal system, it has been observed that "infanticide does not apply to the British principle of equal applicability because it is an offense in which only women are considered the perpetrators."[10]

Infanticide is predominantly committed by a parent of the victim. Although some fathers do kill their young offspring, mothers are most responsible for the killing of infants. According to D. T. Lunde, mothers who commit infanticide are usually "severely disturbed, suffer from extreme bouts of depression and many experience delusions. Before a woman kills her offspring, she is likely to go through a preliminary period when she thinks about how to commit the crime, visualizes the dead child, and considers suicide."[11] A study on infanticide reported that young, unmarried, undereducated mothers were more likely than other mothers to kill their infant children.[12] Poverty, depression, and women experiencing feelings of anomie have also been linked to infanticide.[13]

Recent cases of infanticide can be seen below:

- Between 1986 and 1989, Paula Marie Sims murdered her two infant children. Loralei Sims' skeletal remains were discovered on June 20, 1986, fifteen days after her birth, in a wooded area in Brighton, Illinois. Her sister Heather's corpse was discovered in a garbage can in St. Charles County, Missouri on May 3, 1989, less than two months after she was born. Unable to prove guilt in the first death, Sims was convicted of murder in the death of her second daughter and sentenced to life in prison with no possibility of parole.

- On October 19, 1994, Susan Smith murdered her two young children by drowning them in a lake in Union, South Carolina. With a history of mental illness and a victim of sexual abuse, the 23-year-old Smith was found competent to stand trial. She was convicted on two counts of first-degree murder and sentenced to life in prison.
- Between 1972 and 1985, New Yorker Marybeth Tinning was suspected of murdering her eight young children by suffocation. Initially most of the deaths had been attributed to SIDS, including that of her three-month-old daughter, Tami Lynne, who died on December 20, 1985. After an investigation, Tinning confessed to suffocating three of her children by smothering them with a pillow. She was convicted of second-degree murder in the death of Tami and given a sentence of twenty years to life in prison.[14]
- In 1998, Kimberlee Snyder killed her five-month old daughter in Findlay, Ohio. Using postpartum depression as her defense, she pleaded guilty to involuntary manslaughter and was sentenced to fifteen years behind bars.[15]
- On June 20, 2001, 37-year-old Andrea Yates drowned her five young children in the bathtub of the family's residence in Texas. With a history of depression, Yates pled not guilty by reason of insanity. A jury rejected this, convicting her of capital murder.[16]

THE EXTENT OF INFANTICIDE

How big is the problem of infanticide? No one knows for sure, given the problem of misdiagnosis and other difficulties in determining the cause of child deaths. The U.S. Department of Justice estimated that there are 600 cases of maternal filicide—mothers killing their children—annually.[17] In a study of child fatalities committed by parents, P. Resnick found that most deaths occurred during the first year of life.[18]

In the early 1990s, there were an estimated nine newborn infants per 100,000 killed by parents in the United States.[19] Many such deaths were attributed to unintentional fatal injuries, child abuse, or neglect. Recent data suggests that the number of cases of infanticide involving children age one and under is one the decline.[20] However, overall rates of infanticide have remained relatively stable between 1976 and 1999.

The frightening specter of infanticide was described by Maria Piers:

> A doctoral candidate in the social sciences at one of the large Midwestern universities, who was teaching courses in the social sciences to employees of a large city sewer system, learned from these employees that during the previous year, four corpses of newborns had been found in the sewer screen. The newborns had been thrown directly after birth into the sewers, a pre-

ferred place for children's corpses for millennia. No identification or investigation was attempted in these cases of infant death.[21]

TYPES OF INFANTICIDAL MOTHERS

Researchers have developed typologies of mothers who kill their infants or other progeny. Robert Butterworth, a psychologist, identified eight types of infanticidal mothers as follows:

- **Mentally ill mothers**. Women suffering from serious psychological problems often initiated during childhood or from biological transference. May be acutely psychotic and have difficulty controlling aggression.
- **Retaliating mothers**. Women who are jealous or envious of their newborns because of the attention given by others, which the mother may have lacked herself during childhood.
- **Angry mothers**. Vengeful women whose anger is taken out on their babies, particularly male infants, who may bear the brunt of anger felt toward the father.
- **Depressed mothers**. Studies show that more than one-third of mothers who kill their young children suffer from depression or are suicidal.
- **Unwanted or unexpected mothers**. Mothers with unwanted or unexpected children are at greater risk to kill or abandon their newborns.
- **Merciful mothers**. These women kill their children to protect them from the pain and suffering that life presents or will bring.
- **Batterer mothers**. Women who beat their child to death, often in a fit of rage in response to the child's nonstop wailing.[22]

According to Cheryl Meyer, there are five categories of mothers who murder their offspring:

- Mothers who kill as a result of neglect.
- Mothers who kill from abuse.
- Mothers who perpetrate neonaticide.
- Mothers who have assistance or are coerced in the killing of their child.
- Mothers who intentionally murder their child.[23]

Neonaticide is the killing of a child within twenty-four hours of birth. Research indicates that an estimated one out of three cases of infanticide is neonaticide.[24] The psyche of the neonaticidal woman is described by Steven Pitt and Erin Bale:

> Women who commit neonaticide generally have no plans for the birth or care of their child. They often conceal the pregnancy from both family and friends. Massive denial of the gravid state is a prominent feature . . . [that] can be so powerful that it affects not only the mother's own perception but

those of their family, friends, teachers, employers and even physicians.[25]

WHAT CAUSES MOTHERS TO COMMIT INFANTICIDE?

Why do mothers murder their infants and young children? Like most murderers, there may be a variety of reasons for committing such a crime, ranging from mental illness to economics to violent tendencies to desperation to shame. However, experts on infanticide have concentrated on some antecedents in particular that appear to reflect a high proportion of infanticidal women such as postpartum depression, Munchausen by proxy, and a sense of desperation and helplessness that leads to murder.

Postpartum Depression

Postpartum depression or the "baby blues" is a common occurrence among women after giving birth. Studies show that between 50 and 80 percent of all women suffer from some form of depression following childbirth such as sadness and psychosis.[26] Most of these symptoms are of short duration. Approximately one in five women experience serious symptoms of depression including insomnia, severe mood swings, suicidal ideation, and anorexia.[27] Only two women in every 1,000 become psychotic because of postpartum depression.[28]

The correlation between infanticide and postpartum depression is noted in the American Psychiatric Association's *Diagnostic and Statistical Manual of Mental Disorders* (DSM-IV): "Infanticide is most often associated with postpartum psychotic episodes that are characterized by command hallucinations to kill the infant or delusions that the infant is possessed, but it can also occur in severe postpartum mood episodes without such specific delusions or hallucinations."[29]

According to the DSM-IV, a woman's risk of psychosis resulting from postpartum depression is increased significantly if she has previously experienced psychotic episodes. Researchers have estimated that the odds of recurrence of postpartum depression, whether or not psychosis is present, are anywhere between thirty and eighty-four in 100.[30]

Postpartum depression has been linked to such biological correlates as hormonal levels during pregnancy, while some experts relate postpartum depression to the environment, or an interaction of environmental variables and hormonal influences.[31]

Munchausen Syndrome by Proxy

Some women who kill their infants and young children suffer from Munchausen syndrome by proxy (MBP), a rare mental disorder first brought to light in the 1970s.[32] Victims of MBP often manufacture or fake physical illness in their children, bringing them to doctors or hospitals to be treated. Munchausen parents are almost always mothers who appear to be loving and caring of their children and greatly involved with the medical practitioner in treatment options. Few such mothers give the appearance of being psychotic or otherwise suffering from any serious psychopathology.

According to the DSM-IV, in cases of MBP: "Typically, the victim is a young child and the perpetrator is the child's mother. The motivation for the perpetrator's behavior is presumed to be a psychological need to assume the sick role by proxy."[33] The MBP offender induces or feigns the child victim's disease or illness, then "presents the victim for medical care while disclaiming any knowledge about the actual etiology of the problem."[34]

In cases of MBP, common factors include:

- Continued illness of the child with inconsistent and often confusing symptoms, confounding medical practitioners.
- A recurrence in the child victim's medical treatment.
- The mother typically has some training in a medical field, such as a nurse, or medical knowledge.
- The mother is especially attentive to the child's welfare while under medical care.
- The mother is particularly helpful and cooperative with medical personnel.
- A symbiotic relationship between mother and child.[8]

The extent of Munchausen by proxy-related child homicides is unclear, but appears to be on the rise. Around half of all confirmed MBP cases concern illnesses of the central nervous system such as breathing and sleep-related disorders.[36] Cases of MBP are commonly misdiagnosed as Sudden Infant Death Syndrome (SIDS).

Women who suffer from MBP are generally characterized as having a low self-esteem, and feeling lonely, inadequate, and incompetent—beyond the façade of caring, loving mother. For most, at least part of the motivation is the attention and sense of importance derived from the MBP.

In spite of the seriousness of MBP, surveys reveal that most medical practitioners are not even aware of the disorder, compounding the problem and potential for fatal consequences.[37]

Desperation

Many women who kill their infants do so out of desperation in being confronted with an unplanned, undesirable situation and feeling they have no other viable alternative. Studies indicate that most mothers who fall into this category of child killer tend to be very young, white, single, and with little to no financial resources or family support.[38] Many are also likely to be victims of child abuse and neglect, and are increasingly substance abusers.[39]

Often the desperate mother or mother-to-be is motivated by fear, hopelessness, and shame in deciding to murder her newborn. Secrecy is also a common factor in the scheme of things. Many manage to keep their pregnancy unknown to even family and close friends.

Desperation and despair often lead such mothers to dump their newborns in garbage cans or dumpsters or otherwise abandon them on the streets. The result is usually the same: separation of mother and child, often permanently and, in many cases, fatally.

NOTES

1. Theo Solomon, "History and Demography of Child Abuse," *Pediatrics 51*, 4 (1973): 773-76.
2. *The Holy Bible*, Book of Joshua, 6:17-21.
3. R. Barri Flowers, *Female Crime, Criminals and Cellmates: An Exploration of Female Criminality and Delinquency* (Jefferson: McFarland, 1995), p. 84.
4. Solomon, "History and Demography of Child Abuse," p. 773.
5. C. Morris, *The Tudors* (London: Fontana, 1967).
6. J. E. Oliver, "The Epidemiology of Child Abuse," in Selwyn M. Smith, ed., *The Maltreatment of Children* (Baltimore: University Park Press, 1978), p. 95.
7. Shirley O'Brien, *Child Abuse: Commission and Omission* (Provo: Brigham Young University Press, 1980), p. 5.
8. R. Barri Flowers, *Children and Criminality: The Child as Victim and Perpetrator* (Westport: Greenwood, 1986), p. 4.
9. Carol Smart, *Women, Crime and Criminology: A Feminist Critique* (Boston: Routledge and Kegan Paul, 1977), p. 6.
10. *Ibid.* See also Flowers, *Female Crime, Criminals and Cellmates*, pp. 84-86.
11. D. T. Lunde, "Hot Blood's Record Month: Our Murder Boom," *Psychology Today* 9 (1975): 35-42.
12. Cited in Lawrence S. Wissow, "Infanticide," *New England Journal of Medicine 339*, 17 (1998): 1239.
13. *Ibid.*; R. M. Holmes and S. M. Holmes, *Murder in America* (Thousand Oaks: Sage, 1994), pp. 48-49.

14. R. Barri Flowers and H. Loraine Flowers, *Murders in the United States: Crimes, Killers and Victims of the Twentieth Century* (Jefferson: McFarland, 2001), pp. 123-39.

15. Cited in Mike Tolson, "Criminal Punishment Widely Disparate in Maternal Filicide Cases Such as Yates," http://www.chron.com/cs/ CDA/story.hts/special/drownings/1041253.

16. Houston Chronicle, "January 7 Trial Date is Set for Yates," http://www.chron.com/cs/CDA/story.hts/special/drownings/1073196.

17. Cited in R. Barri Flowers, *Domestic Crimes, Family Violence and Child Abuse: A Study of Contemporary American Society* (Jefferson: McFarland, 2000), p. 25.

18. P. Resnick, "Child Murder by Parents: A Psychiatric Review of Filicide," *American Journal of Psychiatry 126*, 3 (1969): 325-34.

19. Wissow, "Infanticide," p. 1239.

20. FBI, Supplementary Homicide Reports, http://www.ojp.usdoj.gov/ bjs/homicide/children.htm.

21. Maria W. Piers, *Infanticide* (New York: W. W. Norton, 1978), p. 14.

22. Cited in Donnica Moore, "Infanticide," http://www.drdonnica.com/ display.asp?article=3506.

23. Cheryl L. Meyer, "Mothers Who Kill Often Give Warnings," http://www.womensnews.org/article.cfm/dyn/aid/595/context/archive.

24. *Ibid.*

25. Quoted in Charles P. Ewing, *Fatal Families: The Dynamics of Intrafamilial Homicide* (Thousand Oaks: Sage, 1997), p. 87. See also Steven E. Pitt and Erin M. Bale, "Neonaticide, Infanticide, and Filicide: A Review of the Literature," *Bulletin of the American Academy of Psychiatry and Law 23* (1995): 379.

26. Anastasia Toufexis, "Why Mothers Kill Their Babies," *Time* (June 20, 1998), p. 81.

27. "When Do New Mom's 'Baby Blues' Become More Serious Illness?" *Chicago Tribune* (November 27, 1988), p. 3.

28. *Ibid.*

29. American Psychiatric Association, *Diagnostic and Statistical Manual of Mental Disorders*, 4th ed. (Washington: American Psychiatric Association, 1994), p. 386.

30. Eric Lichtblau, "A Long Road for Massip: Postpartum Psychosis: Recovery is Torturous," *Los Angeles Times* (February 3, 1989), p. 1-1.

31. Ewing, *Fatal Families*, pp. 62-63; Marianne Yen, "High-Risk Mothers; Postpartum Depression, in Rare Cases, May Cause an Infant's Death," *Washington Post* (August 23, 1988), p. 18.

32. Ewing, *Fatal Families*, pp. 37-55; Flowers and Flowers, *Murders in the United States*, p. 121.

33. *Diagnostic and Statistical Manual of Mental Disorders*, p. 725.

34. *Ibid.*

35. Ewing, *Fatal Families*, p. 48.

36. *Ibid.*, pp. 53-54.

37. Cited in *Ibid.*, p. 54.

38. Temple Terrace, "A Gift Abandoned," *St. Petersburg Times* (April 14, 1991), p. 5.

39. Flowers, *Female Crime, Criminals and Cellmates*, pp. 87-89.

Chapter 6

PARRICIDE

One of the least studied areas of intrafamilial homicide is parricide, the murdering of one's mother, father, or a like relative. Although parricide is a relatively rare occurrence in modern society, a number of highly publicized cases of parricidal behavior in recent years have placed greater attention on its dynamics, nature, at-risk perpetrators and victims, and ways to prevent it. Parricide is much more likely to be perpetrated by adult offenders, often as a murder-suicide or a reflection of homicidal behavior directed as well at persons outside the family. The parricidal adult often has a history of mental illness. Juvenile parricide, while less common, is often more shocking and devastating because of the age of the offender and characteristics of the offense. Most juveniles who kill their parents are the victims of child abuse, abuse drugs or alcohol, or are described as dangerously antisocial. Parricide itself is often indicative of other family violence, dysfunction, and troubles.

THE NATURE OF PARRICIDE

Parricide is defined as the killing of a parent by a son or daughter. Though historically this form of murder has been taboo in most cultures, it is not a new phenomenon. Episodes of parricide, filicide, fratricide, and multiple suicides spanning three generations in one family are chronicled in the Greek myth of Oedipus.[1] Today, parricide is seen as another example of family violence and homicidal behavior that often results from a history of intrafamilial abuses and dysfunction[2] as well as interrelated variables outside the family.[3] Experts have found that differences exist between adult and juvenile parricide[4] and completed and attempted parricide.[5] Substance abuse is often a factor in parricidal behavior,[6] as is a history of violent behavior and psychiatric troubles,[7] and the use and availability of firearms.[8]

72

Studies show that killers of parents or stepparents are predominantly over the age of eighteen.[9] The adult parricide offender is typically found to suffer from severe mental illness or psychopathy.[10]

Though some juvenile parricide offenders also have a history of mental illness, the typical child murderer of a mother or father is more often a victim of severe child abuse or is considered seriously antisocial.[11] In many instances of juvenile parricide, there are siblings who conspire to murder their mother and/or father.

Recent cases of parricide illustrate this disturbing form of intrafamilial homicide in American society:

- On November 16, 1982, 16-year-old Richard Jahnke, Jr., shot and killed his father in the driveway of the family home in Wyoming. Charged as an accomplice in the murder was his 17-year-old sister, Deborah Jahnke. Both claimed the father had been physically, psychologically, and sexually abusive. Richard Jahnke, Jr. was convicted of manslaughter and sentenced to five to fifteen years in prison. Deborah Jahnke received a three to eight year sentence for aiding and abetting.
- On September 8, 1984, 15-year-old Patrick DeGelleke set ablaze the house of his adoptive parents in Rochester, New York as they slept, killing them. DeGelleke had a history of violence and an uncontrollable temper. He was convicted of murder.
- On February 17, 1986, Matthew Gasparovich, Jr., 15, and his 12-year-old sister, Heidi, shot to death their father as he slept in his home in Iowa. Both were undisciplined and tried to flee to California after the murder. Tried as juveniles, the Gasparovich's were found guilty of patricide and placed in juvenile detention until the age of eighteen.
- On January 1, 1987, following an argument, 16-year-old Sean Stevenson shot and killed his parents, then raped and murdered his 18-year-old sister at their home in Washington. He was found guilty of first-degree murder and aggravated murder and given a life sentence without the possibility of parole.
- On August 20, 1989, Lyle Menendez, 22, and Erik Menendez, 19, shot to death their wealthy parents, José and Mary Menendez in the family's Beverly Hills, California home. Both killers claimed they acted in self-defense following years of physical, sexual, and emotional abuse. The Menendez brothers were convicted of first-degree murder and sentenced to life in prison.
- On July 12, 1993, Herman Dutton, 15, and James Dutton, 12, used a deer rifle to shoot to death their father, Lonnie Dutton, while he slept in the family home in Rush Springs, Oklahoma. Both boys claimed their father had physically and sexually abused them for years. The Dutton's pleaded no contest to the charge of manslaughter and were placed in foster homes.

• On February 27, 1995, Bryan Freeman, 17, and David Freeman, 15, bludgeoned and stabbed to death their parents in the family's home in Pennsylvania. The brothers had neo-Nazi affiliations and violent histories. Both pleaded guilty to murder and were given life sentences with no chance for parole.[12]

HOW OFTEN DOES PARRICIDE OCCUR?

According to Federal Bureau of Investigation (FBI) figures, there were 234 murders in 1999 in which the victim was identified as a father or mother in relationship to the offender.[13] Studies estimate that 300 parents are killed by their progeny annually in the United States.[14]

Despite these numbers and the publicity often generated in cases of parricide, this type of intrafamilial homicide is quite rare. Official data indicates that between 1977 and 1999, parricide constituted less than 2 percent of total homicides committed in the United States.[15] In a review of FBI parricide statistics, Kathleen Heide found that the rate of patricides (the killing of one's father) ranged from 0.7 percent to 1.1 percent of all homicidies, while the rate of matricides (the killing of one's mother) was between 0.6 percent and 0.8 percent of total murders.[16] California parricide data corresponds with that on the national level, accounting for between 0.9 percent and 1.1 percent of the state's homicides.[17]

While the percentage of juvenile cases of parricide are relatively small, juveniles are much more likely to kill their parents than to commit murder in general. Around 10 percent of murders in the United States annually are perpetrated by offenders younger than eighteen years of age.[18] However, according to Heide's study, 34 percent of stepfathers, 30 percent of stepmothers, 25 percent of fathers, and 15 percent of mothers were victims of parricide committed by sons and daughters under the age of eighteen.[19]

CHARACTERISTICS OF PARRICIDE
OFFENDERS AND VICTIMS

Most people who kill their parents are of adult age. It is estimated that more than three-quarters of parricide perpetrators are persons over the age of eighteen.20 The typical parricidal offender tends to have a history of serious psychiatric problems while exhibiting little indication of a background of violence against their parents.[21] Studies show that male parricide offenders are more likely to kill their mothers than fathers; while female parricide offenders tend to murder their mothers.[22] The killing of both parents has been shown to be committed almost wholly by sons.[23]

Researchers have identified other characteristics of parricide offenders as follows:

- Most are white males.
- Most are non-Hispanics.
- More than seven in ten killers of fathers, stepfathers, or stepmothers are under the age of thirty.
- Almost seven out of ten killers of mothers are between the ages of twenty and fifty.
- Most adolescent offenders are between sixteen and eighteen years of age and come from middle and upper-middle class backgrounds.
- Around one in four parricide victims are murdered by a son or daughter younger than eighteen.[24]

Victims of parricide come from all racial, ethnic, and economic backgrounds, and include parents of juvenile and adult parricide offenders. Fathers are more likely to be murdered by offspring than mothers.[25] Parricide experts have found that the typical parent or stepparent victim of parricide is white, non-Hispanic, usually in their forties and fifties.[26] Stepparent victims tend to be younger than parent victims.

TYPES OF ADULT PARRICIDE PERPETRATORS

Most killers of mothers and fathers fall under this category. Adult parricide offenders are most often described in the literature as seriously mentally ill or psychopathic.[27] Researchers have characterized the adult that kills a parent as a paranoid schizophrenic "who is embroiled in a hostile-dependent relationship with the victim."[28] According to psychiatrists, this type of parricide is termed *catathymic homicide*, in reference to:

> chronic emotional tension caused by traumatic experiences, projection of responsibility for the internal tension state onto the external situation, and the perception of violence as the only way out of the situation. The criminal act is perpetrated in a sudden rush of emotional tensions, with little premeditation or deliberation, and thus often leads to judicial verdict of insanity, involuntary manslaughter or simple assault.[29]

The second most common type of adult parricide perpetrator is one who kills a mother or father for sociopathic purposes, such as having a history of violence or receiving insurance payments upon the death. In some instances, the victim may have previously been subjected to parent abuse or elderly exploitation due to dependency.

Parricidal adults often also direct homicidal violence against their family members such as a spouse or children, or persons outside the family, and are frequently suicidal as well.[30]

TYPES OF JUVENILE PARRICIDE PERPETRATORS

Researchers have identified three primary types of juveniles who kill their parents: (1) the severely abused child, (2) the severely mentally ill child, and (3) the dangerously antisocial child.[31] The characteristics of each are described as follows:

- **Severely abused child**. The most common type of adolescent parricide perpetrator who has been the victim of or witness to brutal, chronic abuse in the family and kills in response to this, self-defense, or to protect others from the abuser.
- **Severely mentally ill child**. This type of parricidal child is considered psychotic or seriously mentally ill. Such parricide offenders typically have a history of psychiatric problems, which leads to the murder of a parent.
- **Dangerously antisocial child**. This type of parricide offender kills a mother or father for selfish or deviant reasons. Such parent killers are described in psychiatry as possessing conduct disorders or antisocial personalities, depending on the offender's age and other criteria. The dangerously antisocial child is not considered psychotic.

According to Heide, severely abused adolescent parricide perpetrators are typically diagnosed following the parental murder as suffering from depression or post-traumatic stress disorder (PTSD).[32] Such offenders often experience feelings of sadness, hopelessness, fatigue, difficulties in concentrating, and suicidal ideation.

The dangerously antisocial child who is diagnosed as a conduct-disordered youth motivated to commit parricide for self-serving purposes may often have a history of violent behavior, substance abuse, and involvement with antisocial groups.[33]

WHAT CAUSES A PERSON TO COMMIT PARRICIDE?

Studies show that the causes of or important factors in parricidal behavior include a history of mental illness, child physical or sexual abuse, violent or antisocial conduct, and substance abuse.[34] Greed or profit as a motive has also been shown to motivate some parricide offenders to kill their parents. A good example is that of the Menendez brothers, two young adults who murdered their wealthy parents. In spite of their allegations that they suffered years of abuse from their father and mother, a jury convicted them primarily on the basis of murder for financial gain.

Adult parricide offenders tend to kill in relation to serious psychiatric problems or profit motive, whereas youthful parricide offenders are more likely to kill after being subjected to a pattern of severe parental abusive treatment. More often than not, juvenile parricide involving a sibling conspiracy involves physical, sexual, and/or psychological abuse perpetrated by the murdered parent.

In some cases, child parricide offenders may kill one parent as the unwitting "lethal agent" of the other parent "who unconsciously incites [the child] to kill in order that the [parent] can vicariously enjoy the benefits of the act."[35] L. Bender and F. J. Curran posited that the most common factor in child perpetrated homicide or attempted murder is "the child's tendency to identify himself with aggressive parents, and pattern after their behavior."[36]

Some researchers have found that parricide and other homicide may be related to pent up emotions that explode in homicidal violence before they can be rechanneled. According to B. M. Cormier and colleagues: "Amongst those adolescents who kill within the nuclear group, there is an inability to displace those problems encountered with the parents on to a broader group, such as their peers, where the problem can be defused and new gratifications experienced."[37]

NOTES

1. R. Graves, *Greek Myths* (New York: Penguin, 1962).
2. Neil Websdale, *Understanding Domestic Homicide* (Boston: Northeastern University Press, 1999), pp. 12-13; Kathleen M. Heide, *Why Kids Kill Parents: Child Abuse and Adolescent Homicide* (Thousand Oaks: Sage, 1995).
3. R. Barri Flowers, *Domestic Crimes, Family Violence and Child Abuse: A Study of Contemporary American Society* (Jefferson: McFarland, 2000), pp. 68-70.
4. Heide, *Why Kids Kill Parents*; T. Chaimberlain, "The Dynamics of Parricide," *American Journal of Forensic Psychiatry* 7 (1986): 11-23; Kathleen M. Heide, "Parents Who Get Killed and the Children Who Kill Them," *Journal of Interpersonal Violence* 8, 4 (1993): 531-44.
5. Adam M. Weisman and Kanshal K. Skarma, "Parricide and Attempted Parricide," in U.S. Department of Justice, *The Nature of Homicide: Trends and Changes–Proceedings of the 1996 Meeting of the Homicide Research Working Group* (Washington: National Institute of Justice, 1997), pp. 234-44.
6. Heide, *Why Kids Kill Parents*, pp. 37, 42-43; Michael Maloney, "Children Who Kill Their Parents," *Prosecutor's Brief: California District Attorney's Association Journal 20* (1994): 20-22.

7. Heide, *Why Kids Kill Parents*; Charles P. Ewing, *Fatal Families: The Dynamics of Intrafamilial Homicide* (Thousand Oaks: Sage, 1997), pp. 104-14.
8. R. Barri Flowers, *Kids Who Commit Adult Crimes: A Study of Serious Juvenile Criminality and Delinquency* (Binghampton: Haworth, 2002); T. J. Young, "Parricide Rates and Criminal Street Violence in the United States: Is There a Correlation?" *Adolescence 28*, 109 (1993): 171-72.
9. Heide, *Why Kids Kill Parents*; Weisman and Skarma, "Parricide and Attempted Parricide," p. 234.
10. Kathleen M. Heide, "Dangerously Antisocial Kids Who Kill Their Parents: Toward a Better Understanding of the Phenomenon," in U.S. Department of Justice, *The Nature of Homicide: Trends and Changes—Proceedings of the 1996 Meeting of the Homicide Research Working Group* (Washington: National Institute of Justice, 1997), p. 229.
11. *Ibid.*, pp. 228-30.
12. R. Barri Flowers and H. Loraine Flowers, *Murders in the United States: Crimes, Killers and Victims of the Twentieth Century* (Jefferson: McFarland, 2001), pp. 76, 147-51.
13. U.S. Department of Justice, Federal Bureau of Investigation, *Crime in the United States: Uniform Crime Reports 1999* (Washington: Government Printing Office, 2000), p. 19.
14. Heide, "Dangerously Antisocial Kids Who Kill Their Parents," p. 229; Ewing, *Fatal Families*, p. 103.
15. *Crime in the United States*, p. 19; Weisman and Skarma, "Parricide and Attempted Parricide," p. 234.
16. Heide, "Parents Who Get Killed and the Children Who Kill Them," pp. 531-44.
17. Cited in Weisman and Skarma, "Parricide and Attempted Parricide," p. 234.
18. *Crime in the United States*, p. 14.
19. Heide, *Why Kids Kill Parents*, p. 3.
20. Heide, "Parents Who Get Killed and the Children Who Kill Them."
21. Weisman and Skarma, "Parricide and Attempted Parricide," p. 234.
22. C. E. Newhill, "Parricide," *Journal of Family Violence 64* (1991): 375-94; J. R. Meloy, *Violent Attachments* (Northvale: Aronson, 1992).
23. Weisman and Skarma, "Parricide and Attempted Parricide," p. 235.
24. Ewing, *Fatal Families*, pp. 103-4; Heide, *Why Kids Kill Parents*, p. 3; P. A. Mones, *When A Child Kills: Abused Children Who Kill Their Parents* (New York: Pocket Books, 1991).
25. *Crime in the United States*, p. 19.
26. Ewing, *Fatal Families*, p. 103.
27. Heide, "Dangerously Antisocial Kids Who Kill Their Parents," p. 229.
28. Weisman and Skarma, "Parricide and Attempted Parricide," p. 235.
29. *Ibid.*, pp. 235-36; Meloy, Violent Attachments; L. S. Tucker and T. P. Cornwall, "Mother-Son Folie a Duex: A Case of Attempted Parricide," *American Journal of Psychiatry 134*, 10 (1977): 1146-47.

30. Flowers and Flowers, *Murders in the United States*, pp. 76, 136.
31. Heide, "Dangerously Antisocial Kids Who Kill Their Parents," pp. 228-33; American Psychiatric Association, *Diagnostic and Statistical Manual of Mental Disorders*, 4th ed. (Washington: American Psychiatric Association, 1994); L. Walker, Sudden Fury (New York: St. Martin's Press, 1989); D. Kleiman, *A Deadly Silence* (New York: Atlantic Monthly Press, 1988).
32. Heide, "Dangerously Antisocial Kids Who Kill Their Parents," p. 228.
33. *Ibid.*, p. 230.
34. *Ibid.*, pp. 228-30; Ewing, *Fatal Families*, pp. 103-11; Diana E. Russell, "A Study of Juvenile Murderers of Family Members," *International Journal of Offender Therapy and Comparative Criminology 28* (1984): 177-92.
35. R. Barri Flowers, *Children and Criminality: The Child as Victim and Perpetrator* (Westport: Greenwood, 1986), p. 59. See also D. Sargeant, "Children Who Kill– A Family Conspiracy?" in J. Howells, ed., *Theory and Practice of Family Psychiatry* (New York: Brunner-Mazel, 1971).
36. L. Bender and F. J. Curran, "Children and Adolescents Who Kill," *Journal of Criminal Psychopathology 1*, 4 (1940): 297.
37. Cited in Flowers, *Children and Criminality*, p. 59.

Chapter 7

OTHER INTRAFAMILIAL HOMICIDE

Every year in the United States there are thousands of intrafamilial homicides, or murders involving parents, children, siblings, and entire families. Many of these are the result of child abuse, domestic violence, self-defense, murder-suicide, substance abuse, mental illness, jealousy, rivalry, greed, and other family dysfunction and difficulties. Murderers within the family have been described as "passive and submissive, preferring to avoid open conflict when possible, especially if playing a masochistic role leads to gaining their affection."[1] The suicidal nature of domestic homicide has been noted in the literature in which some victims are believed to "so aggressively provoke violence toward themselves by a family member that they can be viewed as suicides."[2] The complex dynamics of family life can often act as precursors to murder among family members.

The very real threat of bodily harm and lethal intrafamilial victimization led one expert on domestic violence to observe: "The home is a very dangerous place and we have more to fear from close members of our family than total strangers."[3] These sentiments were echoed in an article on family violence in which the authors asserted:

> With the exception of the police and the military, the family is perhaps the most violent social group, and the home the most violent social setting in our society. A person is more likely to be hit or killed in his or her own home by another family member than anywhere else or by anyone else.[4]

Unfortunately, this is all to true when it comes to murder.

DOMESTIC MURDER OF CHILDREN

Filicide–the killing of one's child–is perhaps the saddest form of intrafamilial homicide. According to the Justice Department, in 1999 there were 445 murders in which the victims were identified as sons or daughters of the perpetrator in the United States.[5] Most experts believe that many more children are the victims of murder committed by parents annually, and that the majority of these are caused by or involve child abuse of some type. Every year more than a million children are the victims of substantiated child abuse and neglect in this country.[6] Over three million reports of child maltreatment are investigated by child protective services agencies annually.[7]

Pediatric News reported that one child dies every day from child abuse.[8] Vincent Fontana estimated that 700 children are killed by parents in the United States each year.[9] The National Incidence Study reported that approximately 1,000 children die annually as a result of child abuse or neglect.[10] Sandra Arbetter estimated that there are 600 cases of women alone who murder their children every year.[11]

According to Alex Morales, 3,000 children will die from abuse every year in the United States, with half the victims under the age of one and 90 percent younger than age four.[12] Ray Helfer warned that unless steps were taken to halt the abuse of children, it could result in over 5,000 child deaths per year.[13]

Table 7.1
CHILD FATALITY VICTIMS BY SEX AND AGE, 1997

| Age | | Sex | | |
		Male	Female	Total
0-3	Count	138	106	244
	% within Child Age	56.6%	43.4%	100.0%
	% within Child Sex	77.1%	76.8%	77.0%
4-7	Count	23	18	41
	% within Child Age	56.1%	43.9%	100.0%
	% within Child Sex	12.8%	13.0%	12.9%
8-11	Count	9	5	14
	% within Child Age	64.3%	35.7%	100.0%
	% within Child Sex	5.0%	3.6%	4.4%
12-15	Count	7	4	11
	% within Child Age	63.6%	36.4%	100.0%
	% within Child Sex	3.9%	2.9%	3.5%
16+	Count	2	5	7
	% within Child Age	28.6%	71.4%	100.0%
	% within Child Sex	1.1%	3.6%	2.2%
Total	Count	179	138	317
	% within Child Age	56.5%	43.5%	100.0%
	% within Child Sex	100.0%	100.0%	

Source: U.S. Department of Health and Human Services, *Child Maltreatment 1997: Reports From the States to the National Child Abuse and Neglect Data System* (Washington: Government Printing Office, 1999), p. 6-2.

The National Child Abuse and Neglect Data System (NCANDS) estimated that there were 1,197 child fatalities nationwide in 1997 in which the majority were attributed to child abuse or neglect.[14] The rate of child fatalities among child abuse and neglect victims was 123 per 100,000 child maltreatment victims.

A representative sample of child fatality victims in 1997 accounting for around one-third of all reported fatalities can be seen in Table 7.1. More than three-quarters of the victims were children age three and under, with nearly six in ten such victims male. Overall, 56.5 percent of child fatality victims were male and 43.5 percent female. More than 71 percent of the victims age sixteen and over were female.

Recent cases of filicide can be seen below:

- On May 19, 1983, Elizabeth Downs, twenty-eight, murdered her seven-year-old daughter and tried to kill her two other children in Springfield, Oregon reportedly because they hindered her love life. She was convicted of murder and two counts of attempted murder and sentenced to life in prison plus fifty years.
- On October 26, 1997, Susan Eubanks, thirty-five, shot to death her four young sons in the family home in San Marcos, California. The unemployed nursing assistant had a history of substance abuse and bad relationships. She was convicted of all four murders and sentenced to death.
- On December 4, 1999, Kao Xiong used a high-powered rifle and shotgun to murder five of his seven children before killing himself in the family's apartment in Del Paso Heights, California. The Laos native had argued with his wife prior to the mass filicide-suicide.[15]
- On June 20, 2001, Andrea Yates, thirty-seven, drowned her five young children in the bathtub of their home in Clear Lake, Texas. With a history of severe mental illness, she has pleaded not guilty by reason of insanity.

Characterizing Filicide Perpetrators

According to NCANDS, females are more likely to be the perpetrators of filicide than males. As seen in Table 7.2, of 347 child fatalities detailed in 1997, 62.8 percent of the perpetrators were female, while 37.2 percent were male. Most perpetrators were twenty to twenty-nine years of age, with more than two-thirds female.

In spite of these figures, much of the research indicates that males tend to commit the vast majority of child maltreatment-related homicides.[16] Most of these come as the result of physical child abuse.[17] One study found that 80 percent of child deaths due to trauma of the head and body were perpetrated by male offenders.[18]

Table 7.2

PERPETRATORS OF CHILD FATALITIES BY SEX AND AGE, 1997

Age		Perpetrator Sex		Total
		Male	Female	
19 years or younger	Count	15	30	45
	% within Perpetrator Age	33.3%	66.7%	100.0%
	% within Perpetrator Sex	11.6%	13.8%	13.0%
20 to 29 years old	Count	63	127	190
	% within Perpetrator Age	33.2%	66.8%	100.0%
	% within Perpetrator Sex	48.8%	58.3%	54.8%
30 to 39 years old	Count	26	30	56
	% within Perpetrator Age	46.4%	53.6%	100.0%
	% within Perpetrator Sex	20.2%	13.8%	16.1%
40 to 49 years old	Count	20	16	36
	% within Perpetrator Age	55.6%	44.4%	100.0%
	% within Perpetrator Sex	15.5%	7.3%	10.4%
50 years or older	Count	5	15	20
	% within Perpetrator Age	25.0%	75.0%	100.0%
	% within Perpetrator Sex	3.9%	6.9%	5.8%
Total	Count	129	218	347
	% within Perpetrator Age	37.2%	62.8%	100.0%
	% within Perpetrator Sex	100.0%	100.0%	100.0%

Source: U.S. Department of Health and Human Services, *Child Maltreatment 1997: Reports From the States to the National Child Abuse and Neglect Data System* (Washington: Government Printing Office, 1999), p. 7-3.

While mothers who kill their children are believed to often suffer from severe mental illness or serious depression, such as the aforementioned case of Andrea Yates, according to D. T. Lunde:

> Fathers rarely kill their young children, but when they do, they also build up to the crime, and often have a history of child abuse. Fathers who murder are more likely to kill their teenage sons. These men are marginally adequate husbands and fathers who feel inferior and frustrated by life. Guns and alcohol play significant roles in their lives. Their criminal records, if any, usually involve drinking, drunk driving, and disorderly conduct. They rarely have a history of psychiatric illness. They simply are explosive individuals who kill impulsively.[19]

In a twelve-year study of filicidal men, J. F. Campion, J. M. Cravens, and F. Covan characterized the offenders as having a stressful history, including experiencing domestic violence, child abuse, and broken homes.[20] Three-quarters of the men were found to have had mental or neurological disorders during childhood, while many had been put out of the house due to antisocial behavior or parental mistreatment.

Studies show that the majority of parents who murder their children are in their twenties,[21] with less than 7 percent younger than eighteen years of age.[22] Most filicide offenders kill their victims as the result of injuries inflicted to the head. In a study of child abuse fatalities, Patricia Schloesser and colleagues found that nearly 60 percent of the deaths were caused by head injuries.[23] Similarly, in Richard Krugman's analysis of child maltreatment deaths, 71 percent were due to injuries to the head.[24]

Filicide by shooting is also becoming more common as more offenders gain access to firearms. In Neil Websdale's study of domestic homicide, one in four perpetrators of filicide used a gun to kill their victim.[25]

SIBLING HOMICIDE

Every year more than 100 people are murdered by a sibling in the United States. According to the Uniform Crime Reports, in 1999, there were 104 sibling homicides in this country. Males are most likely to be victims and perpetrators of sibling homicide. Seventy-eight of the homicides were fratricides (the killing of one's brother) and twenty-six were sororicides (the killing of one's sister).[26]

In a recent U.S. Department of Justice survey of homicides in urban counties, 1.5 percent were sibling perpetrated homicides.[27] Over 80 percent of the offenders and victims were adults, while approximately 85 percent of the sibling killers and 73 percent of the victims were male. In nearly 70 percent of cases, the perpetrator-victim were the same sex; and in 65 percent of the sibling homicides, the offender and victim were black. Firearms were used in under 40 percent of the murders.

Recent cases of sibling homicide can be seen as follows:

- In April 1985, Britt Kellum, nine, got into a fight with his eleven-year-old brother before shooting him to death with a 16-gauge shotgun at the family's home near Flint, Michigan. On October 30, 1989, after four years of psychotherapy, Kellum used his father's .38 caliber handgun to kill his six-year-old brother while playing Russian roulette.
- On July 9, 1985, Steven Benson, thirty-four, planted two pipe bombs beneath the family's van outside their Naples, Florida home. The explosion killed his brother and mother and seriously injured his sister. The heir to a tobacco fortune killed out of greed. He was convicted on a number of counts, including two murders, and given two consecutive life sentences.
- On January 3, 1996, Tom Grentz, eighty-seven, used a .25 caliber gun to shoot to death his eighty-five-year-old sister and then himself in the house they shared in Baltimore, Maryland. Both had been seriously ill in recent years.[28]

- On October 26, 1995, Dana Jokela, eighteen, beat to death his twenty-year-old brother, Cary, with a baseball bat at the family's home in Ohio following an argument. There had been a history of violence between the siblings. Jokela pleaded guilty to manslaughter.
- On July 3, 1995, Richard Gibson, thirty-eight, shot to death his forty-one-year-old brother, Allen, following an argument at the house they shared with their father in Detroit, Michigan. The younger Gibson then turned the gun on himself, committing suicide.[29]

Sibling homicide is often a reflection of sibling violence and other family violence and instability. According to the National Crime Victimization Survey, in 1994, there were 138,887 single-offender crimes of violence committed against brothers and sisters.[30] More than 7,000 multiple-offender crimes were perpetrated against siblings. In a study of family violence, Murray Straus and colleagues estimated that based on an "ever happened" premise, some 8.3 million children in the United States have been "beaten up" by a sibling, while 2.3 million have at some point used a gun or knife on a sister or brother.[31]

Reasons Why Siblings Kill Siblings

People commit fratricide and sororicide for various reasons, including a history of bad blood between them, sibling rivalry or abuse, substance abuse, domestic violence, unemployment, relationship problems, and mental illness. The *American Journal of Psychiatry* found that intrafamilial homicidal behavior by children is often associated with extremely violent parents (especially the father), a history of psychomotor seizures and suicidal behavior, and prior psychiatric treatment by the mother.[32] B. M. Cormier and colleagues attributed murder by children within the family as an inability to transfer parental-related problems to the outside world where they might be defused.[33]

The unresolved conflicts and stresses between siblings, often lasting into adulthood, can trigger a homicidal reaction. This may be particularly true when adult siblings live close by or in the same house, as Charles Ewing notes:

> Where adult siblings end up living together and/or under the same roof as their parents, competition among them may continue if not intensify. Even though few adult siblings kill one another, it should come as no surprise that many who do . . . were living with their sibling-victims at the time of the killings.[34]

The relationship between sibling homicide and mental illness has been demonstrated in studies. According to a Department of Justice study, nearly one in five cases of sibling murder involved an offender whose history was characterized by mental illness.[35] Similarly, substance abuse often plays a strong role in homicide between siblings. The study found that over half the offenders and almost 35 percent of the victims had been drinking at the time the murder occurred.[36]

Studies reveal that some cases of sibling homicide are motivated by a history of violent behavior by the perpetrator and other antisocial behavior.[37] Some instance of children killing siblings are classified as accidental killings but are often a reflection of antecedents such as behavioral problems, mental illness, child neglect, or mental illness.[38]

FAMILICIDE

Familicide, or the killing of most or all of one's family, is relatively rare compared to other domestic homicides. There are no national statistics on familicide, however the killing of family in American history has been documented.[39] Websdale points out that "analysis of modern-day familicides emphasize the manner in which socioeconomic pressures and perpetrators' concerns about their social standing compound or supercede psychiatric problems as the primary cause of these tragedies."[40] Notable cases of familicide can be seen below:

- On February 17, 1970, Jeffrey MacDonald, a twenty-six-year-old Army doctor, bludgeoned and stabbed to death his wife and two young children in their Fort Bragg home in Wilmington, North Carolina. In spite of claiming innocence, MacDonald was found guilty of the murders and given three life sentences behind bars.
- On November 13, 1974, Ronald DeFeo, Jr., twenty-three, used a .35 caliber rifle to murder his parents and four siblings at their home in Amityville, New York. Inspiring the movie, *The Amityville Horror*, DeFeo claimed to have been possessed by Satan when committing the mass murder. He was convicted of the murders and sentenced to six consecutive life terms.
- On March 30, 1975, James Ruppert, forty, gunned down eleven members of his family (including his mother) during an Easter Sunday dinner in Hamilton, Ohio. He was convicted of the crimes and received a life sentence in prison.
- On August 3, 1978, Rachal David pushed or forced seven of her children off an eleventh story balcony of a Salt Lake City, Utah hotel and then jumped, killing six of the children and herself. Two days earlier, her husband, wanted by the authorities for fraudulent crimes, had committed suicide.

- On December 28, 1987, Ronald Simmons went on a deadly shooting spree, including the murder of fourteen family members in Russellville, Arkansas. He was found guilty of sixteen counts of murder and put to death by lethal injection.
- On March 19, 1990, Roxanne Jones used a .22 caliber rifle to shoot to death her two teenage sons and young daughter while they slept, before killing herself. Troubled following two stormy marriages, she left several suicide notes.[41]

Characterizing the Familicide Offender

Familicide is committed primarily by adult males, and often ends up with suicide by the perpetrator. According to Ewing, the typical familicide offender is a "white male in his thirties or forties who reacts to extreme stress by killing his wife and child(ren) and then himself. Usually the killings are committed with a firearm that belongs to the perpetrator and has been present in the home for some time."[42]

Researchers have characterized the perpetrator of familicide as often suffering from depression or paranoia and is usually intoxicated.[43] He tends to kill the entire family if he can, including extended family members and even pets. Most familicidal men are unable to handle extreme stress or disruptions in family or outside life. The "dependent-protective" motivation to commit familicide has been identified by some experts on domestic homicide.[44] Peter Marzuk and associates asserted that the perpetrator of familicide-suicide typically likes to control his family and take care of their needs. When his domination is weakened or otherwise undermined, his frustration results in rage that turns homicidal and suicidal.[45] The familicide offender commonly erupts from not only a disintegrating family situation, but loss of control over every aspect of his life and times which reaches an often deadly breaking point.

Although it is rare that females will murder most of or the entire family, as noted earlier it does occur. Such familicide offenders are usually despondent over a lost intimate relationship or a hopeless situation. Most are depressed or suffer from severe mental illness.[46]

Juvenile familicide offenders are predominantly male. As with adult murderers of the family, most juvenile perpetrators commit suicide as part of the mass domestic homicide and are often reacting to extreme stress. Such family killers typically suffer from chronic psychiatric problems and have been victimized by child abuse or other domestic violence.[47]

NOTES

1. R. Barri Flowers, *Children and Criminality: The Child as Victim and Perpetrator* (Westport: Greenwood, 1986), p. 58. See also M. Houts, *They Asked for Death* (New York: Cowles, 1970), p. 241; L. Schultz, "The Victim-Offender Relationship," *Crime and Delinquency 14*, 2 (1968): 135-41.

2. R. Barri Flowers, *Domestic Crimes, Family Violence and Child Abuse: A Study of Contemporary American Society* (Jefferson: McFarland, 2000), p. 62. See also Marvin Wolfgang, "Who Kills Whom," *Psychology Today 3*, 5 (1969): 54-56.

3. M. A. Freeman, *Violence in the Home* (Farnborough: Saxon House, 1979), p. 6.

4. Richard J. Gelles and Murray A. Straus, "Violence in the American Family," *Journal of Social Issues 35*, 2 (1979): 15-39.

5. U.S. Department of Justice, Federal Bureau of Investigation, *Crime in the United States: Uniform Crime Reports 1999* (Washington: Government Printing Office, 2000), p. 19.

6. Flowers, *Domestic Crimes, Family Violence and Child Abuse*, p. 112.

7. Ibid.; John M. Leventhal, "The Challenges of Recognizing Child Abuse: Seeing is Believing," *Journal of the American Medical Association 281*, 7 (1999): 657.

8. "One Child Dies Daily from Abuse: Parent Probably Was Abuser," *Pediatric News 9* (1975): 3.

9. Vincent J. Fontana, *Somewhere A Child is Crying* (New York: Macmillan, 1973).

10. Cited in Pamela D. Mayhall and Katherine Norgard, *Child Abuse and Neglect: Sharing Responsibility* (Toronto: John Wiley & Sons, 1983), p. 98.

11. Sandra Arbetter, "Family Violence; When We Hurt the Ones We Love," *Current Health 22*, 3 (1995): 6.

12. Alex Morales, "Seeking a Cure for Child Abuse," *USA Today 127*, 2640 (1998): 34.

13. Cited in Flowers, *Children and Criminality*, p. 58.

14. U.S. Department of Health and Human Services, *Child Maltreatment 1997: Reports from the States to the National Child Abuse and Neglect Data System* (Washington: Government Printing Office, 1999), p. xiii.

15. R. Barri Flowers and H. Loraine Flowers, *Murders in the United States: Crimes, Killers and Victims of the Twentieth Century* (Jefferson: McFarland, 2001), pp. 76-77, 128-29, 137.

16. Murray Levine, Jennifer Freeman, and Cheryl Compaan, "Maltreatment-Related Fatalities: Issues of Policy and Prevention," *Law and Policy 16*, 449 (1994): 458.

17. *Ibid.*; Flowers, *Domestic Crimes, Family Violence and Child Abuse*.

18. Cited in Levine, Freeman, and Compaan, "Maltreatment-Related Fatalities."

19. D. T. Lunde, "Hot Blood's Record Month: Our Murder Boom," *Psychology Today 9* (1975): 35-42.

20. J. F. Campion, J. M. Cravens, and F. Covan, "A Study of Filicidal Men," *American Journal of Psychiatry 145* (1988): 1141.

21. Levine, Freeman, and Compaan, "Maltreatment-Related Fatalities," p. 458.

22. *Ibid.*

23. Patricia Schloesser, John Pierpont, and John Poertner, "Active Surveillance of Child Abuse Fatalities," *Child Abuse and Neglect 16* (1992): 3-10.

24. Richard D. Krugman, "Fatal Child Abuse: An Analysis of 20 Cases," *Pediatrics 12* (1983-1985): 68-72.

25. Neil Websdale, *Understanding Domestic Homicide* (Boston: Northeastern University Press, 1999), pp. 170-71.

26. *Crime in the United States,* p. 19.

27. U.S. Department of Justice, *Murder in Families* (Washington: Bureau of Justice Statistics, 1994).

28. Flowers and Flowers, *Murders in the United States,* pp. 75, 150.

29. Charles P. Ewing, *Fatal Families: The Dynamics of Intrafamilial Homicide* (Thousand Oaks: Sage, 1997), p. 116.

30. U.S. Department of Justice, Bureau of Justice Statistics, *Criminal Victimization in the United States 1994: A National Crime Victimization Survey* (Washington: Government Printing Office, 1997), pp. 42, 46.

31. Murray A. Straus, Richard J. Gelles, and Suzanne K. Steinmetz, *Behind Closed Doors: Violence in the American Family* (Garden City: Doubleday/Anchor, 1980).

32. Cited in Flowers, *Domestic Crimes, Family Violence and Child Abuse,* pp. 69-70.

33. *Ibid.,* p. 70.

34. Ewing, *Fatal Families,* p. 118.

35. *Murder in Families.*

36. *Ibid.*

37. Ewing, *Fatal Families,* pp. 120-24.

38. *Ibid.,* pp. 124-25.

39. Daniel A. Cohen, "Homicidal Compulsion and the Conditions of Freedom: The Social and Psychological Origins of Familicide in America's Early Republic," *Journal of Social History,* Summer (1995): 725-64.

40. Websdale, *Understanding Domestic Homicide,* p. 18.

41. Flowers and Flowers, *Murders in the United States,* pp. 74-77.

42. Ewing, *Fatal Families,* p. 134.

43. Ibid.; Peter Marzuk, Kenneth Tardiff, and Charles Hirsch, "The Epidemiology of Murder-Suicide," *Journal of the American Medical Association 267* (1992): 3181.

44. Ewing, *Fatal Families,* p. 135; A. L. Berman, "Dyadic Death: Murder-Suicide," *Suicidal and Life Threatening Behavior 9* (1979): 15.

45. Marjuk, Tardiff, and Hirsch, "The Epidemiology of Murder-Suicide," p. 3181.

46. Flowers, *Domestic Crimes, Family Violence and Child Abuse,* p. 68.

47. Ewing, *Fatal Families,* pp. 138-39.

Part III

INTERPERSONAL AND SOCIETAL MURDER

Chapter 8

WORKPLACE HOMICIDE

The focus on violence in the workplace has increased in recent years as seemingly more work-related stresses and other factors have manifested themselves into violent behavior on the job. Particularly disturbing has been the high profile cases of lethal workplace violence in the United States in the 1990s and 2000s. Most of these have been perpetrated by strangers; with many involving former or current workers holding a grudge against an employer or coworker, a vengeful stalker, or someone otherwise venting their frustrations against those in a familiar work setting. Homicidal violence in the workplace has taken on a somewhat new and ominous dimension in the year 2001 with international terrorist attacks of the Pentagon and World Trade Center and biological terrorism in the form of anthrax aimed at news organizations, government offices, and the U.S. postal service. These notwithstanding, workplace violence is relative low in relation to overall violence in society and continues to be largely of a domestic nature. Identifying at-risk victims and offenders and preventative measures continues to be an important undertaking for researchers and policymakers.

IN THE CONTEXT OF WORKPLACE VIOLENCE

The National Crime Victimization Survey (NCVS) defines workplace violence as "violent acts against a person at work or on duty, including physical assaults (rape and sexual assault and aggravated and simple assault) and robbery. Attempts are included with completed victimizations."[1]

How big is the problem of violence in the workplace? In relative terms, workplace violence constitutes only around 11 percent of all nonfatal violent crimes,[2] while fatal workplace violence accounts for about 4 percent of total homicides in the United States.[3] In spite of these figures, workplace violence is a serious problem, affecting millions.

93

Based on data from the NCVS, between 1992 and 1996, there were more than two million workplace violent victimizations in this country each year (see Table 8.1). There were an average of nearly 1.5 million simple assault victimizations annually, accounting for the vast majority of workplace violence. Almost three out of four crimes of violence in the workplace were simple assaults, while nearly two in ten victimizations were aggravated assaults. Homicides accounted for less than 1 percent of the workplace violent victimizations, averaging just over 1,023 murders per year.

Table 8.1
WORKPLACE VIOLENCE VICTIMIZATION, 1992-1996

Type of violence	Annual Average	Percent
Total	2,010,800	100.0
Homicide[a]	1,023	0.05
Rape and sexual assault	50,500	2.5
Robbery	83,700	4.2
Aggravated assault	395,500	19.7
Simple assault	1,480,000	73.6

[a]Homicide data from the FBI's UCR include murder and nonnegligent manslaughter.

Source: U.S. Department of Justice, Bureau of Justice Statistics Special Report, *Workplace Violence 1992-96* (Washington: Government Printing Office, 1998), p. 2.

Other studies have yielded similar results on the magnitude of workplace violence in the United States. For example, a Northwestern National Life survey of physical assaults occurring in the workplace between 1992 and 1993, estimated that there were 2.2 million such assaults.[4]

Some researchers have examined workplace violence in terms of risk factors for victimization,[5] injuries incurred,[6] the frequency of occurrence and circumstances of nonfatal violence in various work settings,[7] and differences between nonfatal and fatal workplace violence.[8]

Characteristics of Workplace Violence

Who are the people who perpetrate and are victimized by workplace violence? Where is workplace violence most likely to occur? Studies show that perpetrators of violence in the workplace are overwhelmingly male, white, and over the age of thirty.[9] As shown in Table 8.2, between 1992 and 1996, males constituted nearly 83 percent of the lone offenders of workplace violence in the United States. Females made up just over 14 percent of single offenders of violence in the workplace.

Table 8.2
CHARACTERISTICS OF PERSONS COMMITTING
WORKPLACE VIOLENCE, 1992-1996

Characteristics of offenders	Percent of victims of workplace violence by lone offenders
Sex	
Male	82.9
Female	14.1
Unknown	2.9
Race	
White	58.4
Black	29.0
Other	8.1
Not ascertained	4.4
Age	
Under 12	1.9
12 to 17	10.0
18 to 20	6.6
21 to 29	29.4
30 or older	47.0
Not ascertained	5.1

Source: U.S. Department of Justice, Bureau of Justice Statistics Special Report, *Workplace Violence 1992-96* (Washington: Government Printing Office, 1998), p. 5.

Nearly six in ten offenders of workplace violence were white, while almost three in ten were black, in disproportion to their population figures. Other races comprised less than 10 percent of the perpetrators.

Workplace violence was most likely to be committed by persons age twenty-one and over. Nearly half the offenders were age thirty and over, while almost 30 percent fell between the ages of twenty-one to twenty-nine.

Studies show that more than two-thirds of violence in the workplace is perpetrated by strangers, though much of the attention is given to violence involving nonstrangers.[10] Researchers have characterized the typical workplace violence offender as follows:

- Has a prior history of violence, especially toward women, children, and animals.
- Is a loner, often withdrawn, and fears change.
- Has emotional problems such as depression and low self-esteem.
- Has a substance abuse problem.
- Has occupation frustrations including losing job or unsteady employment history.

• Has an adversarial association with other people.
• Often obsessed with weapons, violence, a person, job, or zealotry.[11]

Victims of workplace violence are predominantly male, white, non-Hispanic, and between their mid twenties and late forties (see Table 8.3). From 1992 to 1996, males made up more than two-thirds of the victims of workplace violence, compared to female victims constituting about one-third of the total. Male workers are more likely to be the victims of stranger attacks in the workplace, while female workers are more likely to be victimized by someone they know, such as an intimate, acquaintance, or stalker.[12]

Table 8.3
CHARACTERISTICS OF WORKPLACE VIOLENCE VICTIMS, 1992-1996

Victim characteristic	*Percent*
Total	100.0%
Sex	
Male	66.8
Female	33.2
Race	
White	88.6
Black	8.9
Other	2.5
Ethnicity[a]	
Hispanic	6.6
Non-Hispanic	92.1
Age	
Under 12	1.9
12 to 17	10.0
18 to 20	6.6
21 to 29	29.4
30 or older	47.0
Not ascertained	5.1

[a]Ethnicity was unknown for 1.3% of victims of workplace violence.

Source: U.S. Department of Justice, Bureau of Justice Statistics Special Report, *Workplace Violence 1992-96* (Washington: Government Printing Office, 1998), p. 2.

Nearly 90 percent of victims of workplace violence were white, with black victims accounting for less than 9 percent, and other races under 3 percent of victims. More than 92 percent of victims were non-Hispanic.

Around seven out of ten victims of violence in the workplace were between age twenty-five and forty-nine, with nearly four in ten victims age thirty-five to forty-nine.

Violence in the workplace is most likely to occur in law enforcement and retail sales, as seen in Table 8.4. Between 1992 and 1996, an average of 431,200 persons in law enforcement occupations were victims of workplace violence in this country annually. These included police, correctional employees, and private security.

Table 8.4
CHARACTERISTICS OF PERSONS COMMITTING
WORKPLACE VIOLENCE, 1992-1996

Occupation	Annual average number of victims
Medical	160,800
Mental Health	102,500
Teaching	148,800
Law Enforcement	431,200
Retail Sales	331,600
Transportation	76,500
Other or unspecified	758,000

Source: U.S. Department of Justice, Bureau of Justice Statistics Special Report, *Workplace Violence 1992-96* (Washington: Office of Justice Programs, 1998), p. 3.

Retail sales employees accounted for an annual average of 331,600 victims, followed by victims in medical professions and teaching professions, with annual numbers at 160,800 and 148,500, respectively. Occupational victimizations were also reported in mental health and transportation professions. Around 758,000 victims on average were in other or unspecified professions each year.

MURDER IN THE WORKPLACE

Although murder in the workplace represents only a fraction of total homicides in the United States, workplace homicide is the country's fastest growing type of murder.[13] Further, homicide is currently the leading cause of women's death on the job, and the second leading cause of men's workplace deaths.[14] Overall, homicide is the second leading cause of death due to injury occurring at work, according to the Bureau of Labor Statistics.[15]

Lethal violence in the workplace has increasingly become mass murder, giving greater cause for concern. Recent cases of workplace violence in the United States can be seen as follows:

• On August 20, 1982, Carl Brown, a 51-year-old history teacher, entered a Miami, Florida welding machine shop, apparently upset over a bill for work he had done. He unloaded a 12-gauge shotgun, killing eight employees. Brown was killed when a car ran him over.

- On August 21, 1986, Patrick Sherrill, a 44-year-old part-time postal worker, entered an Edmond, Oklahoma post office heavily armed. He shot to death 14 coworkers and wounded six more before killing himself. He was reportedly about to be fired.

- On February 16, 1988, Richard Farley, a 39-year-old software developer obsessed with a coworker, went to a Silicon Valley defense plant's offices in Sunnyvale, California. There, he opened fire, killing seven and wounding four. He was apprehended, convicted, and sentenced to death in the gas chamber.

- On September 14, 1989, Joseph Westbecker, a 47-year-old mentally ill employee of a Louisville, Kentucky printing plant, entered the place with an AK-47 and two semiautomatic weapons. He opened fire, killing seven and injuring 13.

- On June 18, 1990, James Pough, a 42-year-old laborer angry about having his car repossessed, entered a General Motors Acceptance Corporation office in Jacksonville, Florida where he opened fire with a 30-caliber rifle. He killed nine and wounded two others before killing himself.

- On July 29, 1999, Mark Orrin, a 44-year-old day trader entered two Atlanta, Georgia brokerage firms and shot to death nine people and wounded 12 others. He later committed suicide after being surrounded by police. Orrin was reportedly upset after having incurred heavy losses in the stock market.[16]

- On December 26, 2000, Michael McDermott, a 42-year-old computer software technician who was angry over a tax dispute with the Internal Revenue Service and his employer, Edgewater Technology, Inc., went on a deadly shooting rampage at the company in Wakefield, Massachusetts. Armed with an AK-47, shotgun, and semiautomatic pistol, McDermott fatally wounded seven coworkers before he was subdued. He currently awaits trial on seven counts of murder.

- On September 11, 2001, hijacked airliners were crashed into the World Trade Center in New York City and the Pentagon in Washington, D.C. by terrorists. Thousands of people were killed.

The Scope and Nature of Workplace Homicide

Recent data from the National Traumatic Occupational Fatalities (NTOF) Surveillance System reported that between 1980 and 1989, there were nearly 7,600 workers who were homicide victims in the United States. Other findings included:

- Eighty percent of victims were male.

- The homicide rate was three times greater for male workers than female workers.

- Homicide was the leading cause of occupational deaths of women, representing four times as many such deaths as among men.

- Almost half the victims of workplace homicide were between the ages of twenty-five and forty-four.

- The highest rate of occupational homicide was for workers age sixty-five and older.

- Three-quarters of all workplace homicide victims were white.

- Nearly 20 percent of victims of occupational homicide were black.

- Firearms were used in three out of every four workplace homicides.

- Weapons such as knives and other cutting instruments were responsible for less than 15 percent of occupational homicides.[17]

In the BJS report on workplace violence between 1992 and 1996, an estimate of more than 1,000 homicides occurred in the workplace every year, accounting for around one out of every six occupational fatalities.[18]

Firearms are by far the most likely weapon used to commit violence in the workplace. As shown in Figure 8.1, between 1992 and 1996, firearms accounted for nearly 84 percent of the weapons used in occupational homicides. More than 11 percent of the homicides came as the result of a bombing or other weapon such as that which occurred in the 1995 Oklahoma City bombing of the federal building.[19]

Figure 8.1
Weapons Used in Workplace Homicides, 1992-1996[a]

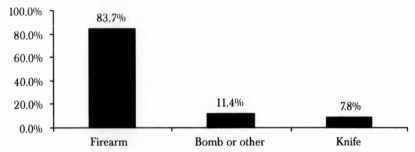

[a] Figures may not add due to rounding.

Source: Derived from U.S. Department of Justice, Bureau of Justice Statistics Special Report, *Workplace Violence, 1992-96* (Washington: Office of Justice Programs, 1998), p. 6.

Workplace homicides are most likely to occur in sales occupations, according to the BJS. Between 1993 and 1996, sales workers were homicide victims 327 times each year on average—more than twice that of the workers in executive/managerial occupations, where the second most homicides occurred. Around seventy law enforcement officers and seventy-four taxi drivers were slain while on duty annually.[20]

Studies of occupational homicide have found the high-risk groups for murder include law enforcement personnel; hotel, motel, and gas station employees; and workers in stores, bars, and restaurants.[21]

Characteristics of Workplace Homicide Victims

Victims of workplace violence can be men, women, and children of all racial and ethnic persuasions and socioeconomic backgrounds as evidenced by the Oklahoma City bombing. However, in general, homicide victims tend to be male, white, and people in their twenties and thirties. Table 8.5 shows workplace homicides in the United States in 1997 and 1998, by victim characteristics. Overall, there were 709 workplace homicides in 1998 compared to 860 in 1997, a decrease of 151. However, occupational murders of females rose from 145 in 1997 to 163 in 1998. Males were more than three times as likely as females to be victims of homicide in the workplace, representing 77 percent of the murdered workers in 1998.

More than half the victims of workplace homicide in 1998 were between the ages of twenty-five and forty-four, a 3 percent increase over 1997. Most victims were thirty-five to forty-four years of age. Nearly two in ten workplace homicide victims were age forty-five to fifty-four. Workers under age twenty-five and age sixty-five and over were the least likely to be victims of workplace homicide.

In 1998, two-thirds of occupational homicide victims were white, while almost two in ten were black, and one in ten Asian. Six percent of victims were Native American or other races. Persons of Hispanic origin constituted 14 percent of victims of workplace violence.[22]

Victims of occupational homicide in 1998 were predominantly likely to be shot to death, as seen in Figure 8.2. Eighty percent of victims died while on duty as a result of use of a firearm, while 9 percent were stabbed, 7 percent hit or beaten, and 4 percent victims of other lethal assaults.

Robbery or other crimes were the primary circumstance for homicides in the workplace in 1998 (see Figure 8.3). Eighty percent died as the result of robbery and other offenses. Fourteen percent of employees were the victims of coworkers, former coworkers, customer or clients; while 6 percent died from murders committed by personal acquaintances such as husbands, ex-husbands, boyfriends, former boyfriends, and other relatives or acquaintances.

Table 8.5

WORKPLACE HOMICIDES, BY VICTIM CHARACTERISTICS, 1997-1998

Victim characteristics	1997 [a]		1998 [a]	
	Number	*Percent*	*Number*	*Percent*
Total	860	100%	709	100%
Employee status				
Wage and salary workers	632	74	521	73
Self-employed[b]	228	26	188	27
Sex				
Male	715	83	546	77
Female	145	17	163	23
Age[c]				
19 years and younger	27	3	19	3
20 to 24 years	60	7	42	6
25 to 34 years	215	25	178	25
35 to 44 years	216	25	199	28
45 to 54 years	171	20	136	19
55 to 64 years	120	14	82	12
65 years and older	51	6	52	7
Not reported	0	–	1	(c)
Race, ethnicity				
White	577	67	470	66
Black	153	18	130	18
Asian or Pacific Islander	92	11	68	10
American Indian, Eskimo, or Aleut	4	(c)	4	1
Other or unspecified	34	4	37	5
Hispanic[d]	101	12	99	14

[a] Detail may not add to total because of the omission of miscellaneous categories and because of rounding.

[b] Includes paid and unpaid family workers, and may include owners of incorporated businesses or members of partnerships.

[c] Less than 0.5%

[d] Persons identified as Hispanic may be of any race; therefore detail will not add to total.

Source: Adapted from U.S. Department of Justice, Bureau of Justice Statistics, *Sourcebook of Criminal Justice Statistics 1999* (Washington: Government Printing Office, 2000), p. 306.

Figure 8.2

Victims of Workplace Homicide, by Type of Offender Attack, 1998

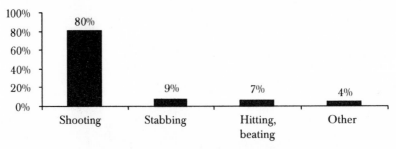

Source: Derived from U.S. Department of Justice, Bureau of Justice Statistics, *Sourcebook of Criminal Justice Statistics 1999* (Washington: Government Printing Office, 2000), p. 306.

Figure 8.3

Victims of Workplace Homicide, by Type of Circumstance, 1998

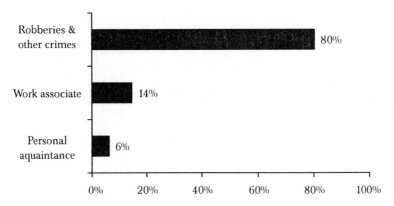

Source: Derived from U.S. Department of Justice, Bureau of Justice Statistics, *Sourcebook of Criminal Justice Statistics, 1999* (Washington: Government Printing Office, 2000), p. 306.

CAUSES OF WORKPLACE HOMICIDE

Workplace homicides are typically caused by stranger robberies and other crimes, vengeful current or former employees, and spouses, ex-spouses, other intimates, and obsessed or stalker killers. However, as we have seen in recent years, the workplace is also a murder target of terrorists, extremists, and others with a personal or political agenda.

Researchers have identified a number of risk factors that may cause or contribute to workplace homicides. These include:

• Job stresses such as termination, demotion, or promotion.
• Personal problems such as divorce, financial losses, or child custody issues.

- Work involving extensive contact or the exchange of money with the public.
- Working alone or with few others around.
- Late night or early morning work.
- Employment in high crime areas.
- Working in government or military occupations.
- Work in high security occupations.
- Work in general public contact professions such as law enforcement or taxi cabs.[23]

According to the National Institute for Occupational Safety and Health:

> Differences between fatal and nonfatal workplace assaults may arise from different distributions of instrumental and expressive violence. It may be that instrumental violence in the workplace (robbery) is more likely to result in a fatal outcome than expressive violence (anger displayed by frustrated customers or clients, or coworkers). The premeditated use of a firearm to facilitate robbery may contribute to more fatal outcomes.[24]

Studies show that occupational homicides can be reduced through adopting various behavioral and environmental standards in high-risk work settings, including:

- Making such high-risk areas more visible.
- The installation of better outside lighting, surveillance cameras, and silent alarms.
- Having more people on duty.
- Keeping only small amounts of cash on hand.
- Nonresistance when encountering a robber.
- Train workers in conflict resolution and responding to issues in a nonviolent manner.
- Routine law enforcement observation of workplace establishments.[25]

NOTES

1. U.S. Department of Justice, Bureau of Justice Statistics Special Report, *Workplace Violence, 1992-96* (Washington: Office of Justice Programs, 1998), p. 1.
2. U.S. Department of Justice, Bureau of Justice Statistics, *Criminal Victimization in the United States 1992: A National Crime Victimization Survey Report* (Washington: Government Printing Office, 1994).
3. D. N. Castillo and E. L. Jenkins, "Industries and Occupations at High Risk for Work-Related Homicide," *Journal of Occupational Medicine 36* (1994): 125-32.
4. Northwest National Life, *Fear and Violence in the Workplace: A Survey Documenting the Experience of American Workers* (Minneapolis: Northwest National Life, 1993).
5. C. A. Bell, "Female Homicides in United States Workplaces, 1980-1985," *American Journal of Public Health 81* (1991): 729-32; G. M. Liss and C. A. Craig,

"Homicide in the Workplace in Ontario: Occupations at Risk and Limitations of Existing Data Sources," *Canadian Journal of Public Health 81* (1990): 10-15.

6. H. P. Davis, A. Honchar, and L. Suarez, "Fatal Occupational Injuries of Women, Texas 1975-1984," *American Journal of Public Health 77* (1987): 1524-27; J. L. Thomas, "Occupational Violent Crime: Research on an Emerging Issue," *Journal of Safety Research 23* (1992): 55-62.

7. See, for example, J. A. Liscomb and C. C. Love, "Violence Toward Health Care Workers: An Emerging Occupational Hazard," *American Association of Occupational Health Nurses Journal 40* (1992): 219-28; R. Erickson, "Convenience Store Homicide and Rape," in U.S. Department of Justice, *Convenience Store Security: Report and Recommendations* (Alexandria: U.S. Department of Justice, 1991), pp. 16-18.

8. Dawn N. Castillo, "Nonfatal Violence in the Work Place: Directions for Future Research," in U.S. Department of Justice, *Trends Risks; and Interventions in Lethal Violence: Proceedings of the Third Annual Spring Symposium of the Homicide Research Working Group* (Washington: National Institute of Justice, 1995), pp. 225-35.

9. *Workplace Violence, 1992-96*, p. 5; National Institute for Occupational Safety and Health, "Preventing Homicide in the Workplace," http://www.cdc.gov/niosh/homicide.html.

10. Cited by U.S. Department of Justice, 1998, http://www.workplace-violence-hq.com/.

11. *Ibid.*

12. *Ibid.*; *Workplace Violence, 1992-96*, p. 4.

13. Cited by U.S. Department of Justice, 1998.

14. *Ibid.*

15. Cited in *Workplace Violence, 1992-96*, p. 6.

16. R. Barri Flowers and H. Loraine Flowers, *Murders in the United States: Crimes, Killers and Victims of the Twentieth Century* (Jefferson: McFarland, 2001), pp. 78-83.

17. "Preventing Homicide in the Workplace."

18. *Workplace Violence, 1992-96*, p. 6.

19. Flowers and Flowers, *Murders in the United States*, pp. 56-57.

20. *Workplace Violence, 1992-96*, p. 7.

21. Castillo, "Nonfatal Violence in the Work Place," p. 229; T. Hales, P. Seligman, C. Newman, and C. L. Timbrook, "Occupational Injuries Due to Violence," *Journal of Occupational Medicine 30* (1988): 483-87.

22. Persons of Hispanic origin may include persons of any race.

23. U.S. Department of Justice, 1998; J. F. Kraus, "Homicides While at Work: Persons, Industries, and Occupations at High Risk," *American Journal of Public Health 77*, 10 (1987): 1285-89.

24. Castillo, "Nonfatal Violence in the Work Place," pp. 229-30.

25. See, for example, S. G. Chapman, *Cops, Killers and Staying Alive: The Murder of Police Officers in America* (Springfield: Charles C Thomas, 1986); W. J. Crow and R. Erickson, *The Store Safety Issue: Facts for the Future* (Alexandria: National Association of Convenience Stores, 1989).

Chapter 9

BIAS-MOTIVATED HOMICIDE

One of the most disturbing areas of homicide in the United States concerns bias-motivated murders. These killings occur primarily due to prejudices by the offender against specific groups in society such as on the basis of race, ethnicity, sexual orientation, or religion. Recent years have seen a number of highly publicized, tragic cases of bias-related homicides. Perpetrators of these crimes are predominantly male, usually young, and they often belong to extremist or hate groups, or otherwise have strong feelings of intolerance or resentment against those targeted.

Bias or hate crimes have long existed in this country, fueled by bigotry and intolerance, along with advances in civil rights. However, it has only been since the early 1990s that a series of laws have been passed to address the national concern over serious and violent criminal behavior motivated by hatred. In spite of this, hate crimes continue to manifest themselves in homicidal violence, including the recent terrorist attacks of hatred directed toward the entire United States population.

WHAT ARE HATE CRIMES?

According to the Department of Justice, a hate crime, also called a bias crime, is "a criminal offense committed against a person, property, or society which is motivated, in whole or in part, by the offender's bias against a race, religion, disability, sexual orientation, or ethnicity/national origin."[1]

An expert on hate crimes defines it as "message crimes. They are different from other crimes in that the offender is sending a message to members of a certain group that they are unwelcome."[2]

The definition of hate crime can vary from state to state. In a study of hate crimes and state definitions, Eve Garber found that "twenty-one states include mental and physical disability . . . twenty-two states include sexual

105

orientation. Three states and the District of Columbia impose tougher penalties for crimes based on political affiliation."[3]

Hate crimes may include any offense motivated by a person's bias such as murder and nonnegligent manslaughter, forcible rape, aggravated assault, simple assault, and intimidation; along with robbery, burglary, larceny-theft, motor vehicle theft, arson, and property destruction, damage or vandalism.

Bias-motivated crime offenders come from every racial and ethnic group, nationality, socioeconomic, and educational background. What they share in common is the willingness to commit criminal acts that are often violent, born out of and sustained by hatred, and related factors aimed at vulnerable victims who conform to the offender's biases.

Homicidal hate crimes are often perpetrated by multiple offenders who share a particular bias toward someone or something a potential victim symbolizes. For instance, in 1998, Aaron McKinney and Russell Henderson beat to death gay college student Matthew Shepard in Laramie, Wyoming. The brutal nature of the attack led to increased efforts to strengthen anti-hate crime legislation.[4]

In September 2001, nineteen men of Middle Eastern descent expressed their hatred against American society and its policies by hijacking four airliners, crashing two into the World Trade Center and another into the Pentagon, causing the deaths of thousands of people (see also Chapter 16).

The vast majority of hate crimes are single-bias incidents, or motivated by a single circumstance or cause. Multiple-bias incidents involving more than one reason for the offense have also occurred.

THE MAGNITUDE OF HATE CRIMES

How large is the scope of hate offenses? Prior to 1990, there was no official national tracking of hate crimes in the United States. Public pressure led Congress to enact the Hate Crimes Statistics Act (HCSA), signed into law in 1990. The Act required the federal government to collect statistics "about crimes that manifest evidence of prejudice based on race, religion, sexual orientation, or ethnicity."[5] In 1994, it was amended by the Violent Crime Control and Law Enforcement Act to include physical and mental disabilities as possible bias-motivations.[6] Data collection on disability-related bias started in 1997.

According to the Uniform Crime Reports, in 1999 there were 7,876 hate crime incidents in the United States reported to the Federal Bureau of Investigation (see Table 9.1). These involved 9,301 offenses, 9,802 victims, and 7,271 known offenders. Single-bias incidents constituted all but five of

Table 9.1

NUMBER OF HATE CRIME INCIDENTS, OFFENSES, VICTIMS, AND KNOWN OFFENDERS, BY BIAS AND MOTIVATION, 1999

Bias motivation	Incidents	Offenses	Victims [a]	Known offenders [b]
Total	7,876	9,301	9,802	7,271
Single-Bias Incidents	7,871	9,291	9,792	7,265
Race	4,295	5,240	5,485	4,362
Anti-White	781	970	996	1,011
Anti-Black	2,958	3,542	3,679	2,861
Anti-American Indian/Alaskan Native	47	49	50	40
Anti-Asian/Pacific Islander	298	363	379	288
Anti-Multi-Racial Group	211	316	381	162
Religion	1,411	1,532	1,686	602
Anti-Jewish	1,109	1,198	1,289	429
Anti-Catholic	36	41	41	18
Anti-Protestant	48	49	50	19
Anti-Islamic	32	34	34	14
Anti-Other Religious Group	151	170	221	98
Anti-Multi-Religious Group	31	35	46	21
Anti-Atheism/Agnosticism/etc.	4	5	5	3
Sexual Orientation	1,317	1,487	1,558	1,376
Anti-Male Homosexual	915	1,025	1,070	1,043
Anti-Female Homosexual	187	216	231	150
Anti-Homosexual	178	205	216	154
Anti-Heterosexual	14	16	16	15
Anti-Bisexual	23	25	25	14
Ethnicity/National Origin	829	1,011	1,040	904
Anti-Hispanic	466	576	588	562
Anti-Other Ethnicity/National Origin	363	435	452	342
Disability	19	21	23	21
Anti-Physical	10	11	13	9
Anti-Mental	9	10	10	12
Multiple-Bias Incidents [c]	5	10	10	6

[a] The term victim may refer to a person, business, institution, or society as a whole.

[b] The term known offender does not imply that the identity of the suspect is known, but only that an attribute of the suspect is identified which distinguishes him/her from an unknown offender.

[c] There were five multiple-bias incidents. Within these incidents, there were ten offenses, ten victims, and six known offenders.

Source: U.S. Department of Justice, Federal Bureau of Identification, *Crime in the United States: Uniform Crime Reports 1999* (Washington: Government Printing Office, 2000), p. 59.

the incidents and ten of the offenses and victims. Known offenders were responsible for 7,265 single-bias incidents and six multiple-bias incidents.

Race was the most likely single bias factor, accounting for 4,295 incidents and 5,240 offenses involving 5,485 victims and 4,362 known offenders. Anti-black hate crime incidents occurred far more than any other racial bias, with 2,958 such incidents and 3,542 offenses.

Religious bias made up the second most incidents, with 1,411 and 1,532 offenses; followed closely by sexual-orientation bias with 1,317 incidents and 1,487 offenses; and ethnicity/national origin bias with 829 incidents and 1,011 offenses. Disability bias accounted for the least amount of single-bias incidents, with nineteen incidents and twenty-one offenses.

There were five multiple-bias incidents in 1999, in which there were ten offenses involving ten victims and six known offenders.

Racial bias accounted for more than 56 percent of the hate crimes reported in 1999 (see Table 9.2). Religion bias comprised 16.5 percent of the offenses, followed by sexual orientation bias at 16 percent, ethnicity/national origin bias at 10.9 percent, disability bias at 0.2 percent, and multiple-bias crimes representing 0.1 percent of all hate crimes. In a 1999 Gallup Poll, more than eight in ten racial, ethnic, and religious minorities and better than three in four homosexuals were afraid of becoming the victim of a hate crime.[7]

Table 9.2
BIAS-MOTIVATED OFFENSES, 1999

Offense	Percent committed
Race	56.3%
Sexual orientation	16.0%
Religion	16.5%
Ethnicity	10.9%
Disability	0.2%
Multiple bias	0.1%

Source: Derived from U.S. Department of Justice, Federal Bureau of Identification, *Crime in the United States: Uniform Crime Reports 1999* (Washington: Government Printing Office, 2000), p. 61.

As seen in Table 9.3, more than two-thirds of the 9,301 hate crime offenses in the United States were crimes against persons. These included such offenses as murder and nonnegligent manslaughter, forcible rape, aggravated and simple assault, and intimidation. Most crimes involved intimidation, followed by assaultive crimes. There were seventeen homicides identified as bias-motivated.

Table 9.3
NUMBER OF OFFENSES, VICTIMS, AND KNOWN OFFENDERS, BY OFFENSE, 1999

Bias motivation	Offenses	Victims[a]	Known offenders[b]
Total	**9,301**	**9,802**	**7,593 (c)**
Crimes against persons	**6,189**	**6,189**	**6,103**
Murder and nonnegligent manslaughter	17	17	28
Forcible rape	6	6	6
Aggravated assault	1,120	1,120	1,482
Simple assault	1,766	1,766	2,267
Intimidation	3,268	3,268	2,308
Other[d]	12	12	12
Crimes against property	**3,082**	**3,583**	**1,444**
Robbery	129	158	275
Burglary	112	132	63
Larceny-theft	103	112	66
Motor vehicle theft	14	14	9
Arson	48	64	22
Destruction/damage/vandalism	2,654	3,078	988
Other[d]	22	25	21
Crimes against society	**30**	**30**	**46**

[a] The term victim may refer to a person, business, institution, or society as a whole.

[b] The term known offender does not imply that the identity of the suspect is known, but only that an attribute of the suspect is identified which distinguishes him/her from an unknown offender.

[c] The actual number of known offenders is 7,271. Some offenders, however, may be responsible for more than one offense and are, therefore, counted more than once in this table.

[d] Includes offenses other than those listed that are collected in NIBRS.

Source: U.S. Department of Justice, Federal Bureau of Identification, *Crime in the United States: Uniform Crime Reports 1999* (Washington: Government Printing Office, 2000), p. 60.

Crimes against persons represented one-third of the offenses reported to law enforcement agencies, with destruction, damage, or vandalism of property accounting for most of the offenses.

In 1999, there were thirty offenses identified as crimes against society involving thirty victims and forty-six known offenders. The total of offenses and victims increased considerably in 2001, with the terrorist and biological attacks on the United States taking several thousand lives.[8]

MURDER CAUSED BY HATE

In 1999, there were seventeen crimes of murder attributed to bias motivation in the United States, representing seventeen victims and twenty-eight identified offenders.[9] In 2001, the victims of hate crimes rose considerably with the terrorist attacks and bioterrorist anthrax attacks resulting in the deaths of thousands. Other homicides in recent years may have been bias-related but were misidentified or have not been solved.

Most bias-motivated homicides in this country are not the work of foreign terrorists or hate groups but are committed by domestic groups or individuals. Notable cases of murder caused by hatred of the victims or what they represented include:

- On June 12, 1963, NAACP activist Medgar Evers was gunned down in front of his home in Jackson, Mississippi. More than three decades later, Byron De La Beckwith, a white supremacist, was convicted of the murder.
- On January 10, 1966, civil rights activist Vernon Dahmer was the victim of a firebombing in Mississippi. After five trials for the murder, former Ku Klux Klan leader Samuel Bowers was convicted in 1998 and sentenced to life in prison. Bowers had previously served time for his role in the 1964 murders of three other civil rights workers.
- On April 4, 1968, civil rights leader Martin Luther King, Jr. was assassinated in Memphis, Tennessee. Arrested and convicted for the murder was James Earl Ray. He was sentenced to 99 years in prison, though he later recanted his guilty plea.
- On April 22, 1970, Rainey Pool, an African American sharecropper was the victim of a fatal mob attack near the town of Louise, Mississippi. Nearly thirty years later, white racists James Caston, Charles Caston, and Hal Crimm were found guilty of manslaughter in Pool's death.
- In June 1998, James Byrd, Jr., an African American, was beaten and dragged to his death in Jasper, Texas. Arrested and convicted for the murder were white supremacists Shawn Berry, John King, and Lawrence Brewer. King and Brewer received death sentences, and Berry was given forty years to life behind bars.
- On October 12, 1998, Matthew Shepard, a gay college student, was viciously attacked in Laramie, Wyoming. He died a few days later. Aaron McKinney and Russell Henderson were arrested and charged with the crime. Both were convicted and given two consecutive life sentences behind bars.
- On November 8, 1998, two Mexican laborers were shot to death in a California border town. Arrested for the crime were teenagers Kenneth Kovzelove and Dennis Bencivenga. Kovzelove pleaded guilty to two counts of first-degree murder and received a sentence of fifty years to life.

Bencivenga pleaded guilty to two counts of manslaughter and was sentenced to fourteen years in prison.[10]

WHO ARE THE PERPETRATORS OF BIAS CRIMES?

The vast majority of hate crimes are committed by young white males.[11] Most are considered "lone wolves" who act in small cells, pairs, or alone.[12] FBI data on known bias-motivated offenders in 1999 shows that 68 percent were white, 16 percent were black, 7 percent other races, and 9 percent were of unknown races (see Figure 9.1).

Figure 9.1
Total Known Offenders of Bias Crimes, by Race, 1999

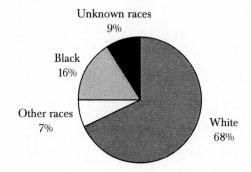

Source: Derived from U.S. Department of Justice, Federal Bureau of Investigation, *Crime in the United States: Uniform Crime Reports 1999* (Washington: Government Printing Office, 2000), p. 6.

Many offenders are either directly or indirectly affiliated with or influenced by hate organizations such as Ku Klux Klan and neo-Nazi groups. According to the Southern Poverty Law Center, there were more than 500 hate groups in existence in the United States in 1998.[13] The Los Angeles based Simon Wiesenthal Center monitors reportedly over 2,100 hate sites operating on the Internet.[14]

Some researchers contend that most perpetrators of hate crimes are not considered "skinheads" or otherwise belonging to a neo-Nazi organization. In a study of 1,459 hate crimes perpetrated in Los Angeles from 1994 to 1995, less than 5 percent of the perpetrators were found to belong to hate organizations.[15]

Young offenders account for a high proportion of the hate crimes committed in the United States. More than half of all bias-motivated murders are committed by persons under the age of twenty-one.[16] Many of these are described as thrill seekers rather than hard core hate offenders. In a Northeastern University study of bias crimes, 60 percent of the perpetrators committed their offenses for the thrill of it.[17]

According to forensic psychologist Karen Franklin, the most widespread and socially acceptable type of hate crime among youthful offenders are those motivated by a sexual orientation bias. She breaks down these offenders into four categories:

- **Ideology assailants** base their bias crimes on negative beliefs and feelings they believe are shared by others in the community or an extremist group they may belong to.
- **Thrill seekers** tend to be adolescent offenders who perpetrate their hate crimes to relieve boredom, for fun and excitement, and as a means to feel power.
- **Peer dynamics** hate crime offenders are often youthful and perpetrate their offense as apart of peer group toughness and acceptance.
- **Self-defense assailants** perceive their actions as in defense of unwanted advances or positions taken such as by homosexuals.[18]

WHAT CAUSES HATE CRIMES?

Hate crimes are caused by various conditions, ideologies, and bigotries. Researchers have found that most bias-motivated offenses are committed by "otherwise law-abiding [citizens] who see little wrong with their actions."[19] Although alcohol and drugs often play a role in hate crime participation, most experts believe that the primary cause of bias offending is individual prejudice, which "colors people's judgment, blinding the aggressors to the immorality of what they are doing. Such prejudice is most likely rooted in an environment that disdains someone who is 'different' or sees that difference as threatening."[20]

The most extreme bias-motivated crimes—such as those involving particularly brutal homicides or other assaultive behavior—tend to be perpetrated by offenders with a history of serious and violent offending or other aggressive behavior.

Some social scientists have related hate crimes to downturns in the economy. Others believe that hate crimes are "sporadic, isolated, uncoordinated, and not tied to economic fluctuation."[21] According to Donald Green, Jack Glaser, and Andrew Rich, who coauthored a study on hate crime: "Rather than economic downturns, neighborhood influxes of ethnically diverse people were most likely to spur bigoted violence. The only time economic hardship relates to hate crime is when established political leaders convince the public that specific groups are to blame."[22] An example of this may be the recent terrorist attack in America in which persons of Middle Eastern origin or Islamic religion became the victims of hate offenders after the terrorists were identified as extremists from the Middle East.

Studies have found that bias-motivated crimes "are not necessarily random, uncontrollable, or inevitable occurrences."[23] On the contrary, most evidence indicates that society and policymakers can create effective strategies for reducing or preventing the occurrence of hate crimes and other types of violence.[24]

HATE CRIME LEGISLATION

A number of laws have been enacted in recent years designed to combat hate crimes. These include the Hate Crimes Prevention Act, the Church Arson Prevention Act, and the Hate Crime Sentencing Enhancement Act.

Hate Crimes Prevention Act

The Hate Crimes Prevention Act of 1999 makes it a crime to interfere with a person's federal right by way of violence or the threat of as a result of the individual's race, ethnicity, gender, religion, national origin, or sexual orientation.[25] The Act provides federal prosecutors greater authority to investigate hate crimes and prosecute offenders.

Church Arson Prevention Act

The Church Arson Prevention Act of 1996 mandated that the collection of hate crime data become a permanent aspect of the FBI's Uniform Crime Reporting Program.[26] The Act created the National Church Arson Task Force whose purpose is to oversee the investigation and prosecution of arson perpetrated at homes of worship across the United States. It also allowed for greater federal jurisdiction for such criminality and a rebuilding recovery fund.

Hate Crime Sentencing Enhancement Act

The Hate Crime Sentencing Enhancement Act is part of the Violent Crime Control and Law Enforcement Act of 1994.[27] The Act allows for longer sentences for hate crime offenses or those motivated by a victim's race, ethnicity, color, gender, sexual orientation, or disability.

NOTES

1. U.S. Department of Justice, Federal Bureau of Investigation, *Crime in the United States: Uniform Crime Reports 1999* (Washington: Government Printing Office, 2000), p. 58.
2. Quoted in Rico Villanueva Siasoco, "Defining Hate Crimes: No Longer a Black and White Issue," http://www.infoplease.com/spot/hatecrirmes.html.
3. *Ibid.*
4. R. Barri Flowers and H. Loraine Flowers, *Murders in the United States: Crimes, Killers and Victims of the Twentieth Century* (Jefferson: McFarland, 2001), p. 181.
5. 28 U.S.C. 534 (1990).
6. *Crime in the United States*, p. 59.
7. George Gallup, Jr. and Alec Gallup, *The Gallup Poll Monthly*, No. 401 (Princeton: The Gallup Poll, 1999), pp. 28-29.
8. From various sources including CNN, NBC, and ABC.
9. *Crime in the United States*, p. 60.
10. Flowers and Flowers, *Murders in the United States*, pp. 178-82.
11. See http://www.civilrights/publications/cause_for_concern/p.10.html; http://www.teemings.com/issue05/hatecrimes.html.
12. Siasoco, "Defining Hate Crimes."
13. *Ibid.*
14. *Ibid.*
15. Cited in American Psychological Association, "Hate Crimes Today: An Age-Old Foe in Modern Dress," http://www.apa.org/pubinfo/ hate/#top.
16. William Lin, "Perpetrators of Hate," *Yale Political Quarterly 19*, 2 (1997): 12.
17. Cited in http://www.civilrights.org/publications/cause_for_concern/ p.10.html.
18. Cited in American Psychological Association, "Hate Crimes Today."
19. *Ibid.*
20. *Ibid.*
21. American Psychological Association, "Study Finds No Evidence That Economic Downturn Spur Hate Crimes," 1998, http://www.apa.org/.
22. *Ibid.*
23. American Psychological Association, "Hate Crimes Today."
24. *Ibid.*
25. 18 U.S.C. 245; as amended by H.R. 1082 (1999).
26. 18 U.S.C. 247 (1996).
27. P.L. 103-322, Sec. 280003 (1994).

Chapter 10

TERRORISM AND MURDER

On September 11, 2001, terrorism and mass murder struck America like never before in its history. That fateful day, nineteen determined foreign terrorists hijacked four United States airliners, crashing two into the twin towers of the World Trade Center and another into the Pentagon, causing the deaths of thousands of innocent victims. This came just over six years after the Oklahoma City bombing, which had been the nation's worst terrorist attack. These and other recent deadly terrorist acts directed toward the United States, including local terrorism, have led to increased antiterrorism measures by the government as well as a general sense of vulnerability to this longtime form of violent and homicidal behavior. Terrorist experts and criminologists are putting forth new efforts in identifying terrorists and terrorist organizations, causes of terrorism, the correlation between terrorism and homicide, and ways to avert disaster before it strikes.

WHAT IS TERRORISM?

Terrorism is a term used to denote acts of terror that instills fear, intimidation, and is often violent and of a political nature. Specifically, the dictionary defines terrorism as "(1) the political use of violence or intimidation and (2) the systematic use of terror especially as a means of coercion."[1] The word *terrorism* originated during the French Revolution in the late 1700s to reflect what was known as the Reign of Terror, in which some revolutionists seized and maintained power through violence.[2]

Over the years, terrorism has been defined by various international organizations, governments, scholars, and experts on terrorism and terrorists. In 1937, the League of Nations Convention defined terrorism as "all criminal acts directed against a State and intended or calculated to create a state of terror in the minds of particular persons or a group of persons or the general public."[3] According to the *World Book*, terrorism is "the use or threat of violence to create fear and alarm. Terrorists murder and kidnap people, set off bombs, hijack airplanes, set fires, and commit other serious crimes. But the goals of terrorists differ from those of ordinary criminals. Most . . . want money or some other form of personal gain. But most terrorists commit crimes to support political causes."[4]

Under Title 22 of the U.S. Code, the term "terrorism" is defined as "premeditated, politically-motivated violence perpetrated against noncombatant targets by subnational groups or clandestine agents, usually intended to influence an audience. 'International terrorism' is terrorism involving the territory or the citizens of more than one country;" while the term "terrorist group" refers to "any group that practices, or has significant subgroups that practice, international terrorism."[5]

In a 1999 United Nations Resolution, terrorism was defined as "criminal acts intended or calculated to provoke a state of terror in the general public, a group of persons, or particular persons for political purposes" while being strongly condemned as "criminal and unjustifiable, whatever the considerations of a political, philosophical, ideological, racial, ethnic, religious or other nature that may be invoked to justify them."[6] Among academics, terrorism has been defined as:

> an anxiety-inspiring method of repeated violent action, employed by (semi) clandestine individual, group or state actors, for idiosyncratic, criminal or political reasons, whereby—in contrast to assassination—the direct targets of violence are not the main targets. The immediate human victims of violence are generally chosen randomly . . . or selectively . . . from a target population, and serve as message generators. Threat- and violence-based communication processes between terrorist (organization), (imperiled) victims, and main targets are used to manipulate the main target (audience(s)), turning it into a target of terror, a target of demands, or a target of attention, depending on whether intimidation, coercion, or propaganda is primarily sought.[7]

Others have been terse but effective in defining terrorism. For example, David Lester and H. A. Cooper note that terrorism "generates a high level of fear in society, has a coercive purpose, and requires a human audience."[8] Whereas Benjamin Wolman's definition of terrorism is "a grave sociopolitical and psychological problem that requires a thorough and responsible analysis."[9]

Perhaps Walter Laquer's broad interpretation of terrorism puts it in a proper definitional context with today's wide ranging, multi causal and motivational terrorism:

> Terrorism . . . has been waged by national and religious groups, by the left and by the right, by nationalist as well as international movements, and it has been state-sponsored. . . . Terrorist movements have frequently consist-

ed of members of the educated middle classes, but there has also been agrarian terrorism, terror by the uprooted and the rejected, and trade union and working-class terror. . . . Terror has been directed against autocratic regimes as well as democracies; sometimes there has been an obvious link with social dislocation and economic crisis, at other times there has been no such connection. Movements of national liberation and social revolution (or reaction) have turned to terrorism after political action has failed. But elsewhere, and at other times, terrorism has not been the consequence of political failure, but has been chosen by militant groups even before other options were tried.[10]

DEADLY TERRORIST ATTACKS AGAINST THE UNITED STATES AND AMERICANS

The incidence of international and domestic terrorist-related deadly attacks against the United States, its citizens, or interests, has risen dramatically in the 1990s and early 2000s. This is primarily due to recent terrorist perpetrated mass murders at the Oklahoma City federal building, New York's World Trade Center, and the Pentagon in Washington, D.C. Other terrorist attacks have also contributed to this alarming trend.

Recent acts of deadly terrorism involving Americans and America include the following:

- In October and November 2001, bioterrorism in the form of inhalation anthrax killed five people in the United States. A total of eighteen people to date have been infected by inhaled or cutaneous anthrax nationwide, believed to have originated from contaminated mail at U.S. postal facilities. As yet, no perpetrators have been identified.
- On September 11, 2001, four American airliners were hijacked by nineteen terrorists, all identified as having Middle Eastern roots. Two planes were crashed into the twin towers of the World Trade Center in New York, causing both to collapse; another plane was crashed into the Pentagon, and the fourth plane went down in Pennsylvania. In all, thousands of people lost their lives, including the hijacker-terrorists. The deadliest terrorist attack in U.S. history was blamed on the Al Qaida terrorist organization, led by its leader, Osama bin Laden.
- On October 12, 2000, terrorists in a boat detonated a bomb outside the U.S.S. Cole in the harbor at Aden, Yemen, killing seventeen sailors and injuring more than thirty others. Those responsible have yet to be brought to justice.
- On August 7, 1998, terrorist bombs exploded at the U.S. Embassies in Nairobi, Kenya and Dar es Salaam, Tanzania, killing 224 people, includ-

ing twelve Americans, and wounding more than 1,000. The attack was blamed on Osama bin Laden and members or associates of his Al Qaida network. On November 4, 1998, a Federal Grand Jury indicated bin Laden on charges in connection with the bombing.

- On June 25, 1996, a fuel truck loaded with explosives detonated outside the Khobar Towers apartment complex in Dhahran, Saudi Arabia, killing nineteen American military personnel and wounding 372 others. On June 21, 2001, fourteen terrorists were indicted for the attack, including thirteen Saudis and one Lebanese.
- On April 19, 1995, a powerful bomb inside a Ryder rental truck exploded outside the Alfred P. Murrah Federal Building in Oklahoma City, Oklahoma. The explosion killed 168 people and injured hundreds of others. Timothy McVeigh, a 29-year-old Gulf War veteran, and Terry Nichols, 40, were charged with what was at the time the country's deadliest act of domestic terrorism. Both men were convicted. McVeigh, sentenced to death, was executed in June 2001. Nichols was sentenced to life in prison.
- Between 1978 and 1995, Theodore Kaczynski, known as the Unabomber, raged a campaign of domestic terror as he mailed homemade bombs to professors, corporations, and computer companies, killing three and injuring twenty-three. The former math professor avoided the death penalty under a plea agreement. He received four consecutive life sentences without the possibility of parole, along with thirty years.
- On February 26, 1993, a truck bomb exploded in the underground parking garage of the World Trade Center in New York, killing six people and wounding more than 1,000. Convicted and imprisoned for the deadly crime were six Islamic extremists, including mastermind Ramzi Yousef, a 29-year-old Kuwati, and his fellow conspirator, Eyad Ismoil, age 26.
- On December 21, 1988, a bomb exploded on Pan Am Flight 103 over Lockerbie, Scotland, killing all 259 on board and eleven on the ground. The jetliner was en route to the United States. Two Libyans were charged with the terrorist attack and were tried in May 2000. One was convicted.
- On October 23, 1983, a truck bomb exploded outside the U.S. Marine headquarters in Beirut, killing 243 American members of a peacekeeping force. No one was ever brought to justice for the mass murder.
- On April 18, 1983, a 2,000-pound bomb in a van exploded at the U.S. Embassy in Beirut, killing sixty-three people inside, including seventeen Americans, and the bomber. Those responsible were never captured.[11]

The vast majority of terrorist-related fatal attacks against Americans are perpetrated by international terrorists. As seen in Table 10.1, between 1981 and 1999, there were 651 Americans killed and 2,226 wounded as a result of international terrorism. However, there were more people murdered in the 1996 Oklahoma City act of domestic terrorism than in all but two individual years of international terrorism between 1981 and 1999.

Table 10.1

CASUALTIES RESULTING FROM INTERNATIONAL TERRORISM,
INVOLVING U.S. CITIZENS, BY TYPE OF CASUALTY, 1981-1999

Year	Total	U.S. citizens	
		Killed	Wounded
Total	2,877	651	2,226
1981	47	7	40
1982	19	8	11
1983	386	271	115
1984	42	11	31
1985	195	38	157
1986	112	12	100
1987	54	7	47
1988	231	192	39
1989	34	16	18
1990	43	9	34
1991	23	7	16
1992	3	2	1
1993	1,011 (a)	7	1,004
1994	11	6	5
1995	70	10	60
1996	535 (b)	25	510
1997	27	6	21
1998	23	12	11
1999	11	5	6

[a] Includes the bombing of the World Trade Center in New York City on Feb. 26, 1983.
[b] Includes the bombing of the Khobar U.S. military housing complex near Dhahran, Saudi Arabia on June 25, 1996.

Source: Adapted from U.S. Department of Justice, Bureau of Justice Statistics, *Sourcebook of Criminal Justice Statistics 1999* (Washington: Government Printing Office, 2000), p. 334.

From 1995 to 2000, seventy-seven Americans were victims of deadly attacks by international terrorists, for an average of thirteen casualties per year.[12] Over the same span, 651 Americans were wounded as a result of international terrorism, for an average of 109 per year. Between 1995 and 2000, North America had the lowest concentration of international terrorist perpetrated attacks with fifteen. However, one coordinated effort in September 2001 by international terrorists led to a higher number of casualties than any previous group terrorist attack.

The vast majority of terrorist attacks against the United States come in the form of bomb attacks (see Table 10.2). Between 1982 and 1997, 81 percent of terrorist incidents targeted against the United States were bombing attacks. Kidnappings, assaults, and assassinations were the second most likely form of terrorist attacks. Commercial establishments were the most likely to be targeted by terrorists and more than twice as likely as military targets and state and federal government buildings.

Table 10.2
TERRORIST INCIDENTS, BY TYPE OF INCIDENT AND TARGET,
UNITED STATES, 1982-1997

	Number
Total	183
Type of incident	
Bombing attacks[a]	147
Malicious destruction of property	4
Acts of sabotage	2
Hostile takeover	4
Arson	8
Kidnapping; assaults; alleged assassinations; assassinations	11
Robbery; attempted robbery	6
Hijacking	1
Type of target	
Private residence/vehicle	18
Military personnel/establishments	33
Educational establishments	6
Commercial establishments	76
State and United States government buildings/property	33
Diplomatic establishments	17

[a] Includes detonated and undetonated devices, tear gas, pipebombs, letterbombs, and firebombs.

Source: Adapted from U.S. Department of Justice, Bureau of Justice Statistics, *Sourcebook of Criminal Justice Statistics 1999* (Washington: Government Printing Office, 2000), p. 334.

TERRORIST ORGANIZATIONS

Although some terrorist attacks are perpetrated by individuals with no particular affiliation to a terrorist group—such as in the case of Timothy McVeigh and Terry Nichols—most terrorists act as part of a terrorist organization. The Central Intelligence Agency recently estimated that there are a minimum of 140 current terrorist organizations worldwide.[13] Table 10.3 lists some of the most well-known terrorist groups.

Believed to be the largest and most deadly is the Al Qaida terrorist organization. Led by Saudi militant Osama bin Laden, Al Qaida is based in Afghanistan but has an international network of Muslim extremists.[14] The

Table 10.3
KNOWN TERRORIST ORGANIZATIONS

Name of Organization	*Location*
Al Qaida	Afghanistan
Armata Corsa	France
Armed Islamic Group (GIA)	Algeria
Aum Shinrikyo	Japan
Basque Fatherland and Liberty (ETA)	Spain
Democratic Front for the Liberation of Palestine (DFLP)	Palestinian
Fatah-Revolutionary Council (Abu Nidal Organization)	Lebanon
Gama'a al-Islamiyya (the Islamic Group, 1G)	Egypt
Hamas (Islamic Resistance Movement)	Palestinian
Harakat al-Mujahedin (HUM)	Pakistan
Hizballah (Party of God)	Lebanon
Irish Republican Army (IRA)	Northern Ireland
Japanese Red Army (JRA)	Japan
Jihad Group	Egypt
Kach and Kahane Chai	Israel
Kurdistan Workers' Party (PKK)	Turkey
Liberation Tigers of Tamil Eelan (LTTE)	Sri Lanka
Manuel Rodriguez Patriotic Front (FPMR)	Chile
Mujahedin-e Khalq Organization (MKO)	Iran
National Liberation Army (ELN)	Columbia
New People's Army (NPA)	Philippines
Palestine Liberation Front (PLF)	Iraq
Palestine Islamic Jihad (PIJ)	Palestinian
Popular Struggle Front (PSF)	Syria
Red Army Faction (RAF)	Germany
Revolutionary Armed Forces of Columbia (FARC)	Columbia
Revolutionary Organization 17 November (17 November)	Greece
Revolutionary People's Liberation Party/Front (DHCP/F)	Turkey
Sendero Luminoso (Shining Path)	Peru
Tupac Armaru Revolutionary Movement (MRTA)	Peru

Source: Terrorist Organizations, http://www.ict.org.il/inter/org.cfm; Crime and Punishment, http://member.compuserve.com/crime/terror.jsp.

terrorist organization's primary objective "is the overthrow of what it sees as the corrupt and heretical governments of Muslim states, and their replacement with the rule of *Sharia* (Islamic Law). Al Qaida is intensely anti-Western, and views the United States in particular as the prime enemy of Islam."[15]

In 1996, Osama bin Laden issued a *fatwa* or religious ruling against the United States, calling upon Muslims to kill Americans. Bin Laden and his Al Qaida network are believed to be behind the September 11, 2001 terrorist attacks on the United States, as well as recent deadly bombings of the U.S.S. Cole ship, and the U.S. Embassies in Africa.

While most terrorism directed against the United States and its citizens is perpetrated by international terrorist organizations, domestic terrorist groups also exist and pose a serious threat. Extremist and hate groups such as the Ku Klux Klan have long orchestrated terrorist attacks on African Americans and other minority groups. Researchers have found that domestic terrorists and antigovernment militias such as The Covenant and the Minnesota Patriots Council have shown an interest in using unconventional weapons such as biological or chemical agents to wage their war on America.[16] Recent deadly anthrax attacks in this country illustrate the potential threats of domestic and international terrorism.

THE ROOTS OF TERRORISM

Terrorism's modern roots can be traced to the dictatorships of Germany's Adolf Hitler, Italy's Benito Mussolini, and the former Soviet Union's Joseph Stalin in the 1930s and 1940s, in which terrorism was used against those who opposed their rule.[17] According to one expert on the justification of such terrorism: "Dictatorial systems believe that the end justifies the means, and they have the right to impose their will on the rest of humankind. . . . They believe they. . .have the right to kidnap, torture, and murder."[18]

Terrorist acts of violence have been used in Northern Ireland by Roman Catholic and Protestant extremist groups "to push for, respectively, the end of or the continuation of, British rule."[19] Since the 1960s, such terrorist groups as the Red Brigades and Red Army Faction formed to destroy their homeland's political and economic systems and establish new ones; while the Palestinian terrorist organizations such as the Hezbollah and Hamas have raged terror campaigns against Israel in hopes of establishing an independent Palestinian state.

More recent terrorist groups such as the Al Qaida network have proven to be even more deadly, violent, and organized in their hatred and political and religious objectives, as evidenced by the September 2001 attack on America.

CHARACTERIZING TERRORISTS

Most terrorists are young, usually poor, men who are easily influenced by radical extremists and their message of hatred towards and violence against groups, governments, and individuals. These terrorists are often willing to die for their cause, whether national or not, making them even more dangerous to innocent people. According to one researcher, "The receptivity of young men to terror's radical message is enormously increased by [the] legacy of conflict, dislocation, and . . . poverty."[20] This is particularly true in the Middle East and South Asia.

However, people from wealthy Western nations can also be sold on the same message. "These people can still powerfully identify with communities elsewhere that they believe have been exploited, victimized, reduced to crushing poverty, or otherwise treated with disrespect."[21]

The perception of victimization and disrespect against a vulnerable group was apparently what motivated Timothy McVeigh to blow up the federal building in Oklahoma City. The terrorist attack came two years after the government's siege against a religious cult in Waco, Texas ended with a fatal fire, killing fifty-eight members of the cult. "In the case of radical Islamic terrorists, such grievances are often expressed as anger over American policy toward Israel and Iraq and American support for 'un-Islamic' Middle Eastern governments."[22]

Most terrorists' actions or reactions often reflect mental instability and the desire to make their mark in a violent and effective way, such as with mail bomber Theodore Kaczynski.[23]

MURDER-SUICIDE TERRORISTS

Many terrorists kill themselves in the process of killing or attempting to kill others, as in the case of the nineteen men who hijacked four airplanes and committed suicide along with murdering more than 3,000 others on September 11, 2001. Although suicide bombers are perhaps most identified with terrorist attacks, experts indicate that the majority of terrorists, "while willing to risk their lives, do not undertake actions that require their deaths in order to succeed. They wish to live after the terrorist act in order to benefit from their accomplishments."[24]

Suicide terrorists, however, have somewhat different motivations in perpetrating suicidal terrorism. Most do not regard their deaths as suicide, per se, bur rather see themselves as martyrs for the cause. Those who run terrorist organizations are seen as "cold and rational, rather than suicidal. For them, suicide terrorism has inherent tactical advantages over 'conventional' terrorism."[25] According to terrorism experts, such advantages include:

- Keeping the operation simple and low-cost, without need for escape routes or rescue operations.
- Can ensure mass casualties and considerable damage, as the suicide bomber need not be concerned with his welfare and safety.
- No concern about captured terrorists being interrogated and revealing information about the network, since the probability of death is high.

• Has a strong effect on the public and government due to the shared grief and feelings of helplessness.

In a survey of terrorist groups who have employed suicide terrorist activities since 1983, it was found that some organizations "that resort to suicide terrorism do so rarely and unsympathetically, while others adopt it as a strategy. It has also been dropped as a tactic when the leaders of terrorist organizations perceive it is counterproductive–either because of massive retaliation or the loss of public sympathy for a cause."[26]

COMBATING TERRORISM IN AMERICA

In general, governments combat terrorism by not giving in to terrorist's demands, enacting tough antiterrorism laws, tightening security at vulnerable targets of terrorists, and going after the terrorists themselves. With respect to the September 11, 2001 terrorist attacks in this country, the federal government has responded through various policy initiatives, heightened security provisions, offering rewards for information leading to the capture of suspected terrorists, and attacking and seeking to bring to justice those believed to be responsible.

Specifically, the following actions have been taken in the war on terrorism to protect America and its citizens:

• **Antiterrorism and Effective Death Penalty Act** was enacted into law in 1996.[27] The Act includes habeas corpus reform, victim restitution, and provisions for stopping the financing of terrorists and barring or deporting alien terrorists.
• **U.S.A. Patriot Act** was signed into law in October 2001.[28] The Act expands the FBI's authority for wiretapping and electronic surveillance, increases penalties for the harboring or financing of terrorists, and increases the number of offenses defined as terrorist acts while imposing stiffer penalties against terrorists. The bill also allows law enforcement new, broad antiterrorism powers, including the ability to search the homes and businesses of people suspected of terrorism and eavesdrop on phone conversations and computer messages.
• **Emergency Supplemental Appropriations Act for Recovery from and Response to Terrorists Attacks on the United States** was enacted in September 2001.[29] The Act provided for emergency supplemental appropriations for the fiscal year for further disaster assistance, antiterrorism initiatives, and assistance in recovering from the terrorist attack of September 11, 2001.

- **Aviation Security Bill** was signed into law on November 19, 2001.[30] The legislation allows for federal oversight of airport passenger and baggage screeners and will eventually make all such workers federal employees. Other provisions include more inspection of checked baggage, fortifying cockpit doors on airliners, and increasing the number of federal marshals on flights.

- **Biological and Chemical Weapons Legislation** has received bipartisan support in the Senate as of November 15, 2001, in response to the threat of biological and chemical terrorist attacks. Important provisions of the bill include $1.1 billion to increase the stockpiles of vaccines in the United States for such diseases as anthrax and smallpox, $1 billion in improving the public health system's ability to respond to chemical or biological attacks, and $1.1 billion to improve detecting procedures of food-borne terrorist attacks.[31]

- **Military Tribunal** became a new weapon in the war on terrorism on November 13, 2001, after President George Bush gave emergency approval for the use of a special military court. The framework of the tribunal would allow the option of trying accused terrorists more quickly and in greater secrecy than in regular criminal courts. Such tribunals could be held abroad, with less evidence needed to convict. American citizens would be excluded from being brought before a military court.[32]

NOTES

1. *American Heritage Dictionary* (New York: Dell, 1994), p. 835; http://www.your-dictionary.com.
2. M. Cherif Bassiouni, "Terrorism," World Book Online Americas Edition, 2001, http://www.cssve.worldbook.compuserve.com/wbol/wbpage/na/ar/co/551940.
3. UN Office for Drug Control and Crime Prevention, "Proposed Definitions of Terrorism," http://www.undep.org/terrorism_definitions.html.
4. Bassiouni, "Terrorism."
5. U.S. Code, Title 22, Sec. 2656 (f); http://jurist.law.pitt.edu/terrorism1.htm.
6. "Proposed Definitions of Terrorism."
7. *Ibid.*
8. David Lester, *Serial Killers: The Insatiable Passion* (Philadelphia: Charles Press, 1995), p. 141; H. A. Cooper, "Terroristic Fads and Fashions," in B. L. Danto and A. H. Kutscher, eds., *The Human Side of Homicide* (New York: Columbia University Press, 1982).
9. Benjamin B. Wolman, *Antisocial Behavior: Personality Disorders From Hostility to Homicide* (Amherst: Prometheus Books, 1999), p. 18.
10. Shoul Bakhash, "The Riddle of Terrorism," http://www.nybooks.com/artiches/4662; Walter Laquer, The Age of Terrorism (New York: Little Brown, 1987).

11. R. Barri Flowers and H. Loraine Flowers, *Murders in the United States: Crimes, Killers and Victims of the Twentieth Century* (Jefferson: McFarland, 2001), pp. 53-57, 81; "Terrorist Attacks on U.S.," http://member.compuserve.com/crime/terrorism.jsp.

12. The Heritage Foundation, "Facts and Figures About Terrorism," http://www.heritage.org/shorts/20010914terror.htm.

13. Cited in Wolman, *Antisocial Behavior*, p. 143.

14. Peter L. Bergen, *Holy War, Inc.: Inside the Secret World of Osama Bin Laden* (New York: Free Press, 2001); Yonah Alexander and Michael S. Swetman, *Usama bin Laden's al-Quada: Profile of a Terrorist Network* (Ardsley: Transnational Publishers, 2001).

15. Terrorist Organizations, "Al-Qu'ada the Base," http://www.ict.org.il/inter_ter/org.cfm. See also Gabriel Weimann and Conrad Winn, *The Theater of Terror: Mass Media and International Terrorists* (New York: Longman, 1994).

16. Gary Ackerman and Cheryl Loeb, "Watch Out For America's Own Extremists," http://cns.miis.edu/pubs/other/watchout.htm.

17. Bassiouni, "Terrorism;" Wolman, *Antisocial Behavior*, p. 141.

18. Wolman, *Antisocial Behavior*, p. 18.

19. Bassiouni, "Terrorism."

20. Thomas H. Dixon, "Why Root Causes Are Important," http://www.pugwash.org/ September11/letter-homerdixon.htm.

21. *Ibid.*

22. *Ibid.*

23. "Kaczynski Gets Life, Says Government Lied," (May 4, 1998), http://www7.cnn.com/US/9805/04/kaczynski.sentencing/index.html.

24. National Center For Policy Analysis, "Suicide Terrorists," http://www.ncpa.org/pi/congress/pd091201e.html.

25. *Ibid.*

26. *Ibid.*

27. P. L. 104-132 (1996).

28. "Bush Signs Antiterrorism Bill Into Law," http://www.cnn.com/2001/US/10/26 /gen.attack.on.terror/index.html.

29. P. L. 107-38 (2001).

30. Associated Press, "Lawmakers Reach Aviation Security Deal," http://www.cnn.com/2001/TRAVEL/NEWS/11/15/rec.aviation.security2ap/index.html.

31. Margaret Garrett, "The Bush White House Will Endorse a $3.25 Billion Senate Bill," http://www.cnn.com/2001/ALLPOLITICS/11/15/bush.bioterror/index.html.

32. Anne Gearan, "Terrorists Could Face Military Trial," http://member.compuserve.com/news/story.jsp?floczff-PLSPLS&id=60816662&dt=2001111480300&w+APO&coview=

Part IV

YOUTH AND MURDER

Chapter 11

YOUTH GANGS AND HOMICIDE

Youth street gangs have long been associated with a disproportionate involvement in homicides and other violent crimes. This is particularly true for racial and ethic minority gangs. The easy availability and possession of modern, sophisticated weapons by gang members is believed to play a major role in youth gang-related homicides, including drive-by shootings and those related to drug dealing and school violence. In spite of the recent migration of gangs to different cities and states across the country and gang rivalries leading to violence, youth gang homicides have declined in general since the 1990s. Yet the number of violent and deadly youth gangs continues to be a problem for law enforcement as well as a barometer for the study of youth violence and homicidal behavior.

DEFINING THE YOUTH GANG

What is a youth gang? Definitions of youth gangs have varied over the years, often relating to the nature and pattern of the gang's activities, particularly with respect to antisocial and violent behavior. Sociologist Frederic Thrasher was one of the first to define the adolescent gang in the 1920s as:

> an interstitial group originally formed spontaneously and then integrated through conflict. It is characterized by. . .meeting face to face, milling, movement through space as a unit, conflict, and planning. The result of this collective behavior is the development of tradition, unreflective internal structure, espirit de corps, solidarity, morale, group awareness, and attachment to local territory.[1]

In the 1970s, Walter Miller, an expert on youth gangs, defined the juvenile delinquent gang as "a group of recurrently associating individuals with identifiable leadership and internal organization, identifying with or

129

claiming control over territory in the community, and engaging either individually or collectively in violent or other forms of illegal behavior."[2]

More recently in the book, *The Adolescent Criminal*, the delinquent youth gang was defined as:

> a loosely organized or disorganized group of juveniles distinguished by colors, race and ethnicity, neighborhood, and principles; and whose delinquent and criminal activities relate to status, respect, revenge, celebrity, satisfaction, and profit, and include murder, gang wars, and drug dealing.[3]

Although youth gangs are typically composed of juvenile members, many may also contain young adults and be affiliated with adult and prison gangs. Most youth gangs are composed of a hierarchy consisting of a core or elite leadership, a group of regular or full-time members, and additional peripheral members. Lewis Yablonsky estimated that 10 to 15 percent of youth gangs include a "hard-core" or elite group that heads the gangs and manages the day-to-day activities, with the other members serving as their subordinates.[4]

YOUTH GANG VIOLENCE

The overall problem of youth gangs and violent activity is of serious concern to law enforcement and often acts as an antecedent to gang-related homicidal behavior. Studies show that youth gang members are disproportionately involved in a high percentage of violent crimes as well as related property and drug offenses.[5] The Program of Research on the Causes and Correlates of Delinquency noted that 30 percent of a sample of youth gang members reported committing 68 percent of violent offenses.[6] Other self-report surveys have shown similar results such as in Denver where 14 percent of the gang sample perpetrated 79 percent of the serious violent crimes;[7] while another survey reported that 14 percent of gang members were responsible for 89 percent of all serious violent offenses.[8] Miller found that gang members accounted for one-third of all crimes of violence, the terrorizing of whole communities, and maintaining a state of siege in many of the urban schools.[9]

Gang norms appear to be a strong factor in the increased level of violence among youth gangs. According to S. H. Decker and B. Van Winkle: "Violence that is internal to the gang, especially during group functions such as an initiation, serves to intensify the bonds among members."[10] In an exploration of youth gangs, James Howell stated that "most gangs are governed by norms supporting the expressive use of violence to settle disputes and to achieve group goals associated with member recruitment, defense of one's identity as a gang member, turf protection and expansion, and defense of the gang's honor."[11]

YOUTH GANG HOMICIDES

Youth gang homicides are defined as homicides involving gang members as victims, perpetrators, or both. Because of the lack of uniformity in defining a gang or gang member from state to state, figures on gang-related homicides are not always consistent. However, national data from several sources indicates that there has been an overall decline in gang homicides in the United States. Between 1991 and 1996, gang involved murders dropped by nearly 15 percent in more than 400 cities across the country, going from 1,748 homicides to 1,492 homicides (see Figure 11.1). Although 32 percent of the cities reported a decline in the number of gang homicides, 29 percent of cities reported an increase, while in 39 percent of cities there was no change.

Figure 11.1
Youth Gang Homicide Trends from 408 American Cities, 1991-1996

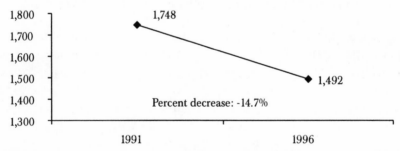

Source: Derived from U.S. Department of Justice, *Youth Gang Homicides in the 1990s* (Washington: Office of Juvenile Justice and Delinquency Prevention, 2000), pp. 1-2.

In a study analyzing data from the National Youth Gang Survey for 1996, 1997, and 1998, covering 1,216 cities with populations of more than 25,000 in which there was a problem with gangs or gang homicides, 237 cities reported gang problems and gang-related homicide statistics (Figure 11.2). A drop in gang homicides over the three years was reported in 49 percent of the cities, while 36 percent of cities showed an increase in gang-related homicides, and 15 percent indicated no change. Overall, the number of gang homicides in the cities in 1996 was 1,293; 1997 had 1,260, and in 1998 there was a total of 1,061 gang-related murders.

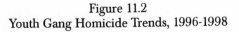

Figure 11.2
Youth Gang Homicide Trends, 1996-1998

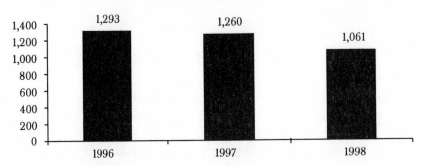

Source: Derived from U.S. Department of Justice, *Youth Gang Homicides in the 1990s* (Washington: Office of Juvenile Justice and Delinquency Prevention, 2001), p. 1.

The highest rate of gang homicides occurred in Chicago and Los Angeles, with 180 and 173 gang-associated homicides, respectively, in 1998. From 1996 to 1998, gang homicides decreased more than twice as much in Los Angeles, dropping 41 percent compared to 19 percent in Chicago.[12]

Youth Gang Versus Nongang Homicides

Studies show some major differences between gang homicides and non-gang homicides with respect to demographic features, situational variables, and interrelated factors.[13] Gang-related homicides were more likely to occur in public settings such as the street, involve strangers, multiple participants, automobiles, a fear of reprisal, and use of firearms.[14] Homicide involved gang members tend to be younger, male, and racial and ethnic minorities than nongang members involved in homicides.

In particular, youth gang homicides are more likely to involve African American and Hispanic offenders and victims than nongang homicides.[15] The vast majority of gang involved homicides are intraracial. In M. W. Klein's study of street gangs, it was found that 92 percent of Los Angeles gang homicides involved African American offenders and victims or Hispanic offenders and victims.[16] However, some studies have found increasing interracial gang homicides and other violence, relating this to territorial issues, drug trafficking, and firearms possession.[17]

Researchers have found that gangs are more likely than their nongang counterparts "to recruit adolescents who own firearms, and gang members are more than twice as likely as nongang members to own a gun for protection, more likely to have peers who own guns for protection, and more likely to carry their guns outside the home."[18] Further, adolescent males who own guns for protection as opposed to sport have been shown to be five times more likely as those not owning a gun for protection to be a member of a gang and three times as likely to perpetrate a serious or violent offense.[19]

Youth Gangs, Guns, and Homicide

A strong relationship exists between youth gangs, guns, and homicides. Most gang-related murders involve the use of a firearm.[20] Studies show that the majority of violent youth gang members either illegally own or are in possession of a gun.[21] An apparent increase in the deadly use of firearms by young members has been attributed to the greater accessibility and use of more sophisticated firearms,[22] as well as the proliferation of lethal weapons by rival gang members.[23] The possession and use of firearms by gang members is a reflection of keeping pace with competing youth gangs, maintaining power, control, and intimidation within gangs and among rival gangs.

Drive-by shootings, in particular, are commonly associated with street gangs, as they once were with organized criminals. These typically occur in inner cities with strong gang affiliations. Research has shown that in drive-by shootings, killing the victim or victims is only a secondary objective to raising fear and intimidating rival gangs.[24] The proportion of gang homicides that are drive-by shootings varies from city to city. For example, between 1989 and 1993, 33 percent of gang homicides in Los Angeles were the result of drive-by shootings, consisting of 590 murders.[25] In a study of Chicago gang-related homicides between 1965 and 1994, only 120 murders or around 6 percent of the total were the result of drive-by shootings.[26]

Youth Gangs and Drug-Related Homicide

There is some evidence of a link between youth gang homicides and a drug-related motive. Studies show that street gangs are becoming increasingly involved with drug offenses including drug trafficking and drug use, which in turn has been both directly and indirectly related to gang violence, migration, and firearm possession.[27]

Homicide violence by youth gangs appears to be tied to a crack cocaine epidemic in the United States. Studies have found an interrelationship between gang involvement in the sale of crack cocaine and drug trafficking, and a rise in violent criminality among youth, such as murder.[28]

However, a number of researchers have found that youth gang homicides are not strongly related to drug offending circumstances. Only 2.2 percent of street gang involved homicides in Chicago from 1965 to 1994 were motivated by drug offenses, according to C. R. Block and colleagues.[29] A similarly small proportion was found by D. M. Kennedy and associates.[30]

Other researchers contend that even an indirect relationship between youth gang homicides and drug crimes such as drug trafficking can still result in an atmosphere in which gang drug-related homicides are not only possible but quite probable.[31]

THE DYNAMICS OF YOUTH GANGS

The Scope of Youth Gangs and Gang Membership

Various estimates over the years have been made on the extent of youth gangs and gang membership in the United States. In the early 1980s, Miller estimated that there were more than 2,000 gangs from nearly 300 jurisdictions, consisting of a membership of almost 100,000.[32] A 1996 estimate placed the figures at approximately 31,000 gangs in some 4,800 jurisdictions, with a membership of almost 846,000.[33]

Youth gangs are most problematic in big cities. In a 1996 survey by the National Youth Gang Center of over 3,000 law enforcement agencies, the highest incidence of gang activity was reported in large cities.[34] Suburban counties were second most likely to have a gang problem, followed by small cities and rural counties. Nearly three-quarters of cities with a population of 25,000 or more reported having youth gangs.

Street gangs are particularly prevalent in some cities with serious gang troubles such as Los Angeles and Chicago. It is estimated that Los Angeles has the most gang members in the United States with over 58,000; while Chicago is estimated to have between 30,000 and 50,000 gang members described as hardcore.[35] The four largest and most violent Chicago gangs–including the Black Gangster Disciples Nation and the Latin Disciples–comprise around 19,000 members while accounting for two-thirds of the city's gang criminality and over half of its gang homicides.[36]

Race, Ethnicity, and Gang Membership

Racial and ethnic minorities are overrepresented among youth gang members. Miller reported that black youths accounted for 47.6 percent of gang members, with Hispanics representing 36.1 percent of membership.[37] In a recent law enforcement survey, 48 percent of youth gangs consisted of African Americans, 43 percent Hispanics, 5 percent whites, and 4 percent Asians (see Figure 11.3).

Figure 11.3
Racial and Ethnic Breakdown of Youth Gangs in the United States

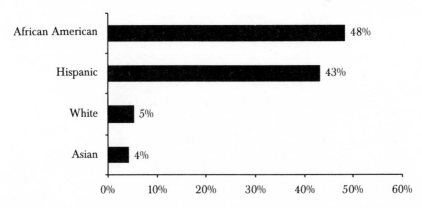

Source: Derived from U.S. Department of Justice, *Youth Gangs: An Overview* (Washington: Office of Juvenile Justice and Delinquency Prevention, 1998), p. 2.

Some studies have found a higher percentage of white youths are involved in street gangs than indicated in previous research. F. Esbensen and D. W. Osgood found that 25 percent of gang membership was white, with 31 percent black, 25 percent Asian, and 15 percent other racial and ethnic groups.[38] Miller noted seven white youth gangs in a large urban area, with many members convicted and imprisoned for serious offenses.[39]

Gender and Youth Gang Involvement

Males constitute the vast majority of youth gang members. Miller found that 90 percent of gang membership was made up of males.[40] An estimated 94 percent of street gangs were male, according to a survey of law enforcement agencies.[41] Some research reports that there may a higher proportion of females involved in gangs than is commonly believed.[42] However, males continue to dominate gang membership and are responsible for most gang violence, including perpetrating virtually all gang-related homicides.

Age and Membership in Youth Gangs

The majority of youth gang members fall between the ages of ten and twenty-four, with the average gang member believed to be about seventeen or eighteen years of age.[43] Gang members tend to be older in cities with a long history of youth gangs, such as Chicago and Los Angeles.[44] According to Miller, in the four cities with the largest gang problem, eight out of ten gang members arrested were between the ages of fourteen and nineteen.[45] Around 4 percent of members were younger than fourteen. Studies reveal that although younger members are becoming more prevalent in youth gangs, a greater increase has occurred in the membership of older persons in gangs.[46]

THEORIES ON YOUTH GANG VIOLENCE

The most influential theories on youth gang crime and violence focus on lower class gangs. Studies indicate that lower class or urban youth gangs are disproportionately involved in serious and violent gang offending.[47] Miller found a relationship between the greater prevalence of lower class populations and more involvement in gangs.[48] This conclusion was generally supported by I. A. Spergel, though noting "it is not clear that either class, poverty, culture, race or ethnicity, or social change per se primarily accounts for gang problems."[49]

Reaction-Formation Theory

The reaction-formation theory was proposed by Albert Cohen.[50] The theory posited that lower class youths resort to gang delinquency as a group response or reaction to an inability to acquire the status established by middle class norms and values. Cohen held that although middle class goals and values are desired by lower class youths—including success, ambition, and talent—they are generally disadvantaged in institutional settings such as school, where they are subject to middle class standards.

These blocked opportunities to attain culturally prescribed goals and conflicts with middle class institutions, Cohen believed, caused lower class youths to deviate in response, which he referred to as "status frustration" or "reaction-formation against a middle class organized status dilemma in which the lower class boy suffers status frustrations in competition with middle status boys."[51] This status frustration is seen as causing many such youths to "band together in juvenile gangs or a delinquent subculture, where they participate in behavior that is nonutilitarian, malicious, negativistic, and hedonistic."[52]

Cohen is credited with being amongst the first to explain delinquent youth group behavior. However, his theory has been criticized by many for its lack of empirical validation, limited evidence to support the notion that lower class youths repudiate the values of the middle class, broad generalizations, and insufficient attention placed on other influences in youth antisocial behavior, such as family, race, and ethnicity.

Opportunity Theory

Opportunity theory of delinquent gangs was put forth by Richard Cloward and Lloyd Ohlin.[53] The theory advanced that an individual's access to legitimate and illegitimate means is highly influenced by the social structure. While differential opportunity is present in reaching culturally prescribed goals through legitimate means, it exists as well in using illegitimate means for achieving socially approved goals.

Opportunity theory explains gang delinquency as a discrepancy between aspirations of lower class youths and what they have access to, with the assumption that "discrepancies between aspirations and legitimate chances of achievement increase as one descends in the class structure."[54] This inability to achieve middle class aspirations results in deep frustration and causes lower class youths to deviate into illegitimate means to achieve these cultural goals.

According to Cloward and Ohlin, it is the social structure within a community that determines the access youths have to "learning structures" and "performance structures." The researchers identify three main types of lower class youth gangs, or subcultural reactions to blocked legitimate or illegitimate means for success: (1) criminal gangs, (2) conflict gangs, and (3) retreatist gangs.

- **Criminal gangs:** youth gangs who take on criminal skills and values acquired from adult and organized criminals. These gangs are motivated primarily by power, material gain, and prestige.
- **Conflict gangs:** youth gangs developed under circumstances in which both legitimate and illegitimate goals are blocked. Membership in conflict gangs enables youths to achieve status, prestige, or a reputation for toughness. The principles of these gangs typically involve fighting, violence, and intergang conflict.
- **Retreatist gangs:** youth gangs formed when youths are denied or reject legitimate or illegitimate means for success. Retreatist youths often become substance abusers and use secondary criminal activities to support habits.

Opportunity theory has been recognized for various delinquent gang subcultures in relation to differential opportunity structures. However, it has drawbacks in its focus on lower class gang delinquency while inadequately accounting for the gang delinquency of other classes and individual delinquency; as well as failure to account for why some communities have different kinds of delinquent youth gangs.

Lower Class Culture Theory

Lower class culture theory was offered by Walter Miller in explaining youth gang delinquency.[55] As opposed to Cohen and Cloward and Ohlin's propositions that lower class gang delinquency is based on a rejection of middle class norms and values, Miller postulated that gang delinquency among the lower class is a reflection of positive attempts by youths to attain goals as established by values or focal concerns of the lower class culture.

Miller identified six such lower class focal concerns, or areas representing the primary concerns of lower class youths: (1) trouble, (2) toughness, (3) smartness, (4) excitement, (5) fate, and (6) autonomy.

- **Trouble** refers to circumstances that lead to undesired involvement with the police.
- **Toughness** is concerned with masculinity, physical superiority, bravery, and daring.
- **Smartness** is the ability to outsmart, outwit, or con others, while avoiding being the victim of dupe or deception.
- **Excitement** concerns the desire for thrills, risks, and avoiding boredom.
- **Fate** refers to interests or beliefs associated with luck, fortunes, and jinxes.
- **Autonomy** is closely related to fate and a desire to be in control of one's own life or destiny.

According to lower class culture theory, the delinquent gang serves as a social setting in which youths can achieve prestige through actions in association with lower class focal concerns.

While Miller's theory of lower class culture is successful in relating differential lower class values to youth gang delinquency, it fails to explain the origins of these focal concerns, or differentiate between lower class offenders and nonoffenders. Further, some critics reject the notion that lower class gang members do not adhere to middle class norms and values.

NOTES

1. Frederic M. Thrasher, *The Gang* (Chicago: University of Chicago Press, 1927), p. 57.
2. Walter B. Miller, *Violence by Youth Gangs and Youth Groups as a Crime Problem in Major American Cities* (Washington: Government Printing Office, 1975).
3. R. Barri Flowers, *The Adolescent Criminal: An Examination of Today's Juvenile Offender* (Jefferson: McFarland, 1990), p. 99.
4. Lewis Yablonsky, *The Violent Gang* (Baltimore: Penguin, 1962), p. 227.
5. S. R. Battin, K. G. Hill, R. D. Abbott, R. F. Catalano, and J. D. Hawkins, "The Contribution of Gang Membership to Delinquency Beyond Delinquent

Friends," *Criminology 36* (1998): 93-115; M. W. Klein, C. L. Maxson, and L. C. Cunningham, "'Crack,' Street Gangs, and Violence," *Criminology 29* (1991): 623-50.

6. T. P. Thornberry, "Membership in Youth Gangs and Involvement in Serious and Violent Offending," in R. Loeber and D. P. Farrington, eds., *Serious and Violent Offenders: Risk Factors and Successful Interventions* (Thousand Oaks: Sage, 1998), pp. 147-66.

7. Cited in Cheryl Maxson, "Gang Homicide," in M. Dwayne Smith and Margaret A. Zahn, eds., *Studying and Preventing Homicide: Issues and Challenges* (Thousand Oaks: Sage, 1999), p. 197.

8. D. Huizinga, "The Volume of Crime by Gang and Nongang Members," paper presented at the Annual Meeting of the American Society of Criminology, San Diego, 1997.

9. Miller, *Violence by Youth Gangs and Youth Groups.*

10. S. H. Decker and B. Van Winkle, *Life in the Gang: Family, Friends, and Violence* (New York: Cambridge University Press, 1996), p. 270. See also U.S. Department of Justice, *Youth Gangs: An Overview* (Washington: Office of Juvenile Justice and Delinquency Prevention, 1998), p. 9.

11. *Youth Gangs,* p. 9. See also J. F. Short, Jr. and F. L. Strodtbeck, *Group Process and Gang Delinquency* (Chicago: University of Chicago Press, 1965); R. Block and C. R. Block, *Street Gang Crime in Chicago* (Washington: National Institute of Justice, 1993).

12. U.S. Department of Justice, *Youth Gang Homicides in the 1990s* (Washington: Office of Juvenile Justice and Delinquency Prevention, 2001), pp. 1-2.

13. *Youth Gangs,* pp. 10-11; Maxson, "Gang Homicide," pp. 197-206; Kelly Damphousse, Victoria E. Brewer, and Cary D. Atkinson, "Gangs, Race/Ethnicity and Houston Homicide in the 1990s," in U.S. Department of Justice, *Proceedings of the Homicide Research Working Group Meetings, 1997 and 1998* (Washington: National Institute of Justice, 1999), pp. 80-92.

14. Klein, Maxson, and Cunningham, "'Crack,' Street Gangs, and Violence," pp. 623-50; C. Rogers, "Gang-Related Homicides in Los Angeles County," *Journal of Forensic Sciences 38,* 4 (1993): 831-34; I. Spergel, "Violent Gangs in Chicago: In Search of Social Policy," *Social Science Review 58* (1984): 199-226.

15. G. W. Bailey and N. P. Unnithan, "Gang Homicides in California: A Discriminate Analysis," *Journal of Criminal Justice 22,* 3 (1994): 267-75.

16. M. W. Klein, *The American Street Gang: Its Nature, Prevalence, and Control* (New York: Oxford, 1995).

17. See, for example, I. A. Spergel, *The Youth Gang Problem: A Community Approach* (New York: Oxford, 1995).

18. *Youth Gangs,* p. 10; B. Bjerregaard and A. J. Lizotte, "Gun Ownership and Gang Membership," *Journal of Criminal Law and Criminology 86* (1995): 37-58.

19. A. J. Lizotte, J. M. Tesoriero, T. P. Thornberry, and M. D. Krohn, "Patterns of Adolescent Firearms Ownership and Use," *Justice Quarterly 11* (1994): 51-73.

20. *Youth Gangs, pp. 10-12; Block and Block, Street Gang Crime in Chicago;* R. Barri Flowers, *Male Crime and Deviance: Exploring its Dynamics, Nature, and Causes* (Springfield: Charles C Thomas, 2003).

21. *Youth Gangs*, p. 12; J. F. Sheley and J. D. Wright, *In the Line of Fire: Youth, Guns and Violence in Urban America* (Hawthorne: Aldine De Gruyter, 1995).
22. Block and Block, *Street Gang Crime in Chicago.*
23. Decker and Van Winkle, *Life in the Gang*, p. 23.
24. H. R. Hutson, D. Anglin, and M. Eckstein, "Drive-by Shootings by Violent Street Gangs in Los Angeles: A Five-Year Review From 1989 to 1993," *Academic Emergency Medicine 3* (1996): 300-3.
25. *Ibid.*
26. C. R. Block, A. Christakos, A. Jacob, and R. Przybylski, *Street Gangs and Crime: Patterns and Trends in Chicago* (Chicago: Illinois Criminal Justice Information Authority, 1996).
27. *Youth Gangs*, pp. 11-12; C. L. Maxson and M. W. Klein, "Defining Gang Homicide: An Updated Look at Member and Motive Approaches," in C. R. Huff, ed., *Gangs in America*, 2nd ed. (Thousand Oaks: Sage, 1996), pp. 3-20.
28. J. A. Inciardi and A. E. Pottieger, "Kids, Crack, and Crime," *Journal of Drug Issues 21* (1991): 257-70.
29. Block, Christakos, Jacob, and Przybylski, *Street Gangs and Crime.*
30. D. M. Kennedy, A. A. Braga, and A. M. Piehl, "The (Un)Known Universe: Mapping Gangs and Gang Violence in Boston," in D. Weisburd and T. McEwen, eds., *Crime Mapping and Crime Prevention* (New York: Criminal Justice Press, 1997), pp. 219-62.
31. *Youth Gangs*, p. 12.
32. Walter B. Miller, *Crime by Youth Gangs and Groups in the United States* (Washington: Office of Justice Programs, 1992).
33. Cited in *Youth Gangs*, p. 1.
34. *Ibid.*, p. 4.
35. National Youth Gang Center, *1995 National Youth Gang Survey* (Washington: Office of Juvenile Justice and Delinquency Prevention, 1997).
36. *Youth Gangs*, p. 4; Block and Block, *Street Gang Crime in Chicago.*
37. Miller, *Violence by Youth Gangs and Youth Groups*, p. 26.
38. F. Esbensen and D. W. Osgood, *National Evaluation of G.R.E.A.T.* Research in Brief (Washington: National Institute of Justice, 1997).
39. Walter B. Miller, "White Gangs," in James F. Short, Jr., ed., *Modern Criminals* (Chicago: Aldine, 1970), pp. 57, 60, 64.
40. Miller, *Violence by Youth Gangs and Youth Groups*, pp. 21-23.
41. Cited in *Youth Gangs*, p. 3.
42. Klein, *The American Street Gang*; Anne Campbell, *Girl Delinquents* (New York: St. Martin's Press, 1981).
43. G. D. Curry and S. H. Decker, *Confronting Gangs: Crime and Community* (Los Angeles: Roxbury, 1998).
44. *Youth Gangs*, p. 2; Klein, *The American Street Gang.*
45. Miller, *Violence by Youth Gangs and Youth Groups*, pp. 21-23.
46. J. W. Moore, "Gangs, Drugs, and Violence," in M. De La Rosa, E. Y. Lambert, and B. Gropper, eds., *Drugs and Violence: Causes, Correlates, and Consequences* (Rockville: National Institute on Drug Abuse, 1990), pp. 160-76; J. J. Hagedorn, *People and Folks: Gangs, Crime and the Underclass in a Rustbelt City* (Chicago: Lakeview Press, 1988).

47. *Youth Gangs,* pp. 2-3; Flowers, *The Adolescent Criminal,* pp. 102-3.
48. Walter B. Miller, "American Youth Gangs: Past and Present," in A. Blumberg, ed., *Current Perspectives in Criminal Behavior* (New York: Knopf, 1974), pp. 410-20.
49. Spergel, *The Youth Gang Problem,* p. 60; *Youth Gangs,* pp. 2-3.
50. Albert K. Cohen, *Delinquent Boys: The Culture of the Gang* (New York: Free Press, 1951); Albert K. Cohen and James F. Short, Jr., "Research on Delinquent Subcultures," *Journal of Social Issues 14,* 3 (1958): 20-37.
51. Cohen, *Delinquent Boys,* pp. 36-44.
52. Flowers, *The Adolescent Criminal,* p. 105.
53. Richard A. Cloward and Lloyd E. Ohlin, *Delinquency and Opportunity: A Theory of Delinquent Gangs* (New York: Free Press, 1960).
54. *Ibid.,* p. 80.
55. Walter B. Miller, "Lower-Class Culture as a Generating Milieu of Gang Delinquency," *Journal of Social Issues 14* (1958): 5-19.

Chapter 12

SCHOOL KILLINGS

In the midst of other types of homicidal violence in society, there has been a rash of fatal school shootings and other school violence in recent years. The mass murder at Columbine High School in 1999 serves as the worst example and has led to increased attention on school violence and at-risk youth by policymakers, criminologists, delinquency experts, and educators. Perpetrators of deadly school violence are predominantly young, suburban males, often with deep-rooted problems that have gone unaddressed. These include pent-up frustrations, a dysfunctional family life, child abuse victimization, mental problems, and, for many, being bullied. Substance abuse is also typically a factor. A gang presence at school can further increase the potential for school shootings and violence. What appears to be the most important correlate to school killings is the availability and use of firearms. Nearly all school fatalities and serious injuries involved guns and other weapons with both students and teachers being potential targets.

DEADLY SCHOOL SHOOTINGS

Although school shootings are not a new phenomenon in America, the recent number of multiple shootings at school has been alarming. Between 1993 and 1999, there have been at least fifteen fatal school shootings with multiple victims across the country.[1] Some of the most deadly school shootings include the following:

- On March 2, 1987, Nathan Ferris, a 12-year-old overweight honor student, took his father's .45 caliber pistol to school in Missouri where he shot to death a classmate who had teased him, before killing himself.
- On January 17, 1989, Patrick Purdy, a 26-year-old drifter, entered the schoolyard of Cleveland Elementary School in Stockton, California.

142

Armed with a semiautomatic AK-47, he opened fire, killing five children and wounding twenty-nine others before killing himself.

- On February 2, 1996, Barry Loukatis, fourteen, walked into Frontier Junior High School in Moses Lake, Washington. Heavily armed, he shot to death two students and a teacher. One of the students had reportedly been verbally abusive to him.
- On February 19, 1997, Evan Ramsey, sixteen, brought a shotgun to Bethel Regional School in Bethel, Alaska. He shot to death a fellow student and the principal, and wounded two others.
- On December 1, 1997, Michael Carneal, fourteen, went on a shooting spree at Heath High School in West Paducah, Kentucky, killing three students and injuring five. His inspiration was the movie, "The Basketball Diaries," in which the main character had a dream about entering a classroom and shooting five students.
- On March 24, 1998, Mitchell Johnson, fourteen, and Andrew Goldman, twelve, entered a middle school in Jonesboro, Arkansas dressed in camouflage. There they opened fire on students and teachers, killing five and wounding ten.
- On May 21, 1998, 14-year-old Kip Kinkel was heavily armed as he entered Thurston High School in Springfield, Oregon. He opened fire, killing two students and wounding twenty-five. Earlier that day, he had committed parricide in killing his mother and father.
- On April 21, 1999, Eric Harris, eighteen, and Dylan Klebold, seventeen, entered Columbine High School in Littleton, Colorado armed with semiautomatic weapons. The two went on a shooting spree, killing thirteen and wounding twenty-five before taking their own lives.[2]

Additionally, there has been a fair share of school shootings in recent years involving a single fatality or the nonfatal injury of victims.[3] Even more disturbing is that the offenders appear to be getting younger. In a study of multiple school killings involving fifteen killers, Kathleen Heide found that more than half the perpetrators were age fourteen or younger.[4] By comparison, nearly 90 percent of juveniles arrested for murder overall in this country are between fifteen and seventeen years of age.[5]

In spite of the tragedy of school shootings and their seemingly increasing numbers, youths are far more likely to be murder victims and offenders away from school. For instance, from 1997 to 1998, a total of 2,752 persons between the ages of five and nineteen were homicide victims in the United States, as shown in Figure 12.1. Of these, only thirty-five were victims of school-related homicides. However, the dynamics of school shootings are similar to those of shootings elsewhere involving young people. Societal violence and its influences can often be a precursor to school shootings and other crime and violence perpetrated at school.

Figure 12.1
Murders of Students at School[a] and of Youths 5 to 19 Years of Age
Away from School, 1997-1998

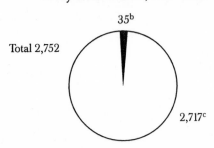

35[b]

Total 2,752

2,717[c]

[a] "At School" includes on school property, on the way to or from school, and while attending or traveling to or from a school-sponsored event.
[b] Student murders at school, July 1, 1997 to June 30, 1998.
[c] Murders of youth ages 5 through 19 away from school, July 1, 1997 to June 30, 1998.

Source: Derived from U.S. Department of Education and Justice, *Indicators of School Crime and Safety 2000* (Washington: Offices of Educational Research and Improvement and Justice Programs, 2000), p. 2.

What are the warning signs for at-risk youth in becoming murderers at school? Experts have found the following traits to exist in many such killers:

- Depression.
- Built-up hostility toward others.
- History of temper tantrums.
- The victim of child abuse.
- A witness to family violence.
- History of problems with alcohol or drugs.
- Disciplinary problems.
- Problems with truancy, school suspensions, or being expelled.
- A strong interest in firearms or explosives.
- Cruelty to animals.
- Obsessed with hate or antigovernment groups.
- Belonging to a gang or antisocial group.
- Involvement with a satanic cult.
- Fascinated with violent games, books, movies, or other violent entertainment.
- Suicidal.
- Blames others for problems experienced.[6]

THE EXTENT OF SCHOOL VIOLENCE

School shootings are representative of the greater problem of school violence occurring at high schools, middle schools, and elementary schools across the country. Various national studies attest to the seriousness of school crime and violence. In a five-year study by the National School Boards Association, 78 percent of school districts reported student assaults against other students and 60 percent reported student assaults against teachers.[7] Sixty-one percent of districts reported school violence involving weapons; while in 82 percent of the districts school violence increased during the period.

According to the Department of Justice's *National Crime Victimization Survey Report*, there were an estimated more than 1.2 million crimes of violence inside school buildings or on school property in the United States in 1995 (see Table 12.1). This constituted 14.2 percent of all reported crimes of violence. There were approximately 280,000 completed acts of school violence and 957,000 attempted or threatened incidents of violence at school.

Table 12.1

SCHOOL CRIMES OF VIOLENCE, BY TYPE OF CRIME, 1995

Type of crime	Total number of incidents	Inside school building/ on school property
Crimes of violence	8,727,230	14.2%
Completed violence	2,515,470	11.1%
Attempted/threatened violence	6,211,770	15.4%
Rape/sexual assault[b]	355,450	4.0% (a)
Robbery	1,039,490	5.7%
Completed/property taken	673,440	5.1%
With injury	196,880	0.0%(a)
Without injury	476,560	7.2%
Attempted to take property	366,050	6.7%
With injury	87,610	12.8% (a)
Without injury	278,440	4.8% (a)
Assault	7,352,290	15.8%
Aggravated	1,622,360	6.4%
Simple	5,729,920	18.5%
Purse snatching/pocket picking	362,100	14.2%
Motor vehicle theft	1,653,820	2.0%
Completed	1,098,280	1.9% (a)
Attempted	555,540	2.2% (a)
Theft	22,006,050	13.3%

[a] Estimate is based on about ten or fewer sample cases.

[b] Includes verbal threats of rape and threats of sexual assault.

Source: Derived from U.S. Department of Justice, *Criminal Victimization in the United States, 1995: A National Crime Victimization Survey Report* (Washington: Office of Justice Programs, 2000), p. 71.

A more comprehensive portrayal of school violence is reflected in the annual National Center for Education and Statistics and Bureau of Justice Statistics' *Indicators of School Crime and Safety*, as seen in Table 12.2. The findings show that in 1998, approximately 2,715,600 school crimes involving stu-

Table 12.2
SCHOOL CRIMES[a] AGAINST STUDENTS 12 TO 18 YEARS OLD,
BY TYPE OF CRIME AND STUDENT CHARACTERISTICS, 1998

Student characteristics	Total[b]	Violent[c]	Serious violent[d]
Total	2,715,600	1,153,200	252,700
Gender			
Male	1,536,100	721,300	144,200
Female	1,179,400	431,900	108,400
Age			
12-14	1,475,100	705,800	162,200
15-18	1,240,500	447,400	90,500
Race/ethnicity			
White, non-Hispanic	1,824,300	785,500	157,100
Black, non-Hispanic	464,000	198,200	48,100
Hispanic	315,100	129,200	42,600
Other, non-Hispanic	105,700	38,100	4,900 (e)
Urbanicity			
Urban	865,000	361,400	99,100
Suburban	1,319,500	548,400	91,700
Rural	531,100	243,400	61,900
Household income			
Less than $7,500	136,500	66,700	21,100 (e)
$7,500-14,999	242,600	146,900	30,400 (e)
$15,000-24,999	428,700	210,400	35,400
$25,000-34,999	351,100	178,200	52,100
$35,000-49,999	361,500	122,400	27,200 (e)
$50,000-74,999	497,400	190,600	45,000
$75,000 or more	453,000	149,500	23,800 (e)

[a] Includes crimes occurring inside or on school property, as well as on the way to or from school.
[b] Includes violent crimes and theft. Due to rounding, totals may not add up.
[c] Includes serious violent crimes and simple assault.
[d] Includes rape, sexual assault, robbery, and aggravated assault.
[e] Estimate based on fewer than ten cases.

Source: Derived from U.S. Department of Education and Justice, *Indicators of School Crime and Safety 2000* (Washington: Offices of Educational Research and Improvement and Justice Programs, 2000), p. 49.

dents twelve to eighteen years old occurred in the United States. Some 1.1 million were violent crimes. Among these, almost 253,000 incidents were characterized as serious violent crimes, including rape, sexual assault, robbery, and aggravated assault.

Victims of violent school crimes were most likely to be male, younger students, white, non-Hispanic, suburban, with a household income of $15,000-$24,999 and $50,000-$74,999.

For seriously violent offenses, the number of female student victims was closer to male student victims than for overall violent crimes; with more serious violent crimes occurring in urban areas than the suburbs or rural areas. Student victims of serious violent crimes tended to most often come from households with incomes of $25,000-$34,999.

The significant relationship between schools and violent crimes was further put in perspective by findings from the Centers for Disease Control and Prevention's Youth Risk Behavior Survey as follows:

- Nearly four in ten high school students engaged in a physical fight within the past year.
- Almost half of male students were in a school fight in the last year.
- More than twice the number of male students as female students were likely to have been in a fight within the past year.
- Around 15 percent of high school students nationwide fought on school property within the last year.
- Racial and ethnic minority students were more likely than white students to be in school fights and to suffer injuries.
- Nearly two in ten students carried a weapon to school in the past month.
- Almost 6 percent of students carried a firearm within the last month.
- Seven percent of high school students were threatened or injured at school with a weapon.
- More than half the middle and high schools across the country reported at least one incident of fighting or unarmed assault during the past year.
- Around one in five middle and high schools reported at least one serious violent crime within the past year.
- Violent school crime is more than twice as likely to occur in cities as rural areas, and more than three times as likely to occur as in small towns.
- Four in ten high school students stayed out of school at least once within the last month out of fear for their safety.[8]

School Violence Against Teachers

Teachers have also been the victims of student perpetrated school violence. According to *Indicators*, between 1994 and 1998, there were an estimated 1.7 million nonfatal crimes directed toward teachers at school (see

Table 12.3). Of these, nearly 669,000 were considered violent crimes and almost 80,000 were classified as serious violent offenses.

Table 12.3
NONFATAL CRIMES AGAINST TEACHERS AT SCHOOL[a],
BY TYPE OF CRIME AND TEACHER CHARACTERISTICS, 1994-1998

Teacher characteristics	Total[b]	Violent[c]	Serious violent[d]
Total	1,755,300	668,400	79,800
Instructional level			
Elementary	630,800	196,800	51,800
Middle/junior high	531,700	250,300	15,400
Senior high	592,900	221,300	12,600
Gender			
Male	514,400	276,300	29,700
Female	1,241,000	392,100	50,100
Race/ethnicity			
White, non-Hispanic	1,488,900	575,400	67,000
Black, non-Hispanic	130,100	48,000	10,500
Hispanic	104,800	38,400	(e)
Other, non-Hispanic	16,200 (f)	4,400 (f)	2,300 (f)
Urbanicity[g]			
Urban	999,300	387,100	48,300
Suburban	469,600	160,900	21,800
Rural	213,700	93,000	9,800

[a] Includes crimes occurring inside or on school property.

[b] Includes violent crimes and theft. Due to rounding, totals may not add up.

[c] Includes serious violent crimes and simple assault.

[d] Includes rape, sexual assault, robbery, and aggravated assault.

[e] No cases were reported.

[f] Estimate based on fewer than ten cases.

[g] Teachers teaching in more than one school in different locales are not included.

Source: Derived from U.S. Department of Education and Justice, *Indicators of School Crime and Safety 2000* (Washington: Offices of Educational Research and Improvement and Justice Programs, 2000), p. 76.

Teachers were most likely to be victims of violent crimes at middle or junior high schools; while being much more likely to experience serious violent crimes at elementary schools than middle or senior high schools.

Female teachers were much more likely to be victims of violent and seriously violent crimes than male teachers. White and urban teachers were predominately more likely to be the victims of any type of violent offenses than other teachers.

Trends in School Violence

Although school shootings and other violence continues to be a serious concern for students and teachers, the incidence of school violence has shown a decline in recent years. From 1992 to 1998, *Indicators* showed that the rate of victimization for violent crimes at school went from forty-eight per 1,000 to forty-three per 1,000 students ages twelve to eighteen.[9] The percentage of students involved in physical fights at school went from 16.2 percent of students in 1993 to 14.8 percent in 1997 (see Table 12.4).

Table 12.4

PERCENTAGE OF STUDENTS, GRADES 9 THROUGH 12, WHO REPORTED
HAVING BEEN IN A PHYSICAL FIGHT ON SCHOOL PROPERTY IN THE
LAST 12 MONTHS, BY STUDENT CHARACTERISTICS, 1993, 1995, AND 1997

Student characteristics	1993	1995[a]	1997[a]
Total	16.2	15.5	14.8
Gender			
Male	23.5	21.0	20.0
Female	8.6	9.5	8.6
Race/ethnicity			
White, non-Hispanic	15.0	12.9	13.3
Black, non-Hispanic	22.0	20.3	19.0
Hispanic	17.9	21.1	19.0
Asian/Pacific Islander	11.7	18.3	8.3
Other, non-Hispanic	18.8	23.0	14.8
Grade			
9th	23.1	21.6	21.3
10th	17.2	16.5	17.0
11th	13.8	13.6	12.5
12th	11.4	10.6	9.5

[a] The response rate for this survey was less than 70 percent and a full non-response bias analysis has not been done to date.

Source: Adapted from U.S. Department of Education and Justice, *Indicators of School Crime and Safety 2000* (Washington: Offices of Educational Research and Improvement and Justice Programs, 2000), p. 61.

While the percentage of female students engaging in fights remained steady from 1993 to 1997, the percentage of male students involved in fights went from 23.5 percent to 20 percent. Among racial and ethnic groups, only Hispanic students showed a rise in the percent participating in physical fighting on school property from 1993 to 1996. Declines in fighting occurred for all grade levels during the span, with ninth grade students more likely than those in other grades to be in physical fights at school.

Other trends supporting a decline in school crime and violence include the following findings:

- Between 1993 and 1997, the percentage of high school students reporting bringing a weapon onto school property dropped from 12 percent to 9 percent.
- From 1995 to 1999, the percentage of students reporting a gang presence at school decreased from about 29 percent to just over 17 percent.
- Between 1995 and 1999, the percentage of twelve to eighteen year old students who avoided places at school dropped from 9 percent to 5 percent.[10]

FACTORS IN SCHOOL SHOOTINGS AND VIOLENCE

Researchers have found a number of factors that play a significant role in school shootings and other violence at school. These include the availability and presence of firearms and other weapons, a gang presence at school, bullying, and the availability, use, and abuse of alcohol and drugs on school property.

Weapons and School Violence

The relationship between school violence and student possession of weapons has been well documented.[11] Virtually all lethal violence at school is closely associated with students carrying, using, or having easy access to guns. The Youth Risk Behavior Survey reported that 61 percent of students said they knew other students who could bring a firearm to school if they chose to.[12] One in four respondents indicated they could easily obtain a gun, while one in five students reported hearing rumors of another student planning to shoot someone from or at school.

A high percentage of students in the United States are likely to carry weapons, according to the research. As seen in Table 12.5, in 1997, more than 18 percent of students in grades nine to twelve reported carrying a weapon such as a gun, knife, or club at some point within the past month alone. Nearly 9 percent of students said they had carried a weapon onto school property within the last thirty days.

Table 12.5
PERCENTAGE OF STUDENTS, GRADES 9 THROUGH 12, WHO
REPORTED CARRYING A WEAPON ON SCHOOL PROPERTY
DURING THE PAST 30 DAYS, BY STUDENT CHARACTERISTIC, 1997

Student characteristics	At any time[a]	On school property[a]
Total	18.3	8.5
Gender		
Male	27.7	12.5
Female	7.0	3.7
Race/ethnicity		
White, non-Hispanic	17.0	7.8
Black, non-Hispanic	21.7	9.2
Hispanic	23.3	10.4
Asian/Pacific Islander	9.2	4.0
Other, non-Hispanic	19.2	10.9
Grade		
9th	22.6	10.2
10th	17.4	7.7
11th	18.2	9.4
12th	15.4	7.0
Ungraded or other	16.7	16.2

[a] The response rate for this survey was less than 70 percent and a full non-response bias analysis has not been done to date.

Source: Adapted from U.S. Department of Education and Justice, *Indicators of School Crime and Safety 2000* (Washington: Offices of Educational Research and Improvement and Justice Programs, 2000), p. 78.

Males were more than three times as likely as females to have carried a gun at any time or on school property in the past month; while black, non-Hispanic, and Hispanic students were more likely than students of other racial and ethnic groups to possess a weapon at any time or at school. More than one in ten Hispanic students reported carrying a gun to school in the last thirty days.

Ninth grade students were the most likely than other students to carry a weapon in the last month on school property or elsewhere. More than two in ten ninth graders reported carrying a weapon at any time, and over one in ten said they took a weapon to school in the past thirty days.

Youth Gangs at School

The increasing presence of youth gangs at school has been strongly related to school shootings, violence, and illicit drug activity.[13] As shown in Table
12.6, more than 17 percent of students twelve to eighteen years of age reported that street gangs were present in their school in 1999. This was an increase
of 2 percent over those reporting a gang presence at school in 1989.

Table 12.6
PERCENTAGE OF STUDENTS, 12 TO 18 YEARS OF AGE, REPORTING
THE PRESENCE OF STREET GANGS AT SCHOOL DURING THE
PAST SIX MONTHS, BY STUDENT CHARACTERISTICS, 1989-1999

Student characteristics	1989[a]	1999
Total	15.3	17.3
Gender		
Male	15.8	17.5
Female	14.8	17.1
Race/ethnicity		
White, non-Hispanic	11.7	13.1
Black, non-Hispanic	19.8	24.7
Hispanic	31.6	28.3
Other, non-Hispanic	25.4	17.9
Grade		
6th	10.3	9.2
7th	16.6	12.0
8th	13.6	12.9
9th	19.6	22.7
10th	16.0	22.1
11th	15.3	19.6
12th	14.2	20.0
Urbanicity		
Urban	24.8	25.1
Suburban	14.0	15.8
Rural	7.8	11.1
Control		
Public	16.4	18.6
Private	4.4	4.4

[a] Includes students ages 12 through 19.

Source: Adapted from U.S. Department of Education and Justice, *Indicators of School Crime and
Safety 2000* (Washington: Offices of Educational Research and Improvement and Justice Programs,
2000), p. 83.

Male and female students were roughly equal in their reporting of gangs at school, with nearly two in ten believing this to be the case in 1999. Black, non-Hispanic, and Hispanic students were far more likely than other students to report a gang presence at school. More than 28 percent of Hispanic students and nearly 25 percent of black students felt there were gangs at school.

Students in higher grades were more likely than those in lower grades to report the existence of gangs at school. More than two in ten students in grades nine and ten believed there were gangs at school, while two in ten twelfth graders reported a school gang presence.

Gangs were more than four times as likely to be reported in public schools as private ones in 1999. A gang presence was much more likely to exist in urban schools than schools in suburban or rural areas. More than one in four students in urban schools believed there were gangs at school.

Researchers have found that youth gangs are involved in a disproportionate level of violent activity.[14] This has been greatly attributed to the availability and use of firearms and access to more sophisticated weapons.[15]

School Bullying

Bullying or being bullied at school is seen by experts as a major factor in violent school behavior. This is particularly true where it concerns school shooting incidents. Research shows that of more than 250 school-related deaths in the United States since 1992, bullying played a role in virtually every incident.[16]

What is bullying? A bully is defined as a person who "directs physical, verbal, or psychological aggression or harassment toward others with the goal of gaining power over another."[17] The act of bullying has been shown to be a persistent problem at school and in communities across the country. An estimated 15 to 30 percent of all students are bullies or the victims of bullying.[18] According to the American Medical Association, roughly 3.7 million youths bully other youths, while more than 3.2 million people are the victims of some form of bullying in the United States each year.[19]

Boys are more likely to be bullies than girls, especially when it comes to physical bullying.[20] The victims of bullies tend to be boys more often than girls, younger students, and those who are physically or socially weak or disadvantaged. Most victims have few friends or confidants and poor social skills and academic difficulties. The rate of fighting by bullies and the victims of bullying tends to be higher than among non-bullying involved children.[21]

Studies indicate that physical bullying tends to increase in elementary school, peaking in middle school, and decreasing in high school.[22] Verbal bullying remains steady throughout. The lack of aggressive response by

schools to bullying is seen as an important part of the problem in both preventing and combating bullying behavior. More than two-thirds of students
who were surveyed believed that school response to bullying has been weak
at best, while about one-quarter of teachers failed to take action when told
about bullying incidents.[23]

ALCOHOL AND DRUG USE BY STUDENTS

The use, abuse, and availability of alcohol and drugs by students is often
cited as a factor in school shootings and violence by researchers.[24] Studies
show that over half of all middle school and high school students in the
United States have had at least one drink within the last year, while almost
half of all high school seniors have used one or more illegal drugs in their
lifetime.[25] In a 1993-1994 survey of middle and high school students undertaken by the Parent Resource Institute for Drug Education (PRIDE), a strong
correlation was found between alcohol and marijuana use and such violent
behavior as carrying a firearm to school and a threat of harm to another individual.[26] Other researchers' findings have supported a significant relationship
between youth violence and alcohol and drug use and abuse.[27]

Male students are much more likely to have ever used alcohol or drugs
than female students, as well as to have used at school.[28] In one study of student drug use, male students were found to be more than twice as likely as
female students to have used marijuana while at school, and were more likely to have used alcohol on school property.[29]

Figure 12.2

Percentage of Students, Grades 9-12, Reporting Drugs Were Made Available to
Them on School Property During the Past 12 Months, by Sex, 1997

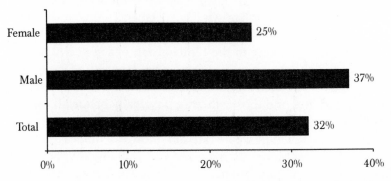

Source: Adapted from U.S. Department of Education and Justice, *Indicators of School Crime and Safety
2000* (Washington: Offices of Educational Research and Improvement and Justice Programs, (2000),
p. 42.

The availability of illegal drugs at school has also been associated with school violence, street gangs, drug dealing, and other adolescent antisocial behavior.[30] As shown in Figure 12.2, in 1997, almost one-third of students in grades nine through twelve nationwide reported that illicit drugs were offered, given, or sold to them on school property within the last year.

Male students were more likely than female students to report the availability of drugs at school. Nearly four in ten male students said they had been offered, given, or sold illegal drugs at school, compared to one in four female students.

NOTES

1. R. Barri Flowers and H. Loraine Flowers, *Murders in the United States: Crimes, Killers and Victims of the Twentieth Century* (Jefferson: McFarland, 2001), pp. 183-87; Kathleen M. Heide, "1998 Keynote Address: School Shootings and School Violence: What's Going on and Why?" in U.S. Department of Justice, *Proceedings of the Homicide Research Working Group Meetings, 1997 and 1998* (Washington: National Institute of Justice, 1997), pp. 116-30.
2. Flowers and Flowers, *Murders in the United States*, pp. 183-87.
3. *Ibid.* See also R. Barri Flowers, *Kids Who Commit Adult Crimes: A Study of Serious Juvenile Criminality and Delinquency* (Binghampton: Haworth, 2002).
4. Heide, "1998 Keynote Address," p. 117.
5. Kathleen M. Heide, *Young Killers: The Challenge of Juvenile Homicide* (Thousand Oaks: Sage, 1999).
6. R. Barri Flowers, *Male Crime and Violence: Exploring the Dynamics, Nature, and Causes* (Westport: Greenwood, 2002).
7. Cited in R. Barri Flowers, *The Victimization and Exploitation of Women and Children: A Study of Physical, Mental and Sexual Maltreatment in the United States* (Jefferson: McFarland, 1994), p. 111.
8. Flowers, *Kids Who Commit Adult Crimes.*
9. U.S. Department of Education and Justice, *Indicators of School Crime and Safety* (Washington: Offices of Educational Research and Imprisonment and Justice Programs, 2000), p. 4.
10. *Ibid.*, pp. 28, 35.
11. Flowers, *Kids Who Commit Adult Crimes*; Flowers and Flowers, *Murders in the United States*, pp. 183-87; J. F. Sheley and J. D. Wright, *In the Line of Fire: Youth, Guns, and Violence in America* (New York: Aldine de Gruyter, Inc., 1995).
12. Youth Risk Behavior Survey, http://www.Alfred.edu/teenviolence/ potential_violence.html.
13. *Indicators of School Crime and Safety*, pp. 28, 35; U.S. Department of Justice, *Youth Gangs: An Overview* (Washington: Office of Juvenile Justice and Delinquency Prevention, 1998).

14. J. C. Howell, "Gangs and Youth Violence," in J. C. Howell, B. Krisberg, J. D. Hawkins, and J. J. Wilson, eds., *A Sourcebook: Serious, Violent and Chronic Juvenile Offenders* (Thousand Oaks: Sage, 1995), pp. 261-74; T. P. Thornberry and J. H. Birch, *Gang Members and Delinquent Behavior* (Washington: Office of Justice Programs, 1997).

15. Sheley and Wright, *In the Line of Fire*; C. R. Block and R. Block, "Street Gang Crime in Chicago," in M. W. Klein, C. L. Maxson, and J. Miller, eds., *The Modern Gang Reader* (Los Angeles: Roxbury, 1995), pp. 202-11.

16. Cited in Flowers, *Male Crime and Violence.*

17. Andrea Cohn and Andrea Carter, "Bullying: What Schools and Parents Can Do," National Association of School Psychologists, http://www.guideancechannel.com/details.asp?index=508&cat=1.

18. *Ibid.*

19. Cited in *Ibid.*

20. *Ibid.*; Flowers, *Male Crime and Violence.*

21. Cohn and Carter, "Bullying: What Schools and Parents Can Do."

22. *Ibid.*

23. *Ibid.*

24. Heide, "1998 Keynote Address," p. 124; R. Barri Flowers, *Drugs, Alcohol and Criminality in American Society* (Jefferson: McFarland, 1999), pp. 99-111.

25. Cited in Flowers, *Drugs, Alcohol and Criminality in American Society*, pp. 100, 104.

26. Cited in Heide, "1998 Keynote Address," p. 124.

27. See, for example, D. S. Elliot, D. Huizinga, and S. Menard, *Multiple Problem Youth: Delinquency, Substance Abuse, and Mental Health Problems* (New York: Springer-Verlag, 1989).

28. Flowers, *Drugs, Alcohol and Criminality in American Society*, p. 108; *Indicators of School Crime and Safety*, pp. 38-42.

29. Flowers, *Drugs, Alcohol and Criminality in American Society*, pp. 104-10.

30. *Ibid.*; R. Barri Flowers, *The Adolescent Criminal: An Examination of Today's Juvenile Offender* (Jefferson: McFarland, 1990), pp. 94-97.

Part V

TYPES OF KILLERS

Chapter 13

SEXUAL KILLERS

A high percentage of murderers can be termed sexual killers. These are killers whose crimes are motivated by sexual needs or gratification, sexual jealousy, sexual perversions, childhood sexual victimization, or other sex-related factors. Many who kill are driven by sexual impulses or sexually fantasize about murdering people or someone in particular. Sexual sadist killers associate sexual pleasure with violence and inflicting pain on victims. The relationship between the sexual deviant, sexual predator, or pedophile and murder is often reflected in intimate homicides, rape-murders, child murders, serial killings, and some mass murders. Sex-related killers typically abuse alcohol or drugs, come from violent and sexual abusing families, and exhibit other characteristics that may predispose them to homicidal and violent behavior.

WHAT IS SEXUAL MURDER?

Sexual murder reflects homicides with a sexual theme, nature, or character. The dictionary defines sexual as "(1) of sex, sexuality, the sexes, or the sex organs and their functions, and (2) implying or symbolizing erotic desires or activity;"[1] while defining homicide as "(1) the killing of one person by another or (2) a person who kills another."[2] As such, sexual murder can be defined as "homicide in which there is a sexual element, motivation, relationship, or perversion involved such as rape, molestation, prostitution, intimacy, battering, and sexual jealousy."[3]

According to the book, *Sexual Homicide: Patterns and Motives*, sexual homicide refers to the "killing of a person in the context of power, sexuality, and brutality."[4] The authors further describe sexual homicide as "murders with evidence or observations that indicate that the murder was sexual in nature."[5]

Murders that are sexually motivated usually fall under the category of *lust murder*, also referred to as erotophonophilia.[6]

The *Diagnostic and Statistical Manual of the American Psychiatric Association (DSM III-R)* places sexual deviance under the term paraphilia, which is characterized as:

> arousal in response to sexual objects or situations that are not part of normative arousal activity patterns and whose essential features are intense sexual urges and sexually arousing fantasies generally involving non-human objects, the suffering or humiliation of one's self or one's partner, or children or other non-consenting persons.[7]

Paraphilic acts that are commonly involved in sexual murders include rape, incest, sadism, voyeurism, exhibitionism, fetishism, homosexuality, bestiality, coprolagnia, and urolagnia.

Studies show that sexual homicides often involve children, intimates, sex workers, serial and ritual murders.[8] In their study of lethal violence in Chicago over a twenty-year period, Carolyn Block and Antigone Christakos described sexually-based homicide syndromes, or homicides based on the perpetrator's primary motive or goal when the crime of murder occurred. These included rape homicides, confrontations involving spouses, ex-spouses, romantic partners, or other intimates; and murder-suicide pacts.[9] Other research has supported a relationship between sexual factors and circumstances and homicidal behavior.[10]

THE EXTENT OF SEXUAL MURDER

Assessing the true extent of sexual homicides can be difficult, given the often multiple and overlapping motivations and circumstances attributed to homicides, as well as limitation of official and other data. According to the Federal Bureau of Investigation's Uniform Crime Reports, there were an estimated 14,088 murders committed in the United States in 1998, for which supplementary data was provided (see Table 13.1).

There were 279 identified sex-related murders, including those involving rape, prostitution and commercialized vice, other sex offenses, and romantic triangles. Overall, males outnumbered females as victims of sex-related homicides. However, females were far more likely to be murdered in crimes involving rape or prostitution or commercialized vice.

Sexual factors may often play a role in murders in which the primary circumstance was believed to be alcohol- and/or drug-related. Studies show that sexual homicides often involved substance abuse on the part of the perpetrator, victim, or both.[11] Other types of homicide-related violent offenses

Table 13.1

SEXUAL MURDER CIRCUMSTANCES, BY SEX OF VICTIM, 1998

Circumstances	Total muder victims	Male	Female	Unknown
Total murders	14,088	10,606	3,419	63
Felony-type total	2,491	1,999	485	7
Rape	61	5	56	—
Prostitution and commercialized violence	14	4	10	—
Other sex offenses	20	11	9	—
Other than felony type total	7,135	5,213	1,917	—
Romantic triangle	184	142	42	—
Total sex-related	279	162	117	—

Source: U.S. Department of Justice, Federal Bureau of Investigation, *Crime in the United States: Uniform Crime Reports, 1998* (Washington: Government Printing Office, 1999), p. 21.

and property crimes can also reflect a sexual nature, such as robbery-rape murders and burglary-rape murders.[12]

Some criminologists believe that there may be far more sex-related homicides than indicated in official data. In 1999, there were nearly 4,000 murders in which the circumstances were unknown.[13] Studies suggest that a high number of these may have been sexual murders.[14]

Long-term murder trends reveal that there are hundreds of homicides that are sexual in nature each year. According to the FBI's Supplemental Homicide Reporting program, between 1976 and 1994 there were an estimated 4,807 murders involving rape or other sexual offenses in the United States.[15] This represented around 2 percent of all murders committed. However, these figures do not include some types of sex-related murders.[16]

Figure 13.1
Sex-Related Homicides, 1994-1999

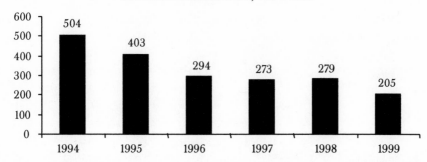

Source: Derived from U.S. Department of Justice, Federal Bureau of Investigation, *Crime in the United States: Uniform Crime Reports 1994-1999* (Washington: Government Printing Office, 1995-2000).

More recent years indicate that sex-related murders are on the decline (see Figure 13.1). Between 1994 and 1999, the number of sexual murders dropped by 299. On average, there were 326 identified murders of a sexual nature committed in this country each year.

It is important to note that although most murders are solved or cleared by law enforcement agencies, many sexual homicides are not solved. For instance, in 1999, the clearance rate for murder in the United States was 69 percent. This left more than 30 percent of homicides unsolved, including those involving sexual circumstances.[17]

CHARACTERISTICS OF SEXUAL MURDERERS AND VICTIMS

Who are the offenders and victims of sexual homicides? What are the circumstances of sex-related murders? Characteristics of sexual assault murderers between 1976 and 1994 can be seen in Table 13.2. Sexual killers were predominantly male, white, and between eighteen and twenty-four years of age. Ninety-five percent of sexual assault killers were male compared to nearly 87

Table 13.2

CHARACTERISTICS OF SEXUAL ASSAULT MURDERERS, 1976-1994

Offender characteristic	Murders	
	All	Sexual assault
Sex		
Male	86.6%	95.0%
Female	13.4	5.0
Race		
White	47.8%	58.0%
Black	50.3	39.9
Other	1.9	2.1
Age		
12 or younger	0.2%	0.1%
13-17	8.1	9.9
18-24	30.1	39.1
25-29	18.0	22.5
30-39	23.1	21.1
40-49	11.1	5.4
50-59	5.4	1.5
60 or older	3.9	0.4
Average Age	31 years	26 years

Source: Derived from U.S. Department of Justice, Bureau of Justice Statistics, *Sex Offenses and Offenders: Executive Summary* (Washington: Government Printing Office, 1997), p. 3.

percent of all murderers, while 58 percent of sex killers were white, compared to almost 48 percent of all killers.

Blacks were disproportionately represented as sex offender murderers, constituting nearly 40 percent of the total. However, this was lower than the more than 50 percent of overall murderers identified as black.

Sexual assault murderers and total killers tended to be mostly between eighteen and thirty-nine years of age. Nearly four in ten murders involving a sexual assault were committed by killers between the age of eighteen and twenty-four.

In an FBI analysis of sexual killers, half were found to come from families with criminal histories, while more than half had mental illness in the family.[18] More than two-thirds of sexual murderers had families in which at least one member had a problem with alcohol, one-third had a family member with a drug problem, and half of the killers came from families in which someone had a sexual problem. Around two-thirds of sexual murderers' childhood was characterized by mental illness, with nearly half being the victims of physical, sexual, or emotional abuse. Most had cold, unsympathetic, uncaring parents.

Many sexual killers had violent, rape, or sadistic childhood fantasies, and often displayed cruelty to other children or animals. They have been characterized by criminologists as having highly negative mental states, including anger, frustration, hostility, agitation, and excitement.[19] Sexual murderers often regard the world as "unjust [and] desire to be strong, powerful and in control, and favor autoerotic sexual activitites."[20]

The characteristics of victims of sexual assault murders between 1976 and 1994 can be seen in Table 13.3. Victims were predominantly female, white, and young. More than eight in ten victims of sexual assault homicides were female. This compares to all murders in which less than one in four victims were female.

Whites constituted nearly seven in ten victims of sexual assault murders, compared to just over half of all murder victims; while almost three in ten sexual assault-murder victims were black, and under 3 percent were of other races.

Most victims of sexual assault homicides were under the age of thirty. Nearly six in ten victims were age twenty-nine and younger, with more than two in ten victims of sexual homicides between the ages of eighteen and twenty-four. Nearly 15 percent of victims were age twelve and younger. Sexual assault-murder victims tended to be younger than total murder victims.

The majority of sexual assault homicides are intraracial in nature. Around eight in ten such murders involve victims and perpetrators are of the same race[21] Sex-related homicides are twice as likely as homicides in general to involve strangers; however, they are equally likely to involve persons who are acquaintances in some fashion.[22]

Table 13.3

CHARACTERISTICS OF SEXUAL ASSAULT MURDER VICTIMS, 1976-1994

Victim characteristic	Murders	
	All	Sexual assault
Sex of victim		
Male	76.4%	18.0%
Female	23.6	82.0
Race of victim		
White	51.7%	68.4%
Black	46.3	28.9
Other	2.0	2.7
Age of victim		
12 or younger	10.1%	14.8%
13-17	4.6	9.7
18-24	21.3	21.7
25-29	15.7	12.3
30-39	22.0	14.2
40-49	11.7	8.3
50-59	6.9	5.3
60 or older	7.7	13.7
Average Age	32 years	32 years

Source: Derived from U.S. Department of Justice, Bureau of Justice Statistics, *Sex Offenses and Offenders: An Analysis of Data on Rap and Sexual Assault* (Washington: Government Printing Office, 1997), p. 29.

TYPES OF SEXUAL KILLERS

Intimate Killers

The relationship between sexual intimacy and homicide has been strongly supported through studies and official data. According to the Bureau of Justice Statistics, there were nearly 52,000 women and men killed by an intimate between 1976 and 1996 in the United States.[23] FBI figures show that in 1999 alone, there were 1,274 murders of wives, husbands, girlfriends, and boyfriends.[24] Studies reveal that an estimated three out of every ten women murdered in this country are victims of intimate homicides.[25] About one in five female murder victims are killed by a spouse or ex-spouse; while one-third of all intimate murders in the United States are perpetrated by the victim's boyfriend or girlfriend.[26]

The male intimate is primarily responsible for partner homicides, often motivated by sexual issues such as jealousy, desire, adultery, or separation.[27]

This is especially true for spousal homicides. Women are the victims of uxoricide, or death perpetrated by a husband, more than any other type of murder.[28] Although women who murder intimates largely do so in self-defense from an abusive mate, there are cases in which women kill husbands, boyfriends, or ex-intimates out of sexual jealousy, revenge, or involvement with another man.[29]

In a study of intrafamilial homicides in Detroit, it was found that cohabitating spouses were eleven times more likely to be killed by a spouse than were family members by another relative living in the residence.[30] Other studies have found that noncohabitating spouses are also vulnerable to spouse homicide. In a comparison of uxoricide rates in several countries, including Canada and Australia, Margo Wilson and Martin Daly reported that the risk of uxoricide increased following a separation.[31]

Researchers have further found that the risk of uxoricide increased with male sexual proprietary jealousy toward young fertile wives.[32] This jealousy has been related to such issues as the wife's physical attractiveness, sexual rivals, and possible new sexual partners.

Serial Killers

Serial murders have long been associated with sexual themes. Such notable examples include Jack the Ripper, who murdered prostitutes in Victorian England; Ted Bundy, who raped and murdered as many as forty women across the United States in the 1970s; Gerald and Charlene Gallego, who abducted, sexually assaulted, and killed ten young women in California, Nevada, and Oregon in the late 1970s and early 1980s as part of their "sex slave" fantasies; and "lust killer" Jerry Brudos who raped, mutilated, and murdered women in Oregon during the late 1980s.[33]

According to experts, most serial killers are sexual deviants, often with a history of physical and sexual abuse. J. S. Brown postulated that some sexual serial killers are psychotic, while some psychotic serial killers are sexually motivated in perpetrating their crimes.[34] P. A. Jenkins characterized serial killers as sexual psychopaths or paranoid schizophrenic offenders.[35] David Lester wrote about lust serial murderers who experience sexual arousal and pleasure in association with their killings.[36]

The FBI found that sexually motivated serial murderers were more likely to be organized than disorganized and tended to have more victims.[37] (See Chapter 14 for further discussion on serial killers.)

Signature Killers

Another type of sexual murderer is the signature killer. This category of serial killer differs from others in that the perpetrator tends to leave a "calling card" or psychological signature behind unique to him at every crime scene. In a study of signature killers, Robert Keppel and William Birnes describe the signature serial killer as "psychologically compelled to leave [his imprint] to satisfy himself sexually."[38] The FBI Behavioral Sciences Unit's John Douglas characterized the sexual serial killer's signature as "the person's violent fantasies which are progressive in nature and contribute to thoughts of exhibiting extremely violent behavior."[39]

Signature murderers are thought to represent the greatest subtype of serial murderers, "driven by such a primal psychological motivation to act out the same crime over and over again that their patterns become obsessive. All signature murderers seek some form of sexual gratification, and their crimes are expressions of the ways they satisfy that need."[40]

Anger has been shown to be an important factor in sexual signature murders. Keppel and Birnes noted two types of anger-motivated signature killers: (1) anger-retaliation killer and (2) anger-excitation killer.[41]

The anger-retaliation killer is characterized by sexual violence and overkill, typically involving the use of more than one weapon, whereas the anger-excitation killer's signature tends to be more sadistic, characterized by "a prolonged, bizarre, ritualistic assault on the victim."[42]

The anger-driven signature killer often begins as a retaliatory murderer and evolves to an excitation killer over the course of his murders, depending on the degree of anger. The murderer's signature tends to reflect "one or more of the components of sadism, control, humiliation, progression of violence, posing, torture, overkill, necrophilia, and cannibalism."[43]

Sexually Sadistic Killers

Sadism is defined as sexual gratification through inflicting pain and suffering upon others. A high percentage of sexual killers are sadists, associating sexuality with cruelty and violence.[44] Indications of such deviant behavior often manifest themselves early in the sexual sadist's life, such as sexually violent fantasies and cruelty to animals.

Sexually sadistic killers are mostly white males who are in their twenties and thirties, and are often "intelligent, personable, sociable and seldom have criminal records. They suffer from gender-identity conflicts and a sense of purposelessness. The latter results in frequent changes in jobs, location, roles, and goals."[45] The background of this type of sex killer includes a history of substance abuse, child sexual and physical abuse, and broken homes.

Many mass and serial murderers are sexual sadists, according to researchers. Almost one in five serial killers examined by Jack Levin and James Fox based on FBI files and newspaper reports were characterized as sexual sadists.[46] In their study of sexually sadistic killers, R. R. Hazelwood, P. E. Dietz, and J. Warren, found that 43 percent had participated in homosexual acts during adulthood, while 20 percent had perpetrated sexual crimes such as voyeurism and exhibitionism.[47] Dietz identified one type of serial killer as a psychopathic sexual sadist, positing that every known serial killer with ten or more victims was a male diagnosed with antisocial personality disorder and possessing sexually sadistic tendencies.[48]

Researchers have identified a number of factors that relate to the formation of sexually sadistic tendencies, including:

- Genetic transmission of behavioral traits.
- Abnormal hormonal levels that can negatively influence aggression and sexual behavior.
- Dysfunctional child rearing practices, such as child sexual abuse and maternal promiscuity.
- Psychiatric disorders, such as antisocial personality disorder and bipolar affective disorder.[49]

NOTES

1. R. Barri Flowers, *Sex Crimes, Predators, Perpetrators, Prostitutes, and Victims: An Examination of Sexual Criminality and Victimization* (Springfield: Charles C Thomas, 2001), p. 3.
2. *Ibid.*
3. *Ibid.*
4. Robert K. Ressler, Ann W. Burgess, and John E. Douglas, *Sexual Homicide: Patterns and Motives* (New York: Lexington Books, 1988), p. 1.
5. *Ibid.*, p. xiii. See also R. K. Ressler, A. W. Burgess, C. R. Hartman, J. E. Douglas, and A. McCormack, "Murderers Who Rape and Mutilate," *Journal of Interpersonal Violence 1* (1986): 273-87.
6. J. Money, "Forensic Sexology," *American Journal of Psychotherapy 44* (1990): 26–36.
7. American Psychiatric Association, *Diagnostic and Statistical Manual of Mental Disorders*, 3rd ed. (Washington: American Psychiatric Association, 1987). See also Dawn Fisher, "Adult Sex Offenders: Who Are They? Why and How Do They Do It?" in Tony Morrison, Marcus Erooga, and Richard C. Beckett, eds., *Sexual Offending Against Children: Assessment and Treatment of Male Abusers* (New York: Routledge, 1994), p. 7.
8. Flowers, *Sex Crimes, Predators, Perpetrators, Prostitutes, and Victims*, p. 4.
9. Carolyn R. Block and Antigone Christakos, "Chicago Homicide From the Sixties to the Nineties: Major Trends in Lethal Violence," in U.S. Department

of Justice, *Trends, Risks, and Interventions in Lethal Violence: Proceedings of the Third Annual Spring Symposium of the Homicide Research Working Group* (Washington: National Institute of Justice, 1995), pp. 26-29.

10. See, for example, R. Barri Flowers, *Domestic Crimes, Family Violence and Child Abuse: A Study of Contemporary American Society* (Jefferson: McFarland, 2000), pp. 62-64, 78-80; R. E. Dobash, R. Dobash, M. Wilson, and M. Daly, "The Myth of Sexual Symmetry in Marital Violence," *Social Problems 39,* 1 (1992): 71-91; A. W. Burgess, C. R. Hartman, R. K. Ressler, J. E. Douglas, and A. McCormack, "Sexual Homicide," *Journal of Interpersonal Violence 1* (1986): 251-72.

11. Flowers, *Sex Crimes, Predators, Perpetrators, Prostitutes, and Victims,* p. 5; Flowers, *Domestic Crimes, Family Violence and Child Abuse,* p. 61.

12. Block and Antigone, *Trends, Risks, and Interventions in Lethal Violence,* p. 28.

13. U.S. Department of Justice, Federal Bureau of Investigation, *Crime in the United States: Uniform Crime Reports 1999* (Washington: Government Printing Office, 2000), p. 19.

14. Flowers, *Sex Crimes, Predators, Perpetrators, Prostitutes, and Victims,* pp. 5-6; B. S. Cormier and S. P. Simmons, "The Problem of the Dangerous Sexual Offender," *Canadian Psychiatric Association 14* (1969): 329-34.

15. U.S. Department of Justice, Bureau of Justice Statistics, *Sex Offenses and Offenders: An Analysis of Data on Rape and Sexual Assault* (Washington: Government Printing Office, 1997), p. 28.

16. The figures exclude such sexual murders as those involving prostitution and commercialized vice.

17. *Crime in the United States,* p. 23.

18. U.S. Department of Justice, Federal Bureau of Investigation, "The Men Who Murdered," *FBI Law Enforcement Bulletin 54,* 8 (1985): 2-6.

19. Ressler, Burgess, and Douglas, *Sexual Homicide,* pp. 45-56.

20. David Lester, *Serial Killers: The Insatiable Passion* (Philadelphia: Charles Press, 1995), p. 51.

21. *Sex Offenses and Offenders,* p. 30.

22. Flowers, *Sex Crimes, Predators, Perpetrators, Prostitutes, and Victims,* p. 7.

23. U.S. Department of Justice, Bureau of Justice Statistics Factbook, *Violence by Intimates: Analysis of Data of Crimes by Current or Former Spouses, Boyfriends, and Girlfriends* (Washington: Government Printing Office, 1998), p. 6.

24. *Crime in the United States,* p. 19.

25. *Violence by Intimates,* p. v.

26. *Ibid.,* p. 6.

27. Flowers, *Domestic Crimes, Family Violence and Child Abuse,* pp. 61-64, 90-91; A. L. Kellermann and J. A. Mercy, "Men, Women and Murder: Gender-Specific Differences in Rates of Fatal Violence and Victimization," *Journal of Trauma 33* (1992): 1-5.

28. Flowers, *Sex Crimes, Predators, Perpetrators, Prostitutes, and Victims,* pp. 9-10.

29. R. Barri Flowers and H. Loraine Flowers, *Murders in the United States: Crimes, Killers and Victims of the Twentieth Century* (Jefferson: McFarland, 2001), pp. 140-41.

30. Martin Daly and Margo Wilson, "Homicide and Kinship," *American Anthropologist 84* (1982): 372-78.

31. Margo I. Wilson and Martin Daly, "Spousal Homicide Risk and Estrangement," *Violence and Victims 8* (1993): 3-15.
32. Cited in Flowers, *Sex Crimes, Predators, Perpetrators, Prostitutes, and Victims,* p. 10.
33. Flowers and Flowers, *Murders in the United States,* pp. 86-106.
34. J. S. Brown, "The Historical Similarity of 20th Century Serial Sexual Homicide to Pre 20th Century Occurrences of Vampirism," *American Journal of Forensic Psychiatry 12,* 2 (1991): 11-24.
35. P. A. Jenkins, "A Murder 'Wave'?" *Criminal Justice Review 17,* 1 (1992): 1-19.
36. Lester, *Serial Killers,* pp. 74-77.
37. Cited in *Ibid.,* pp. 81-82.
38. Robert D. Keppel and William J. Birnes, *Signature Killers: Interpreting the Calling Cards of the Sexual Murderer* (New York: Pocket Books, 1997), p. 5.
39. *Ibid.*
40. *Ibid.,* p. 23.
41. *Ibid.,* pp. 59, 89-94.
42. *Ibid.,* p. 189.
43. *Ibid.,* p. 89.
44. Flowers, *Sex Crimes, Predators, Perpetrators, Prostitutes, and Victims,* pp. 10-11; D. T. Lunde, *Murder and Madness* (New York: Norton, 1979); R. Barri Flowers, *The Sex Slave Murders* (New York: St. Martin's Press, 1996); R. Langevin, M. H. Ben-Aron, P. Wright, V. Marchese, and L. Handy, "The Sex Killer," *Annals of Sex Research 1* (1988): 263-301.
45. Lester, *Serial Killers,* p. 59; R. G. Rappaport, "The Serial and Mass Murderer," *American Journal of Forensic Psychiatry 9,* 1 (1988): 39-48.
46. Jack Levin and James A. Fox, *Mass Murder* (New York: Plenum, 1985).
47. R. R. Hazelwood, P. E. Dietz, and J. Warren, "The Criminal Sexual Sadist," *FBI Law Enforcement Bulletin 61* (1992): 12-20.
48. P. E. Dietz, "Mass, Serial and Sensational Homicides," *Bulletin of the New York Academy of Medicine 62* (1986): 477-91.
49. Lester, *Serial Killers,* pp. 90-93; Money, "Forensic Sexology," pp. 26-36; L. B. Schlesinger and E. Revitch, "Sexual Dynamics in Homicide and Assault," in L. B. Schlesinger and E. Revitch, eds., *Sexual Dynamics of Anti-Social Behavior* (Springfield: Charles C Thomas, 1983).

Chapter 14

SERIAL KILLERS

Perhaps the most frightening killer outside the family is the serial killer. Although this type of murderer constitutes only a small percentage of total killers, the multiple and often violent or sadistic killings perpetrated by the serial murderer command far more attention by criminologists, law enforcement, researchers, writers, and the media. The literature is replete with terrifying tales of infamous serial killers such as Jack the Ripper, Albert Fish, John Wayne Gacy, Ted Bundy, Henry Lucas, and Gerald Gallego. Contrary to popular belief, these killers are generally not insane but are more often than not sociopaths and sexual deviants who tend to derive sadistic pleasure from the act of killing and the attention multiple murders generates. While most serial killers are male, females have also shown the capacity and willingness to commit serial murders, though often for different reasons, such as money and love. The serial killer will often kill until apprehended or killed, typically taunting pursuers, and seems to draw upon society's worst fears in committing heinous and violent serial murders.

WHAT IS A SERIAL KILLER?

The phrase "serial killer" was first introduced in the 1980s in reference to killers who kill a series of persons over a course of time. This differs from a "mass murderer" who kills a number of people at one time and place, or an individual that kills one or two people at any time then stops or is stopped for good. The serial killer normally targets and systematically kills victims one by one until no longer able to, usually due to being captured by authorities.

Various criminologists have defined the serial killer, based on methodology, the number and type of victims, the length of time between murders, and other criteria.[1] S. A. Egger defined serial murder as occurring when one or

170

more persons, predominantly male, perpetrates a second murder at a different time.[2] In general, most experts on serial murder require that a minimum
of three murders must be committed at different times and usually different
places for a person to qualify as a serial killer.[3] R. M. Holmes and S. T.
Holmes proposed that there must be at least a thirty-day period between the
first and last killings for the perpetrators to fit the definition of a serial killer.[4]

Law enforcement authorities tend to define the serial killer as "a nomadic,
sexual sadist who operates with a strict pattern of victim selection and crime
scene behavior."[5] Others have focused on motivational factors in defining the
serial murderer. For instance, James Fox and Jack Levin note that the serial
killer "acts as a result of some individual pathology produced by traumatic
childhood experiences."[6]

Some researchers prefer to define the serial murderer by excluding or
including certain types of killers and motivations. Egger's definition omits
female serial killers, while requiring that the killer and victim be strangers to
one another and that the killing is not motivated by material gain.[7] F.
Browning and J. Gerassi documented cases of serial killers considered pro-
fessional criminals or belonging to organized crime, as well as those financially or politically motivated or for business purposes.[8] David Lester noted
that different studies of serial killers excluded such multiple murderers as
hospital or nursing home staff killers or landlord murderers motivated by
financial gain from killing residents.[9]

THE MAGNITUDE OF SERIAL MURDER

Although much attention has been given to serial murder and its specter
in society, how big is the problem? The often unsolved cases of serial killing,
unknown victims of serial killers, and differing interpretations of what constitutes a serial murderer or murder, has made it difficult, if not impossible,
to know the magnitude of this crime at any given time. In the 1980s, the
Justice Department estimated that as many as 5,000 people are victims of
serial murder every year.[10] Some criminologists have supported this figure.[11]

Others have suggested that the numbers of victims of serial killers are far
lower. In an examination of serial killers from 1978 to 1983, as listed in the
New York Times Index, Egger found there to be fifty-four such murderers who
had killed at least four people, or a minimum of 216 victims.[12] E. W. Hickey
estimated that between 1975 and 1995, there were 153 serial murders who
totaled up to 1,400 victims, or less than 100 victims a year.[13]

Fox and Levin argued that serial killings likely accounted for under 1 percent of the homicides in the United States.[14] In 1999, there were an estimated 15,533 persons murdered nationwide.[15] One percent would amount to

155 victims of serial murder annually. In spite of the low figure, given that the number of perpetrators of such homicides is likely much smaller, the significance of serial murder is obvious and the concern of law enforcement and the public not without merit.

Infamous examples of American serial killers and their horrific crimes include the following:

- **David Berkowitz**, calling himself the "Son of Sam," began a thirteen-month reign of terror in New York City in 1976. He used a .44 caliber pistol to randomly shoot to death six people while wounding seven more. He was tried and convicted of multiple murders and sentenced to 365 years in prison.

- **Theodore "Ted" Bundy** is believed to have sexually assaulted and murdered as many as forty females in five states between 1974 and 1978. Thought by many criminologists to be the prototype of the modern sexual serial killer, Bundy was tried in Florida for the murders of sorority sisters, convicted, and sentenced to death. He was executed in the electric chair in 1989.

- **Andrew Cunanan** bludgeoned or shot to death five men over several states between April and July 1997, including Italian designer Gianni Versace. The 27-year-old gay hustler's murder spree led to one of the biggest manhunts in United States history. Cunanan committed suicide as the police closed in on him while hiding out in a houseboat in Miami, Florida.

- **Jeffrey Dahmer** murdered as many as seventeen young males in the early 1990s in Wisconsin and Ohio. The 31-year-old cannibal drugged, strangled, and dismembered his victims. He was brought to trial in both states and received sixteen life sentences. In 1994, Dahmer was beaten to death by another inmate while serving his term in Wisconsin.

- **John Wayne Gacy** sexually assaulted and murdered thirty-three boys between 1972 and 1978 in Illinois. The convicted sex offender and clown buried most of the victims under his house. He was arrested, tried, and convicted, receiving a death sentence. In 1994, Gacy was executed by lethal injection.

- **Henry Lee Lucas** claimed to have murdered at least 200 people across the country over a seventeen-year period during the 1970s and 1980s. Years earlier, he had stabbed to death his mother. Lucas was convicted of eleven murders and sentenced to death in Texas, before having his sentence commuted to life in prison.

- **Richard Ramirez**, dubbed the "Night Stalker," murdered at least thirteen people in California between 1984 and 1985. The Satan worshipper also raped and mutilated his victims. He was convicted on all thirteen counts of murder and sentenced to death.

- **Angel Maturino Resendiz** is suspected of murdering as many as twenty-four people between 1997 and 1999, who lived near railroad tracks in the United States and Mexico. He turned himself in to authorities in Texas in July 1999. Resendiz was found guilty of capital murder in 2000 and sentenced to death.
- **Arthur Shawcross** murdered as many as thirteen people during the 1970s and 1980s, often torturing, mutilating, and dismembering them. Two of his victims were children. Shawcross is currently serving a 250-year prison term for the murders of his last eleven female victims.
- **Robert Yates** is believed to have slain as many as seventeen women in Washington between 1990 and 1998. Most of the victims were prostitutes and homeless women. The 48-year-old Army veteran pled guilty to thirteen of the murders and was sentenced to 408 years behind bars.
- **The "Zodiac Killer"** is thought to have killed anywhere from five to forty-nine people in California between 1968 and 1974. The unknown serial killer boasted of the murders, often sending letters to newspapers and signing them with the zodiac symbol. Some believe the killer is still active.[16]

CHARACTERIZING THE SERIAL KILLER

The vast majority of serial killers are white males, usually with a sexual motivation for their killings. Though few have been found to be certifiably insane, most are believed to be sociopaths, sadists, and possess some degree of mental illness or instability.[17] J. S. Browne postulated that some sexual serial killers may also be psychotic and, conversely, some psychotic serial killers may also be sexually motivated in their murders.[18] D. T. Lunde asserted that most serial killers are schizophrenic or sadist murderers.[19] R. M. Holmes and J. E. DeBurger characterized most serial killers as psychopathic.[20]

R. G. Rappaport advanced in his study of serial killers that rather than having a sexual motivation, per se, most serial homicides are "an attempt to cope with an internal conflict, a way to achieve relief from psychological pain, primarily by demonstrating power and mastery over others."[21]

Researchers have found the typical serial murderer to be a white male, twenty-five to thirty-five years old, often a loner though many are married, intelligent, and charming.[22] Victims are most often white women, though minority women and children are also at risk for victimization.

Most serial killers tend to have a history of violence, child physical and sexual abuse, substance abuse, dysfunctional families, and involvement with the criminal justice system.[23] In an FBI analysis of serial murderers, single and double sexual killers, the following characteristics emerged:
- All were male, with most white and a first or second born.

- Most grew up in homes with both parents present.
- Half came from families where members had a history of criminality.
- More than half the killers had family members with psychiatric problems.
- Two-thirds of the murderers had childhood psychiatric problems.
- Most had dominant mothers, while half the killers' relationship with their mothers was described as uncaring.
- The majority described disciplinary practices as hostile and abusive.
- Many were victims of sexual, physical, or psychological abuse.
- Many were cruel to animals and other children during childhood.
- Fantasies played a role in the deviant behavior of many of the killers.
- Killers became more organized with the experience of each subsequent murder.[24]

Based on a review of literature on serial killers, D. Sears further characterized the typical serial murderer as:

- Raised in a home absent of nurturing and stability.
- Using fantasies to escape the realities of life, turning into sexual and violent fantasies.
- Not possessing a psychiatric disorder.
- Self-centered and requiring attention.
- Intelligent and often successful academically or professionally.
- Having a fascination with police investigations.
- Using alcohol or drugs before perpetrating the crime.[25]

TYPES OF SERIAL KILLERS

A number of criminologists have identified different types of serial murderers. Rappaport found there to be five kinds of serial killers:

- **Spree killers**–people who kill a series of victims during a continuous span of murders.
- **Functionaries of organized criminality**–killers such as hit men for the Mafia, gang members, mercenaries, and terrorists.
- **Custodial killers**–people such as medical personnel or foster parents who poison or asphyxiate victims for financial gain, revenge, or altruism.
- **Psychotic killers**–people who are delusional or hallucinational in their serial murders.
- **Sexually sadistic killers**–murderers who derive pleasure through inflicting pain and torture on their victims.[26]

A similar typology of serial killers was established by P. E. Dietz.[27]

Holmes and DeBurger suggested four types of serial murderers including visionary killers, mission-oriented killers, hedonistic killers, and control-oriented killers:

- **Visionary killers** act in response to commands to kill from voices in their head or visions.

- **Mission-oriented killers** consciously decide to murder a certain category of individuals deemed unworthy of being alive, such as prostitutes.

- **Hedonistic killers** kill for the thrill or pleasure derived from the act. This category includes lust killers.

- **Control-oriented killers** are motivated by being in control of the victim in deciding life and death, when, where, and how they will kill.[28]

Holmes later added a **predatory serial killer** type as a person who hunts for victims to kill for recreation or sport.[29]

Two types of serial murderers were identified by P. Jenkins in his study of English serial killers between 1940 and 1985.[30] **Predictable killers** had a long and often violent history of juvenile offending. **Respectable killers** had no violent history of crime prior to reaching their twenties; they were motivated by a significant crisis in middle life, with the abuse of alcohol also a factor.

According to D. J. Gee, there are three types of serial murderers: (1) those who secretly hide the corpses of victims and attempt to conceal the murders; (2) killers who serial murder victims but the deaths are not recognized initially as homicides; and (3) murderers who do not seek to conceal their crimes or hide the victims.[31] Jack the Ripper is a perfect example of the latter type serial killer.

Some serial killers perpetrate their crimes as part of a team of two or more killers. This is particularly true when involving male-female multiple murderers or strong-weak killer pairs or groups.[32] A good example of the latter are the serial killer partners of Dean Corll and Elmer Henley. With Henley, seventeen, acting as the 33-year-old Corll's accomplice, the two combined to rape, torture and murder thirty-two boys in Pasadena, Texas in the early 1970s.[33]

In Jenkins' study of serial killers in the United States from 1971 to 1990, he found that there were fifty-eight serial murder cases. Twelve of these indicated involvement of multiple killers.[34] He described four types of partner or group serial killers: (1) dominant-submissive pairs, (2) equally dominant teams, (3) extended family or group of killers, and (4) organized or ceremonial social units or groups.

The Female Serial Killer

Although female serial killers are rare, they do exist, and have a long history.[35] Most female serial murderers tend to be motivated by monetary or material gain, often through murdering successive husbands or persons under their care. These types of serial killers are known as *Black Widows*. Many female serial killers act in tandem with male serial killers, usually their husbands or lovers.

Infamous examples of female serial killers include the following:

- **Belle Gunness** is believed to have murdered as many as forty-nine people between 1896 and 1908 in Illinois and Indiana. Dubbed "Lady Bluebeard," the Black Widow killed two husbands, a number of her children, and two suitors. She was motivated primarily by collecting insurance payments or robbery. Gunness is thought to have died in a fire at her farmhouse in 1908, though some believe she survived and continued her murderous ways well beyond that.
- **Dorothea Puente** murdered as many as twenty-five tenants living in her boarding house in Sacramento, California in 1988. The 59-year-old ex-con killed her victims for their Social Security checks. Puente was tried and convicted for three of the murders and sentenced to life in prison without the possibility of parole.
- **Aileen Wuornos** killed at least seven men in Florida between 1989 and 1990. The 33-year-old prostitute, who had a history of child sexual and physical abuse and alcoholism, claimed to have killed the men—all johns— in self-defense. She was tried and convicted of murdering her first victim and sentenced to death.
- **Martha Beck** and **Raymond Fernandez** murdered as many as twenty women between 1947 and 1949 in several Southeast states. The killer couple, dubbed the "Lonely Hearts Killers," lured victims through lonely hearts clubs and newspaper advertisements, stealing from them and killing them by poisoning, bludgeoning, and strangling. Beck and Fernandez were tried and convicted on multiple murder counts, and sentenced to death. They were executed in Sing Sing prison's electric chair in 1951.
- **Gwendolyn Graham** and **Catherine Wood** suffocated five elderly nursing home patients and attempted to kill five others in Michigan in 1987. The lesbian serial murderers were motivated by sexual thrills. Wood pled guilty to second-degree murder and Graham was convicted on five counts of homicide and sentenced to life in prison without parole.
- **Charlene Gallego** and **Gerald Gallego** abducted, sexually assaulted, and murdered ten people in three Western states between 1978 and 1980. The married serial killers were motivated by fulfilling "sex slave" fantasies. Charlene, who lured most of the victims to their deaths, plea bargained for

a reduced sentence of sixteen years and eight months behind bars. Gerald Gallego was convicted in California and Nevada for four murders and sentenced to death both times.[36]

In a study of female serial killers worldwide from 1580 to 1990, K. Segrave found that the typical killer perpetrated her initial murder at the age of thirty-one, continuing to kill for five years, before being caught. On average, the female serial murderer killed seventeen people, with poison and arsenic the most common weapons of choice.[37] Victims were most likely to be those most vulnerable, such as children, the elderly, and ill people.

Holmes and Holmes described five types of female serial killers:

- **Visionary serial killers**–women who kill in response to directives to kill from voices in their head or visions.

- **Comfort-oriented serial killers**–females who murder for financial or material benefit.

- **Hedonistic serial killers**–women who kill for sexual gratification.

- **Power-seeking serial killers**–females who kill for the thrill and power gained through having full control over life and death for the victim.

- **Disciple serial killers**–women who kill under the command or desire of a charismatic leader.[38]

THEORIES ON SERIAL KILLING

Criminologists have long theorized on the causes of multicidal, sexual, and sadistic killings. E. Leyton held that serial homicides are a "personalized form of social protest in which killings are an act of revenge by the killer for what he perceives as his social exclusion from society."[39] J. Caputi posited that the serial murderer reflects "an extreme in the latest expression of male supremacy which has always involved the raping and killing of women."[40]

In his review of theories of violent behavior, Sears observed that serial murderers are typically diagnosed as psychopaths–breaking down into two types: *primary psychopaths* and *secondary psychopaths*.[41] Primary psychopaths feel no anxiety, fear, or guilt for their actions; while secondary psychopaths perpetrate antisocial acts as a result of "emotional conflicts or inner distress," and often feel fear and anxiety.[42]

According to Lunde, serial killers can be described as sexual sadists and paranoid schizophrenics.[43] F. Wertham's notion of a *catathymic crisis* describes the repetitive nature of a serial killer's actions based upon an initial idea of perpetrating violence and the urge to follow through on the desire or fantasy, and finally actual culmination of murder. These stages are then repeated in serial killing.[44]

The relationship between serial murder and sexual sadism has been established by a number of researchers. R. A. Prentky and colleagues noted the role of violent sexual fantasies and sexual deviance in serial homicide.[45] John Money advanced that sexual sadism was a brain disease caused by genetic factors, hormonal abnormalities, child-rearing factors, and psychiatric disorders such as antisocial personality disorder and disassociative disorders.[46]

In his research on serial killers, Joel Norris profiled such murderers as often having a history of head trauma, genetic brain abnormalities, sexual assault, sexually deviant behavior, suicidal ideation, ritualistic behavior, compulsivity, substance abuse, physical and emotional abuse, and feeling inadequate and powerless.[47]

NOTES

1. James A. Fox and Jack Levin, "Serial Murder: Myths and Realities," in M. Dwayne Smith and Margaret A. Zahn, eds., *Studying and Preventing Homicide: Issues and Challenges* (Thousand Oaks: Sage, 1999), pp. 79-96; David Lester, *Serial Killers: The Insatiable Passion* (Philadelphia: Charles Press, 1995), pp. 10-17.
2. S. A. Egger, "A Working Definition of Serial Murder and the Reduction of Linkage Blindness," *Journal of Police Science and Administration 12* (1984): 348-57.
3. Lester, *Serial Killers*, pp. 10-13.
4. R. M. Holmes and S. T. Holmes, *Murder in America* (Thousand Oaks: Sage, 1994).
5. Fox and Levin, "Serial Murder," p. 80.
6. *Ibid.*
7. Egger, "A Working Definition of Serial Murder;" S. S. Egger, "Serial Murder," in S. A. Egger, ed., *Serial Murder* (New York: Praeger, 1990).
8. F. Browning and J. Gerassi, *The American Way of Crime* (New York: Putnam, 1980).
9. Lester, *Serial Killers*, p. 14.
10. Fox and Levin, "Serial Murder," p. 81.
11. *Ibid.*; Egger, "A Working Definition of Serial Murder;" R. M. Holmes and J. E. DeBurger, *Serial Murder* (Thousand Oaks: Sage, 1988).
12. Egger, "A Working Definition of Serial Murder."
13. E. W. Hickey, *Serial Murderers and Their Victims*, 2nd ed. (Belmont: Wadsworth, 1997).
14. Fox and Levin, "Serial Murder," p. 82.
15. U.S. Department of Justice, Federal Bureau of Investigation, *Crime in the United States: Uniform Crime Reports 1999* (Washington: Government Printing Office, 2000), p. 14.
16. R. Barri Flowers and H. Loraine Flowers, *Murders in the United States: Crimes, Killers, and Victims of the Twentieth Century* (Jefferson: McFarland, 2001), pp. 86-105.
17. *Ibid.*; Fox and Levin, "Serial Murder," pp. 83-85; R. M. Holmes and J. E. DeBurger, "Profiles in Terror," *Federal Probation 49*, 3 (1985): 53-61.
18. J. S. Browne, "The Historical Similarity of 20th Century Serial Sexual Homicide to Pre-20th Century Occurrences of Vampirism," *American Journal of Forensic Psychiatry 12*, 2 (1991): 11-24.

19. D. T. Lunde, *Murder and Madness* (New York: Norton, 1979).

20. Holmes and DeBurger, "Profiles in Terror."

21. Lester, *Serial Killers*, p. 59. See also R. G. Rappaport, "The Serial and Mass Murderer," *American Journal of Forensic Psychiatry 9*, 1 (1988): 39-48.

22. Holmes and DeBurger, "Profiles in Terror;" F. H. Leibman, "Serial Murderers," *Federal Probation 53*, 4 (1989): 41-45; R. R. Hazelwood, P. E. Dietz, and J. Warren, "The Criminal Sexual Sadist," *FBI Law Enforcement Bulletin 61*, 2 (1992): 12-20.

23. Lester, *Serial Killers*, pp. 48-60; Hazelwood, Dietz, and Warren, "The Criminal Sexual Sadist," pp. 12-20; Robert K. Ressler, Ann W. Burgess, and John E. Douglas, *Sexual Homicide: Patterns and Motives* (New York: Lexington Books, 1988).

24. U.S. Department of Justice, Federal Bureau of Investigation, "The Men Who Murdered," *FBI Law Enforcement Bulletin 54*, 8 (1985): 2-6.

25. D. Sears, *To Kill Again* (Wilmington: Scholarly Resources, 1991).

26. Rappaport, "The Serial and Mass Murderer," pp. 39-48.

27. P .E. Dietz, "Mass, Serial and Sensational Homicides," *Bulletin of the New York Academy of Medicine 62* (1986): 477-91.

28. Holmes and DeBurger, *Serial Murder*.

29. R. M. Holmes, "Human Hunters," *Knightbeat 9*, 1 (1990): 43-47.

30. P. Jenkins, "Serial Murder in England, 1940-1985," *Journal of Criminal Justice 16* (1988): 1-15.

31. D. J. Gee, "A Pathologist's View of Multiple Murder," *Forensic Science International 38* (1988): 53-65.

32. Flowers and Flowers, *Murders in the United States*.

33. *Ibid.*, p. 164.

34. P. Jenkins, "Sharing Murder," *Journal of Crime and Justice 12* (1990): 125-48.

35. Flowers and Flowers, *Murders in the United States*, pp. 109-16, 143-45; R. Barri Flowers, *The Sex Slave Murders* (New York: St. Martin's Press, 1996).

36. *Ibid.*

37. K. Segrave, *Women Serial and Mass Murderers* (Jefferson: McFarland, 1992).

38. Holmes and Holmes, *Murder in America*.

39. Lester, *Serial Killers*, pp. 85-86. See also E. Leyton, *Hunting Humans* (London: Penguin, 1989); E. Leyton, *Compulsive Killers* (New York: New York University Press, 1986).

40. Lester, *Serial Killers*, p. 85. See also J. Caputi, *The Age of Sex Crime* (Bowling Green: Bowling Green State University Press, 1987).

41. Sears, *To Kill Again*.

42. *Ibid.*

43. Lunde, *Murder and Madness*.

44. F. Wertham, "The Catathymic Crisis," *Archives of Neurology and Psychiatry 37* (1937): 974-78.

45. R. A. Prentky, A. W. Burgess, F. Rokous, A. Lee, C. Hartman, R. Ressler, and J. Douglas, "The Presumptive Role of Fantasy in Serial Sexual Homicide," *American Journal of Psychiatry 146* (1989): 887-91.

46. J. Money, "Forensic Sexology," *American Journal of Psychotherapy 44* (1990): 26–36.

47. Joel Norris, *Serial Killers* (New York: Anchor, 1989).

Chapter 15

MASS MURDERERS

Recent years have seen a rash of mass murders in the United States, including school shootings, workplace murders, and terrorist attacks—resulting in thousands of lost lives, all told. Although mass murder is not a new phenomenon, more individuals with various motivations and hostilities seem to be driven toward committing this type of homicide these days, often with devastating results. Understanding the rational or irrational behavior of the mass murderer and warning signs may make it easier to identify such persons and prevent their crimes.

WHAT IS MASS MURDER?

The term *mass murder* generally refers to a number of murders committed at the same time in the same location by one or more killers. Researchers differ on how many murders should constitute mass murder. Some criminologists such as R. M. Holmes and J. E. DeBurger,[1] and E. Hickey,[2] and Thomas Petee and colleagues[3] contend that a minimum of three murders need to be committed in a single crime of homicide for it to be considered a mass murder. Others such as R. Hazelwood and J. Douglas believe there must be at least four victims to qualify as a mass murder crime.[4] P. E. Dietz maintained that mass murder should include the wounding of five persons and the death of no less than three.[5]

As it is, most mass murderers that come to our attention commit many more murders than three or four. Consequently, the mass murderer tends to be synonymous with a massive slaughter of innocents. One of the most glaring examples is the bombing of the Alfred P. Murrah Federal Building in Oklahoma City, Oklahoma in 1995. Orchestrated by Timothy McVeigh and Terry Nichols, it was a mass murder that took 168 lives and injured hundreds.[6]

180

Not all mass murders occur at the same time and location, or necessarily involve the same perpetrators. For instance, in the worst case of terrorist mass murder to ever hit the United States in September 2001, nineteen killers were involved in the hijacking of four airliners, resulting in the mass murder of more than 3,000 people in different locations at different times, though clearly one coordinated effort (see Chapter 10).

Mass murder is at once a crime of violence and typically an act of hatred and vengeance–designed to get maximum results from the homicidal aggression.

THE NATURE OF MASS MURDER

In spite of the multiple killings perpetrated by mass murderers that often make the headlines and perhaps have the most profound effect on the public, the fact is that mass murder accounts for only a relatively small number of murders or homicides in the United States. This notwithstanding, the sheer numbers of potential victims of mass murderers, as illustrated above, ensure that it will always be of special interest to criminologists and lawmakers.

Mass murderers are predominantly male, often white, and tend to direct their multicidal behavior against those they are connected to in some way, such as intimates, family members, or coworkers. The motivation is usually related to anger, revenge, and a desire to commit suicide. Most mass murders involve the use of weapons of mass destruction such as high-powered firearms or bombs.

Notable recent episodes of mass murder in the United States can be seen as follows:

- On May 20, 1984, Michael Silka, a twenty-five-year-old drifter, went on a deadly shooting spree in Manley Hot Springs, Alaska, killing eight people and tossing their bodies in to the Tanana River. He was shot to death by police but not before adding a state trooper as his ninth mass murder victim.
- On December 7, 1987, David Burke, a vengeful minded ex-airline employee, boarded a Pacific Southwest Airlines plane and forced it to crash into a California hillside, killing all forty-three people on board. The murder-suicide resulted in new federal rules for security procedures involving airline personnel.
- On October 16, 1991, George Hennard, a thirty-five-year-old loner, drove his pickup truck through the window of a cafeteria in Killeen, Texas. He then opened fire, killing twenty-two people and injuring twenty others

before committing suicide. At the time, the crime was considered the worst mass murder in the nation's history.

- On July 18, 1994, James Huberty, a heavily armed forty-one-year-old unemployed security guard, entered a McDonald's restaurant in San Ysidro, California. He opened fire and killed twenty before being shot to death by a police sniper. It was believed at the time to be the worst single-day mass murder in U.S. history.
- On September 15, 1999, Larry Ashbrook, a forty-seven-year-old unemployed loner, burst into a Baptist church in Fort Worth, Texas and shot to death eight people, wounding several others, before killing himself. It was called the worst mass murder in the city's history.[7]

Although there have been very few female mass killers, some women have perpetrated this type of crime. In most cases of female mass murder, it has involved the killing of family members. Examples of recent mass murders committed by females include:

- On October 30, 1985, Sylvia Seegrist, a twenty-five-year-old with a history of mental problems, entered a shopping mall in Delaware County, Pennsylvania, wearing camouflage pants and combat boots. Armed with a semiautomatic rifle, she shot to death three people and wounded seven others. She was found guilty of first-degree murder and given three life sentences in prison.
- On October 26, 1997, Susan Eubanks, a thirty-five-year-old divorced former nursing assistant with a history of substance abuse, shot to death her four young sons in their home in San Marcos, California. She was convicted on all murder counts and sentenced to death.
- On March 23, 1998, Megan Hogg, a twenty-seven-year-old suffering from depression, suffocated her three young daughters in their home in Redwood City, California. After failing at a suicide attempt, she was charged with three counts of murder, pleading no contest, and sentenced to twenty-five years to life in prison.
- On September 3, 1998, Khoua Her strangled to death her six children in their St. Paul, Minnesota apartment. The twenty-five-year-old Laos immigrant plea bargained for a sentence of fifty years in prison.[8]

WHERE AND HOW MASS MURDERS OCCUR

Where do most mass murders take place and under what circumstances? Contrary to the recent spate of school mass murders and terrorist attack mass killings directed toward government buildings or the government itself, most multiple murders involving three or more victims occur at restaurants.

According to a study of factors in public mass murders committed between 1965 and 1998 in the United States, nearly 17 percent took place at a restaurant, just over 14 percent in a retail or grocery store, and almost 13 percent in a government office or other facility. Less than 9 percent of mass murders occurred at a school or college.[9] Around one in four mass murders were described as taking place at an "other" location.

The place where a mass murder occurs appears to be less related to the location itself than the perpetrators and the particular motivations for the mass killings or significance of the setting. For instance, intimate or family-related mass murder is likely to take place at a residence or other location most accessible or appropriate to the offender. Whereas a mass killer in the workplace will likely choose the location in relation to his present or previous employment and grievances to that effect.

The weapon of choice for most mass murderers is a handgun. In more than one out of four mass killings occurring between 1965 and 1998, a handgun was used by the perpetrator(s). In nearly nine in ten cases of mass murder, some form of firearm was used, and often more than one type.[10] Studies show that in most mass murders, the offenders used weapons that were legally purchased, as opposed to banned firearms such as assault weapons.[11]

Although recent murder-suicide mass killings have received much media attention, more often than not mass murderers do not commit suicide as part of the crime. From 1965 to 1998, nearly 60 percent of mass murder episodes ended with the killer or killers fleeing the scene of the crime.[12] Just over 15 percent of the mass killers committed suicide, while just under 15 percent were arrested after the incident.

TYPES OF MASS KILLERS

Researchers have identified various character traits and motivational characteristics of the mass murderer. According to R. M. Holmes and S. T. Holmes, there are five types of mass killers:

- **Disciples** mass murder after being ordered to kill by a persuasive, dominating leader such as a Charles Manson type.

- **Family annihilators** mass murder most or all of their family. They are often the family patriarch or oldest son with a history of depression and substance abuse.

- **Pseudocommandos** are usually a single assailant who stockpiles weapons of mass murder, then targets a particular place to carry out the crime.

- **Disgruntled employees** tend to target a current or former place of work and commit mass murder against a supervisor and other employees they may hold a grudge against, while also killing others randomly.

- **Set-and-run** mass killers use something such as a bomb or poison to inflict maximum casualties, while watching the events take place out of harm's way.[13]

Psychiatrist Paul Mullen puts mass murderers into two distinct categories: (1) those whose primary motive is to commit suicide, and (2) those whose primary desire is to kill people as punishment to society or the government for not recognizing or dismissing their entitlements or talents.[14] He found that the following characteristics could be found in both types of mass killers:

- A fascination with weapons and paraphernalia dealing with militarism.

- Depression.

- Unable to establish intimate relationships.

- Obsessive behavior.

- Narcissistic inclinations.

- Attracted to other mass murderers.

THE CAUSES OF MASS MURDER

What causes one to commit mass murder? Some experts believe that most mass murderers suffer from severe mental illness. In a study of forty mass murderers and serial killers, D. T. Lunde concluded that virtually all of the offenders could be termed as insane.[15] David Lester contended that mass murderers tend to be characterized as having "a serious psychiatric disturbance."[16]

Criminologists generally assert that while mass killers lack "normal psychosocial and emotional responses, they typically are not mentally ill."[17] Instead, most mass murderers are aware of their actions, which are often planned in advance, and are motivated by revenge, hostility, hopelessness, and/or suicidal tendencies.

In studying mass murders in other cultures, Mullen noted in particular the murder-suicide phenomenon first addressed in the Malaysian archipelago:

> The mass murderer in this situation is typically young, male and isolated, and usually has experienced some loss of face or humiliation. And when they decide that life is not worth living, they don't just kill themselves . . . instead, they take a sword or hatchet and run down the street, killing apparently at random until they themselves are struck down and killed. In this way, causing the death of others and ending lives restores faith. This model–

in which you die and vindicate yourself–becomes very attractive to other angry, suicidal and humiliated young men.[18]

In Western societies, mass murderers have similar characteristics. Generally speaking, mass killings are most likely to occur in domestic or intrafamilial circumstances, with the motives being jealousy, depression, and a desire to commit suicide. Drug or alcohol abuse is often a factor. However, many mass murderers in recent years have directed their desire to kill against random targets, making for an even more frightening prospect.

Research has shown that the media itself may play an important role in the onset of mass murder. While there has not been a dramatic shift in the use and availability of firearms in the United States or the degree of social and psychological concerns that may lend to mass killings, media coverage of mass murder events has intensified as media outlets battle to see who can deliver the most detailed, sensationalistic coverage. This type of increasingly prolonged saturation and attention given to the mass murderer often inspires copycats or others seeking such attention and infamy. A study of seven mass murders found media reporting to be a significant factor in five of the mass killings.[19]

NOTES

1. R. M. Holmes and J. E. DeBurger, *Serial Murder* (Thousand Oaks: Sage, 1988).
2. E. Hickey, *Serial Killers and Their Victims* (Pacific Grove: Brooks/Cole, 1991).
3. T. A. Petee, K. G. Padgett, and T. S. York, "Debunking the Stereotype: An Examination of Mass Murder in Public Places," *Homicide Studies 1*, 4 (1997): 317-37.
4. R. Hazelwood and J. Douglas, "The Last Murder," *FBI Law Enforcement Bulletin 49*, 4 (1980): 1-8.
5. P. E. Dietz, "Mass, Serial, and Sensational Homicides," *Bulletin of the New York Academy of Medicine 62* (1986): 477-91.
6. R. Barri Flowers and H. Loraine Flowers, *Murders in the United States: Crimes, Killers and Victims of the Twentieth Century* (Jefferson: McFarland, 2001), pp. 56-57.
7. *Ibid.*, pp. 78-83.
8. *Ibid.*, pp. 141-43.
9. Thomas A. Petee, "Situational Factors Related to Public Mass Murder Incidents: 1965-1998," in U.S. Department of Justice, *Proceedings of the Homicide Research Working Group Meetings, 1997 and 1998* (Washington: National Institute of Justice, 1999), pp. 154-56.
10. *Ibid.*, p. 154.
11. *Ibid.*, p. 155.
12. *Ibid.*

13. R. M. Holmes and S. T. Holmes, "Understanding Mass Murder," *Federal Probation 56*, 1 (1992): 53-61.

14. Cited in Brenda Harkness, "Portraying a Mass Killer," http://www.mnash.edu.au/pubs/ montage/Montage_97_02/killer.html

15. D. T. Lunde, *Murder and Madness* (New York: Norton, 1979).

16. David Lester, *Serial Killers: The Insatiable Passion* (Philadelphia: Charles Press, 1995), p. 65.

17. Quoted in Harkness, "Portraying a Mass Killer."

18. *Ibid.*

19. Belinda Parsons, "Mass Murder," http://www.theage.com.au/daily/98061/new/ news26.html

Chapter 16

SELF-KILLERS

Suicide, or the intentional killing of oneself, is one of the leading causes of death in the United States. More than 30,000 people die each year as a result of suicide, or approximately twice as many people are murdered. Teenagers are especially at high risk for suicide. Suicidal ideation, or thoughts about committing suicide, is fairly common in this society among all age, social, racial, and ethnic groups. Most who contemplate suicide fail to succeed or never seriously try. However, there are millions of Americans who have attempted to kill themselves at some point.

Many suicidal persons are also homicidal, or vice versa. It is not uncommon for certain types of murderers to kill themselves as well, particularly intrafamilial or intimate killers, mass murderers, and terrorist killers. Most murder-suicides are driven by factors such as control or loss of control, anger, revenge, making a statement, or an act of desperation. In rare instances, murder-suicides may be considered mercy killing or a suicide pact between two or more people who wish to die due to serious illness or other severe problems.

Depression is the leading cause of suicide. However, other factors can play an important role in self-murder such as the presence of firearms, substance abuse, child abuse, domestic violence, unemployment, and lack of a support group or adequate resources in dealing with suicidal ideation.

WHAT IS SUICIDE?

Suicide, or self-killing, is the follow through of a decision or intention to end one's life. It has been called a "permanent solution to a temporary problem."[1] However, there are various definitions attached to suicide due to its complexities, motivations, interpretations, misdiagnosis, subjectivity, and, in

187

many cases, inconclusive analysis of the dead person's intent or mindset at the time of death.

The term *suicide* originated in the Seventeenth century from the Latin "sui (general) of oneself" and English "-cide" defined at "the act or an instance of taking one's own life voluntarily and intentionally, especially by a person of years of discretion and of sound mind."[2] Since then, the word suicide has been synonymous with such terms as "self-murder," "self-slaughter," "self-killing," and "self-destruction."

Even before the act was termed suicide, the Greeks once described suicidal behavior as "'to break up life,' 'to grasp or seize death,' 'to do violence to oneself,' [or] 'to leave the light.'"[3] In the Nineteenth century, Emile Durkheim defined suicide as "the termination of an individual's life resulting directly from a positive or negative act of the victim himself which he knows will produce this fatal result."[4]

More recently, the World Health Organization defined suicide as simply "a suicidal act with a fatal outcome," with such an act being defined as "self-injury with varying degrees of lethal intent."[5] A medical definition was established by the Centers for Disease Control and Prevention in certifying death as caused by suicide. Commonly used by medical examiners, coroners, scientists, and officials in public health, it defined suicide as "death from injury, poisoning, or suffocation where there is evidence (either explicit or implicit) that the injury was self-inflicted and that the decedent intended to kill himself [or] herself."[6]

According to suicide researcher Kay Jamison: "Suicide is the anchor point on a continuum of suicidal thoughts and behaviors. This continuum is one that ranges from risk-taking behaviors at one end, extends through different degrees and types of suicidal thinking, and ends with suicide attempts and suicide."[7]

The term *attempted suicide* has been somewhat ambiguous in its meaning as interpretations on what constitutes "attempted" can vary. In seeking to establish a general consensus on attempted suicide, many clinicians, scientists, and researchers over the past two decades have effectively replaced the term with *parasuicide*, meaning "deliberate self-harm," defining it as:

> An act with non-fatal outcome, in which an individual deliberately initiates a non-habitual behavior that, without intervention from others, will cause self-harm, or deliberately ingests a substance in excess of the prescribed or generally recognized therapeutic dosage, and which is aimed at realizing changes which the subject desired via the actual or expected physical consequences.[8]

THE SCOPE OF SUICIDE

By most accounts, suicide is a serious problem globally. The World Health Organization estimated that 1.8 percent of the fifty-four million deaths in 1998 worldwide was the result of suicide.[9] This means there were nearly one million suicides that year. In the United States alone, there are more than 30,000 suicide deaths annually, according to the American Association of Suicideology.[10] A person commits suicide in this country every seventeen minutes, or eighty-four times a day. It is estimated that anywhere from ten to twenty-five suicides are attempted for every suicide that is completed.[11]

In 1997, the rate of suicide in the United States was 11.41 per 100,000 population. Table 16.1 shows the suicide rate by age, sex, and race for each age group. Males were more than four times as likely to commit suicide as females, while whites were twice as likely to commit suicide as blacks. When considering race and sex, white males had the highest suicide rate, followed by other males. Black females had the lowest rate of suicide, followed by females of other races.

Among teenagers, the suicide rate was highest for males and whites. The rate of suicide for white males age fifteen to nineteen was nearly five times that of white females, and almost six times higher than that of black females. Male teens other than blacks had the second highest suicide rate, while black male teens were significantly more likely to commit suicide than female teens of any race.

Overall, the suicide rate tended to be highest in older persons. However, the rate of suicide among blacks and black males peaked in the age twenty to twenty-four range.

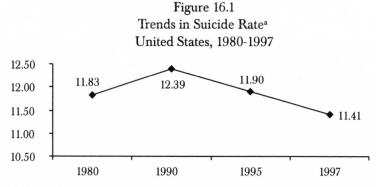

Figure 16.1
Trends in Suicide Rate[a]
United States, 1980-1997

[a] Per 100,000 population.

Source: Derived from U.S. Department of Justice, Bureau of Justice Statistics, *Sourcebook of Criminal Justice Statistics 1999* (Washington: Government Printing Office, 2000), p. 308.

Table 16.1

SUICIDE RATE,[a] BY AGE, SEX, AND RACE, UNITED STATES, 1997

Age	Total	Sex		Race			Race and Sex					
							White		Black		Other	
		Male	Female	White	Black	Other	Male	Female	Male	Female	Male	Female
Total	11.41	18.69	4.42	12.43	6.19	7.44	20.24	4.87	10.94	1.90	11.43	3.67
10-14	1.59	2.36	0.79	1.67	1.36	1.09	2.48	0.82	1.88	0.83	1.94	0.20
15-19	9.45	15.16	3.38	9.96	7.12	8.59	15.97	3.51	11.36	2.75	13.87	3.19
20-24	13.61	23.04	3.69	13.94	11.62	14.30	23.40	3.82	21.48	1.98	21.87	6.61
25-29	14.36	23.90	4.75	15.21	10.63	11.46	25.02	5.12	19.40	2.57	18.27	5.00
30-34	14.29	23.41	5.21	15.27	10.46	8.65	24.68	5.70	19.18	2.73	13.28	4.32
35-39	15.06	23.68	6.47	16.39	8.57	9.08	25.37	7.25	14.97	2.90	15.42	3.12
40-44	15.55	24.06	7.17	17.09	8.05	7.31	26.08	8.06	14.27	2.61	10.91	4.06
45-49	15.17	23.32	7.29	16.69	6.64	7.97	25.44	8.04	10.96	3.01	11.36	4.99
50-54	14.16	21.41	7.28	15.46	5.33	7.99	23.16	8.01	8.92	2.42	11.73	4.64
55-59	14.48	23.40	6.23	15.68	6.12	10.06	24.98	6.90	11.71	1.77	16.17	4.56
60-64	12.37	21.29	4.41	13.32	5.68	8.15	22.71	4.74	10.46	2.09	13.75	3.49
65-69	13.22	23.85	4.28	14.10	6.10	10.57	25.25	4.55	12.01	1.68	17.92	5.16
70-74	15.71	29.39	5.13	16.66	7.01	10.50	31.15	5.33	14.12	2.13	13.86	8.03
75-79	18.45	37.35	5.16	19.67	5.76	12.55	39.70	5.48	12.97	1.21	20.87	6.50
80-84	20.61	47.04	5.16	21.70	6.47	20.72	49.56	5.33	16.24	1.40	33.37	11.37
85+	20.79	60.35	4.86	22.00	5.81	22.81	64.96	4.91	17.52	0.97	27.77	19.69

[a] Per 100,000 population in each age group.

Source: Derived from U.S. Department of Justice, Bureau of Justice Statistics, *Sourcebook of Criminal Justice Statistics 1999* (Washington: Government Printing Office, 2000), p. 308.

In general, the rate of suicide has dropped in the United States in recent years. As seen in Figure 16.1, between 1980 and 1997, the suicide rate in this country went from 11.83 to 11.41 per 100,000 population. The rate of suicide rose during the span for persons between the ages of ten and nineteen (see Figure 16.2). Teenagers are especially at high risk to attempt or commit suicide. According to one study, teen suicide in North America had risen by more than 300 percent over the past thirty years.[12]

Figure 16.2
Trends in Suicide Rate[a] for Persons Age 10-19, 1980-1997

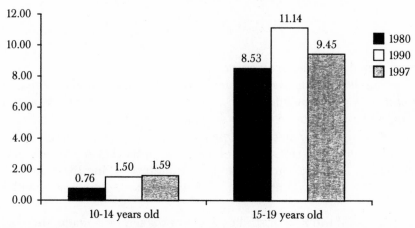

[a] Per 100,000 population in each age group.

Source: Derived from U.S. Department of Justice, Bureau of Justice Statistics, *Sourcebook of Criminal Justice Statistics 1999* (Washington: Government Printing Office, 2000), p. 308.

Parasuicide rates in the United States are inconsistently reported due to privacy issues. However, in a comprehensive government survey of parasuicide rates between 1980 and 1985, around 3 percent of respondents had ever attempted suicide.[13] Nearly six in ten who had tried to kill themselves at some point were women, while the rate of prevalence for attempts was significantly higher among individuals twenty-five to forty-four years of age than persons over the age of forty-four.

Other data on suicide and suicidal persons show that:

- Suicide occurs more often than homicide.
- Suicide is the second leading cause of death for females and fourth for males worldwide.
- There is an attempted suicide in the United States every forty-two seconds.
- Women survive attempted suicides more often than men.

- A teenager commits suicide every 100 minutes.
- Daily, four persons between the ages of fifteen and twenty-four kill themselves.
- Female teenagers are twice as likely to attempt suicide as male teenagers.
- The rate of suicide is highest for persons age seventy and over.
- Fifteen percent of people with depression take their own lives.
- Sixty percent of suicides are committed at home.
- Two-thirds of completed suicides occur after a previous suicide attempt.
- Forty percent of people who kill themselves leave a suicide note.[14]

SUICIDAL IDEATION

How often do people seriously contemplate committing suicide or attempt to kill themselves? Estimates on suicidal thoughts have ranged from a low of 3.5 percent of the population with respect to recent thoughts, to around 19 percent when questioned about suicidal thoughts over the past twelve months, to a high of 53 percent of people who had ever considered the possibility of committing suicide.[15] The latter suggests that more than half the population has at least contemplated the notion of taking their own lives at one time or another, with about one in five considering the notion within the last year.

In one of the largest studies ever conducted on suicide, the National Institute of Mental Health reported that 11 percent of the 18,500 respondents had thought about killing themselves at some stage in their lives, while 3 percent had tried to commit suicide on at least one occasion.[16] Other surveys of adults in the general population found that between 5 and 15 percent had ever contemplated suicide.[17]

Although men are four times more likely than women to kill themselves, women attempt to commit suicide two to three times more often than men.[18] Women have been found to suffer from depression twice as much as men, which is believed to manifest itself in more suicidal ideation and suicide attempts.[19] Battered women are especially at risk for suicidal ideation and attempted suicide. Studies by M. D. Pagelow[20] and J. J. Gayford[21] found that half of the battered women in their samples had thought about committing suicide; while E. Stark and A. Flitcraft reported that one in ten of their sample group of abused women had attempted suicide, with half of these battered women seeking to kill themselves on more than one occasion.[22] In the latter study, it was found that more than one in four attempted suicides by females (that hospitals were aware of) involved intimate partner violence.

Research on college and high school students has yielded rates on suicidal ideation among young adults. In a comprehensive nationwide study of undergraduate college students undertaken by the 1995 National College Health Risk Behavior Survey, researchers found that 10 percent of the students had thought about committing suicide on a serious level, with 7 percent having developed a plan to kill themselves.[23] Studies in the United States, Europe, and Africa have shown that mild to serious suicidal thoughts occur in anywhere from 20 to 65 percent of all students in college.[24]

Suicidal ideation among high school students may be even more common. According to the 1997 Youth Risk Behavior Surveillance Survey, which questioned over 16,000 students in grades nine to twelve between the ages of fifteen to eighteen, 20 percent had seriously contemplated attempting to take their own lives in the last year, with 16 percent having created a plan to that effect.[25] In surveys of high school students in New York and Oregon, rates of suicidal ideation were more than 50 percent and 20 percent, respectively.[26] Other North American and European studies have yielded similar findings on thoughts of suicide among boys and girls.[27]

TEENAGERS AND SUICIDE

Suicide by teenagers is a major source of concern by mental health professionals and experts on youth. Suicide is the third leading cause of death among persons between the ages of fifteen and twenty-five and the sixth leading cause for persons between the ages of five and fourteen.[28] More teenagers and young adults die as the result of suicide than from such means as heart disease, stroke, cancer, AIDS, birth defects, influenza, and pneumonia put together.

An estimated 500,000 teenagers attempt suicide every year, with around 5,000 successful in killing themselves.[29] Nearly twice as many youth die as a result of suicide than from natural causes.

According to studies, male teenagers age seventeen to nineteen who drink alcohol are at the greatest risk to commit suicide.[30] More than one in two teen victims of suicide abused drugs or alcohol.[31]

Teenage runaways and prostitutes face a particularly high risk for attempting or committing suicide. In a study of runaways in youth shelters, Carol Canton and David Shaffer found that 50 percent had seriously considered or attempted suicide.[32] Nearly seven out of ten girl prostitutes and almost four in ten boy prostitutes have attempted suicide.[33]

Gay teenagers are also at high risk for suicide. Some studies have reported that around one-third of all teenage suicide victims in the United States every year are homosexual males or females.[34] Gay and lesbian youth are two to three times as likely to complete attempted suicide as other youth.

Most teens that kill themselves do so out of depression, loneliness, hope-lessness, or isolation, with substance abuse often a factor. Warning signs for teen or adult suicide include:

- Talking about committing suicide.
- Difficulty with eating or sleeping.
- Drastic behavioral changes.
- Withdrawing from friends or social activities.
- Loss of interest in school, hobbies, or work.
- The recent breakup of a relationship or death in the family.
- Having attempted suicide previously.
- Abuse of alcohol or drugs.
- A preoccupation with death or dying.

MURDER-SUICIDE

Murder-suicide tends to occur most often in an intimate or intrafamilial setting. It is unclear just how many murder-suicides take place each year in the United States, as some are misidentified, unknown, or unclassified as such in homicide statistics. In a study of homicide followed by suicide occurring in Kentucky between 1985 and 1990, Sherry Currens and colleagues found that homicide-suicides represented 6 percent of the total homicides over the span.[35]

A male intimate is typically the perpetrator in murder-suicides. In Stuart Palmer and John Humphrey's study of offender-victim relationships in criminal homicide-suicides in North Carolina from 1972 to 1977, 94 percent were perpetrated by males.[36] Similarly, Marvin Wolfgang's analysis of twenty-four homicide-suicides in Philadelphia found that 92 percent were committed by men.[37] Most victims of murder-suicide are female. In the Currens and associates study, 73 percent of the homicide victims were women.[38]

Spouse battering is often a precursor to domestic partner murder-suicide, in conjunction with offender jealousy, anger, depression, psychological factors, and substance abuse.[39] In his examination of homicide followed by suicide, Steven Stack found that the risk of suicide after a homicide was significantly higher if the victim was intimately involved with the offender, an ex-intimate, or the child of the offender.[40]

Murder-suicide is also common in suicide pacts where one person kills another, then his or herself as part of a jointly agreed-upon ending of life. Mercy killing-suicide can occur when perpetrators, usually elderly, take an ill spouse's life, and then out of guilt, loneliness, depression, and/or fear of consequences, commit suicide.[41]

Intrafamilial homicide-suicide may sometimes result in the murder of one's entire family before the killer, usually an adult male, takes his own life. Other interpersonal murder-suicides include those perpetrated in the workplace by disgruntled current or ex-employees.

Mass murders typically involve murder-suicide in which the killer or killers wish to make a violent statement, express rage, or achieve martyrdom while escaping apprehension through the act of suicide. A good example is the Columbine High School massacre in 1999, in which Eric Harris and Dylan Klebold killed thirteen and wounded twenty-five others before turning their guns on themselves before authorities could close in. Mass murder-suicide is also typically perpetrated by terrorists who kill themselves because it is often the only way to assure completing the crime with maximum effectiveness. This was painfully illustrated with the September 2001 terrorist attack on the United States, in which nineteen men hijacked four airliners and crashed them, killing thousands, including themselves (see Chapter 10).

SUICIDE METHODS

Self-killers take their own lives through a variety of means, dependent upon the suicidal individual's frame of mind, accessibility to the desired method of suicide, state of health, knowledge, intent, fears, morals, and other considerations. However, use of firearms is by far the most common method of committing suicide in the United States (see Figure 16.3). Firearms account for around 60 percent of all suicides, while about 25 percent are committed by strangulation and drug or poison overdoses, with the other 15 percent of suicides committed by inhaling gases or vapors, cutting, falling, and drowning.

Figure 16.3
Suicide Methods in the United States

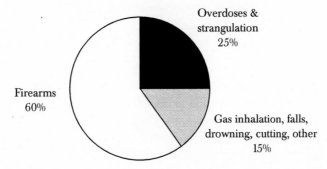

Source: Data derived from Kay R. Jamison, *Night Falls Fast: Understanding Suicide* (New York: Vintage, 199), p. 138.

Figure 16.4 breaks down suicide methods by gender. Sixty-four percent of males take their own lives by use of handguns or other firearms; 14 percent commit suicide by strangulation, suffocation, or hanging; and 10 percent by inhalation of gases or vapors. Around 12 percent of males commit suicide by drug overdose or other methods.

Figure 16.4
Suicide Methods, by Gender

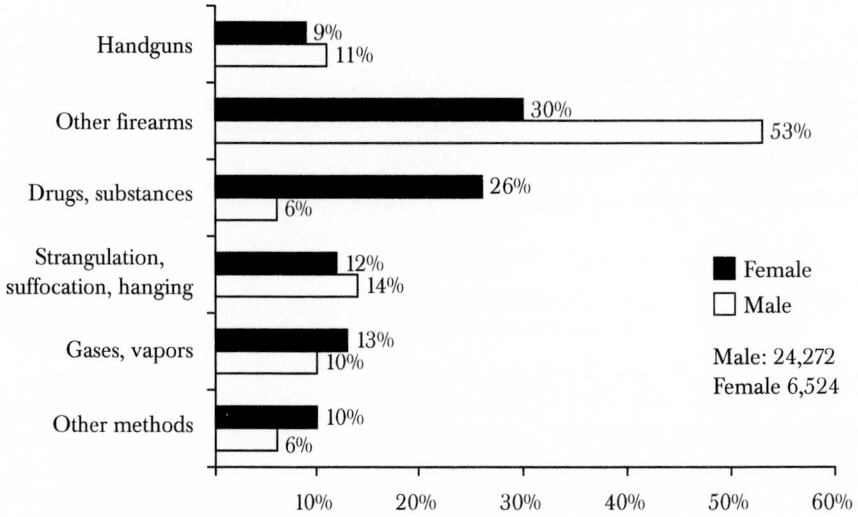

Source: National Center for Health Statistics, Division of Vital Statistics

Females are much less likely than males to commit suicide with firearms. However, firearms are the most common method of suicide for females, constituting about 39 percent of suicides. Twenty-six percent of females end their lives by overdosing on drugs or other substances, with 13 percent choosing to die by inhaling gases or vapors, and 12 percent committing suicide by strangulation, suffocation, or hanging. Around 10 percent of females take their lives through other means.

Age can also be an important factor in the method chosen to commit suicide, especially among young suicidal persons. According to research:

- Sixty-four percent of young men kill themselves with firearms.
- Twenty percent of young women take their own lives with firearms.
- Eighteen percent of young men end their lives by hanging.
- Fifty-three percent of young women commit suicide by drug overdose or poison.[42]

Figure 16.5
Firearm Involved Suicide Attempts, 1993-1997

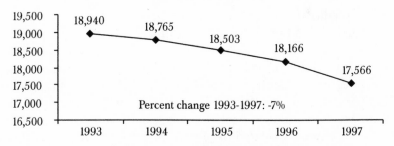

Source: U.S. Department of Justice, Bureau of Justice Statistics Selected Findings, Firearm Injury and Death from Crime, 1993-97 (Washington: Office of Justice Programs, 2000), p. 7.

Suicide by firearms is on the decline. As shown in Figure 16.5, between 1993 and 1997, firearm-related suicides decreased 7 percent, going from 18,940 to 17,566. A much more dramatic decline can be seen in attempted suicides involving firearms over the same span, which dropped 45 percent in 1997 to 3,100 from the 1993 figure of 5,600 (see Figure 16.6).

Figure 16.6
Firearm Involved Suicide Attempts, 1993-1997

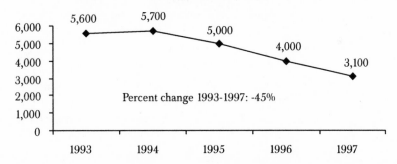

Source: U.S. Department of Justice, Bureau of Justice Statistics Selected Findings, Firearm Injury and Death from Crime, 1993-97 (Washington: Office of Justice Programs, 2000), p. 7.

In discussing various factors that may be involved in the method chosen to commit suicide, Jamison noted the importance of "the type and degree of psychopathology. . . . Severely mentally ill patients are more likely than others to immolate themselves, leap in front of trains, or choose particularly bizarre and self-mutilation ways to die."[43] She also contended that revenge, anger, symbolism, and suggestion could all play roles in the suicide method and circumstances thereof.

SUBSTANCE ABUSE AND SUICIDE

A strong correlation exists between suicidal persons and substance abuse. Studies show that a high percentage of individuals who commit suicide have a history of alcohol or drug abuse and are often under the influence of substances at the time of death.[44] More than half of teenage suicide victims had problems with drugs or alcohol; while over one-third of all young persons who took their lives were diagnosed with substance abuse problems.[45] According to research, mood disorders combined with drug and alcohol abuse are most commonly related to suicide as are psychiatric disorders and possession of firearms.[46]

In his study on suicide, Mark Williams found that

> alcohol and substance abuse represent major risk factors for suicide right across the life-span. . . . The number of years somebody who completes suicide has typically been abusing alcohol is between twenty and twenty-five, possibly because as alcoholism progresses, it destroys those factors known to protect against suicide. . . . Alcohol and substance abuse raises the risk of suicide as soon as the abuse starts.[47]

Aside from the illicit drug abuse, prescription drug dependency has also been shown to increase the risk of suicide. Persons dependent on prescription drugs are twenty times more likely to commit suicide as the population at large.[48] While those addicted to prescription drugs have a higher suicide rate than alcoholics, people who are alcohol dependent account for far more cases of suicide.[49]

Drug and alcohol abuse are often a reflection of mental illness or coping with it. "Independently or together they can precipitate acute episodes of psychosis.... Substance abuse loads the cylinder with more bullets. By acting to disinhibit behavior, drugs and alcohol increase risk taking, violence, and impulsivity. For those who are suicidal or potentially so, this may be lethal."[50]

DEPRESSION AND SUICIDE

The relationship between depression and suicide is well documented.[51] Depression is defined as a "condition of feeling sad or despondent" and characterized by "an inability to concentrate, insomnia, and feelings of dejection and hopelessness."[52] Untreated, depression is seen by experts as the number one cause of suicide. The National Institute of Mental Health reports that 15 percent of people who suffer from a major depressive disorder such as depression, manic-depression, and schizophrenia, kill themselves if their affliction goes untreated or they are unresponsive to treatment.[53] This represents a thirty-five times greater rate of suicide than in the general population.

According to the *Diagnostic and Statistical Manual of Mental Disorders* (DSM-IV): "The most serious consequence of a major depressive disorder is attempted or completed suicide. Motivations for suicide may include a desire to give up in the face of perceived insurmountable obstacles or an intense wish to end an excruciatingly painful emotional state that is perceived to be without end."[54] Studies show that the severity of the depressive state is directly correlated to risk of suicide. Severe depression is far more likely to result in suicide than milder forms of depression.[55]

When depression is combined with substance abuse, the risk of attempted or completed suicide is even higher.[56] Alcohol and/or drugs can both facilitate ending one's life and act as an antecedent in dependency that may foster conditions that lead to suicide. The accessibility of alcohol and legal and illegal drugs, along with guns, and untreated depressive disorders are seen as highly contributory to the suicide rate.

High-risk groups for depression-related suicide ideation, attempts, and actual suicide include females, pregnant women, teenagers, and the elderly.[57] Suicide tends to be more common as well among talented writers and artists, as well as persons successful in business or the scientific community. In most cases, depression, manic-depression, and substance abuse have been shown to be highly instrumental in such suicides.[58]

DOCTOR-ASSISTED SUICIDE

There is growing interest among the public in doctor-assisted suicide, or a doctor prescribing lethal medications to help a person—usually terminally ill—to end their life. According to a 1999 Gallup Poll, 61 percent of the national sample believed that doctor-assisted suicide should be allowed for terminally ill patients or those in severe pain.[59] This was 4 percent more than a 1997 poll. Males tend to be more in favor than females, whites more than minorities, and young people more than older ones, for the legalization of doctor-assisted suicide.

Currently, Oregon's physician-assisted suicide law, in effect since voters passed the initiative in 1994, is the only such law in the United States. To date, at least seventy terminally ill Oregonians have used the law to take their lives.[60] However, the federal government is seeking to undermine the state's doctor-assisted suicide law by suggesting that the law violates the Controlled Substances Act, regulating the manufacture, distribution, and dispensation of certain drugs. As of this writing, Oregon and the government are using the courts to settle the issue and set precedence for the future of physician-assisted suicide in this country.

There have been cases of physicians circumventing the law in assisting patients to commit suicide. Perhaps the best known example is Doctor Jack Kevorkian. The retired Michigan pathologist known as "Dr. Death" is believed to have assisted in the suicides of more than 130 terminally ill people.[61] In 1999, Kevorkian was convicted of second-degree murder and delivery of a control substance in the death of a man suffering from Lou Gehrig's disease. He was sentenced to ten to twenty-five years in prison.

NOTES

1. "How to Cope with Suicidal Thoughts and Feelings–In Yourself and Others," http://www.healingfromdepression.com/suicidal.htm.
2. YourDictionary.com, http://yourdictionary.com/cgi-bin/mw.cgi.
3. Kay R. Jamison, *Night Falls Fast: Understanding Suicide* (New York: Vintage, 1999), p. 26.
4. Quoted in Mark Williams, *Cry of Pain: Understanding Suicide and Self-Harm* (New York: Penguin, 1997), p. 19. See also Emile Durkheim, *Le Suicide* (Paris: Alcain, 1897).
5. Quoted in Jamison, *Night Falls Fast*, p. 27.
6. *Ibid.*
7. *Ibid.*, p. 34.
8. Williams, *Cry of Pain*, p. 69.
9. Cited in Jamison, *Night Falls Fast*, p. 48.
10. Cited in Al Tompkins, "A Thoughtful Look at Suicide," (July 17, 2000), http://www.flepioa.org/suicide.htm.
11. Ibid.; Jamison, *Night Falls Fast*, p. 46.
12. "Suicide," http://www.travestyproductions.com/deadend/suicide_notes/stats.html##how
13. Williams, *Cry of Pain*, pp. 75-76.
14. "Suicide;" Jamison, *Night Falls Fast*, pp. 48-49.
15. Williams, *Cry of Pain*, pp. 77-78; R. D. Goldney, "Suicidal Ideation in a Young Adult Population," *Acta Psychiatrica Scandinavica* 79 (1989): 481-9.
16. Cited in Jamison, *Night Falls Fast*, pp. 35-36.
17. *Ibid.*
18. *Ibid.*, pp. 46-47; Williams, *Cry of Pain*, p. 77.
19. Jamison, *Night Falls Fast*, pp. 46-47, 109.
20. M. D. Pagelow, *Family Violence* (New York: Praeger, 1984).
21. J. J. Gayford, "Wife Battering: A Preliminary Survey of 100 Cases," *British Medical Journal 1* (1975): 194-97.
22. E. Stark and A. Flitcraft, "Violence Among Intimates: An Epidemiological Review," in V. B. Van Hasselt, R. L. Morrison, A. S. Bellack, and M. Hersen, eds., *Handbook of Family Violence* (New York: Plenum, 1988), pp. 293-317.
23. Cited in Jamison, *Night Falls Fast*, p. 36.

24. *Ibid.*

25. *Ibid.*, pp. 36-37.

26. *Ibid.*, p. 37.

27. Cited in *Ibid.*

28. "Suicide is a Teenage Epidemic," http://www.jaredstory.com/teen_epidemic. html.

29. *Ibid.*

30. "Suicide."

31. *Ibid.*

32. Cited in R. Barri Flowers, *The Prostitution of Women and Girls* (Jefferson: McFarland, 1998), p. 93.

33. Ibid., p. 87; Clare Tattersall, *Drugs, Runaways, and Teen Prostitution* (New York: Rosen, 1999), p. 31.

34. Tattersall, *Drugs, Runaways, and Teen Prostitution,* p. 31; Williams, *Cry of Pain,* p. 33; J. Harry, "Sexual Identity Issues," in *Report of the Secretary's Task Force Report on Youth Suicide,* Vol. 2 (Washington: Department of Health and Human Services, 1989), pp. 131-42.

35. Cited in Neil Websdale, *Understanding Domestic Homicide* (Boston: Northeastern University Press, 1999), pp. 16-17.

36. Stuart Palmer and John A. Humphrey, "Offender-Victim Relationships in Criminal Homicide Followed by Offender's Suicide, North Carolina, 1972-1977," *Suicide and Life-Threatening Behavior 10,* 2 (1980): 106-18.

37. Marvin E. Wolfgang, "An Analysis of Homicide-Suicide," *Journal of Clinical and Experimental Psychopathology and Quarterly Review of Psychiatry and Neurology 19,* 3 (1958): 208-18.

38. Websdale, *Understanding Domestic Homicide,* pp. 16-17.

39. *Ibid.*, p. 17; R. Barri Flowers, *Domestic Crimes, Family Violence and Child Abuse: A Study of Contemporary American Society* (Jefferson: McFarland, 2000), pp. 61-67, 71-78; Milton Rosenbaum, "The Role of Depression in Couples Involved in Murder-Suicide and Homicide," *American Journal of Psychiatry 147,* 8 (1990): 1036-39.

40. Steven Stack, "Homicide Followed by Suicide: An Analysis of Chicago Data," *Criminology 35,* 3 (1997): 435-53.

41. Peter M. Marzuk, Kenneth Tardiff, and Charles S. Hirsh, "The Epidemiology of Murder-Suicide," *Journal of the American Medical Association 267,* 23 (1992): 3179-83; Patricia W. Easteal, *Killing the Beloved: Homicide Between Adult Sexual Intimates* (Canberra: Australian Institute of Criminology, 1993).

42. "Suicide."

43. Jamison, *Night Falls Fast,* pp. 141-42.

44. *Ibid.*, pp. 50, 102, 126-27; Williams, *Cry of Pain,* pp. 40-41; Flowers, *The Prostitution of Women and Girls,* pp. 87, 93.

45. "Suicide;" Jamison, *Night Falls Fast,* p. 50; Williams, *Cry of Pain,* pp. 41, 231.

46. Jamison, *Night Falls Fast,* pp. 47, 103-4.

47. Williams, *Cry of Pain,* pp. 40-41.

48. Jamison, *Night Falls Fast,* p. 102.

49. *Ibid.*
50. *Ibid.*, p. 127.
51. *Ibid.*, pp. 126-28, 180, 190; Williams, *Cry of Pain*, pp. 126-29.
52. *The American Heritage Dictionary* (New York: Dell, 1994), p. 232.
53. "How to Cope with Suicidal Thoughts."
54. *Ibid.* See also *American Psychiatric Association, Diagnostic and Statistical Manual of Mental Disorders,* 4th ed. (Washington: American Psychiatric Association, 1994).
55. Jamison, *Night Falls Fast*, pp. 110-14.
56. *Ibid.*, pp. 110-11, 123-28.
57. *Ibid.*, pp. 46-47, 50, 103.
58. *Ibid.*, pp. 180-81.
59. George Gallup, Jr. and Alec Gallup, *The Gallup Poll Monthly*, No. 402 (Princeton: The Gallup Poll, 1999), p. 37.
60. Cited in Ashbel S. Green, "State Wins Time to Defend Suicide Law," http://www.oregonlive.com/news/oregonian/index.ssf?/xml/story.ssf/html.
61. R. Barri Flowers and H. Loraine Flowers, *Murders in the United States: Crimes, Killers and Victims of the Twentieth Century* (Jefferson: McFarland, 2001), pp. 107-8, 204.

Part VI

EXPLANATIONS FOR MURDER

Chapter 17

CRIMINAL HOMICIDE THEORIES

Theories on criminal homicide and other violent behavior can generally be broken down into three categories: (1) those who subscribe to free will or the conscious and voluntary choice of behavior, (2) a deterministic view of violence, or the notion that such behavior is the result of biological, psychological, and sociological factors independent of free will, and (3) a critical approach to criminality, which is less concerned with explaining crime and violence, per se, but rather how society interprets such actions and responds to it.

Although there is strong individual support over the notion of free will in explaining deviant behavior, modern criminology has, for the most part, moved away from this school of thought, preferring instead to focus primarily on biological, psychological, and social-cultural determinants of homicidal and violent behavior. Critical criminology is less relied upon in terms of explaining violent criminality, though is somewhat more effective in understanding social policy and the criminal justice system in relation to crime.

CLASSICAL THEORIES OF CRIMINALITY

The origins of the classical criminology school of thought are commonly believed to be the writings of Cesare Beccaria in the Eighteenth century. In his 1764 essay, *On Crimes and Punishment*, Beccaria advanced that "people were by nature, inherently rational (capable of logical thought), intelligent (capable of creative thought), hedonistic (motivated by pain/pleasure), and self-determining (free willed)."[1] He believed behavior to be "freely chosen based on assessments of the pain/pleasure or cost/benefits of the actions."[2]

With respect to criminal behavior, Beccaria saw this as a matter of choice. In short, the answer to the prevention or deterrence of crime was to "make the punishment fit the crime," or "increase the pain/cost of an action to the point where it overwhelms its possible pleasure/benefits."[3] Beccaria observed that such punishment for criminal actions should not only be in response to the particular offense and its severity but also be doled out swiftly and surely, "since even the severest punishment has no deterrent quality if it can be escaped."[4]

The classical perspective on criminality lost credibility in the Nineteenth century as a preeminent means of explaining criminal behavior. This was due largely to its propositions of free will in determining one's involvement in criminal actions, along with the progression of "physical and medical science...and [discovery of] an increasing number of ways in which human beings were not self-determining."[5]

Classical criminology theories reemerged in the Twentieth century with more sophisticated approaches, such as *criminological economic theories*,[6] *deterrence theories*,[7] and *rational choice theories*.[8] However, while such theories rely primarily on the individual's own free will or choice in behavior, there is also the recognition that other factors beyond the person may play a role in the perpetration of violent and other types of crimes.

POSITIVISTIC THEORIES OF CRIMINALITY

A positivistic approach in explaining criminal behavior as an alternative to classical criminology gained strength in the Nineteenth century. Positivistic criminology assumed that human behavior was to some extent influenced "by factors which were largely outside the control of any specific individual."[9]

Within this school of thought lies two particular types of determinism, or the belief that every act or decision made is the inevitable result of certain antecedents aside from human will: *individual determinism* and *social-cultural determinism.*

Individual determinism attributes human behavior to influences "largely located inside the individual, either in [one's] physical/biological nature or [one's] mental/psychological processes."[10] Whereas, social-cultural determinism posits that crime is not a consequence of "flawed people but rather...a flawed society."[11] Within this context, homicide offenders and other criminals "are seen as being primarily influenced by social or cultural factors, which are, again, largely outside their control."[12]

BIOLOGICAL THEORIES ON CRIME AND VIOLENCE

The biological-positivistic school of thought in explaining criminal behavior was pioneered by Italian physician Cesare Lombroso. Highly influenced by the work of Charles Darwin, Lombroso, who was called the "father of criminology," introduced his *theory of atavism* in the 1876 book *L'Uomo Delinquente.*[13] He argued that criminals were throwbacks to earlier genetic forms and, as such, could be differentiated from noncriminals by physical stigmata. This perspective has been essentially dismissed as methodologically flawed, among other reasons. Although Lombroso would later modify some of his hypotheses, the basic tenet of his work remained.

Other early biological perspectives on criminality included *body type theories* and *hereditary theories.* In the 1930s and 1940s, such criminologists as Ernest Hooten,[14] William Sheldon,[15] and Sheldon and Eleanor Glueck[16] postulated that certain body types were characteristic of criminals. For example, Hooten believed that tall, heavy men were more likely than other body types to be murderers; whereas Sheldon and the Gluecks advanced that certain somatotypes such as mesomorphics—characterized as aggressive, assertive, muscular and hard—were disproportionately likely to engage in delinquent or criminal behavior.

Hereditary theories attributed criminal behavior or genetically transmitted mental or physical defectiveness or deficiencies. Such theorists as Richard Dugdale[17] and Henry Goddard[18] examined the long histories of criminality, feeblemindedness, and other aberrant behavior in some families. Like atavism theory, body type theories and early hereditary theories have been rejected as unscientific and otherwise weak.

Twin, Adoption, and Fosterling Studies

More recent biological theories have shown greater promise in understanding criminal behavior. *Twin studies* have linked antisocial behavior to genetic traits found in identical twins, in particular. Studies by Johannes Lange[19] and Karl Christiansen[20] found that the rate of criminal *concordance*—a genetic term referring to the degree in which twins or related pairings demonstrate a specific behavior or condition—was much greater among identical than fraternal twins. In a review of twin studies, Hans Eysench asserted that heredity is "beyond any doubt . . . an extremely important part in the genesis of criminal behaviour."[21]

Similarly, *adoption and fosterling studies* have explored the relationship between the criminality of adopted or foster children and the criminal behavior of their biological and adoptive or foster parents. The most significant research in this area was conducted by Bernard Hutchings and Sarnoff Mednick. In examining 1,145 male adoptees and the same number of non-adoptees, controlling such factors as age, sex, and the occupations of fathers, it was concluded that adoptees were nearly twice as likely as nonadoptees to have criminal records, and that the biological fathers of adoptees were three times more likely to be involved in criminal activity than either the adoptive fathers or fathers of the control group.[22]

In an even more comprehensive study of adoptees, Mednick, W. F. Gabrielli, and Hutchings, in comparing conviction records of 14, 427 adoptees to the conviction records of their biological and adoptive parents, concluded the genetic transmission of criminal tendencies increased the probability of children becoming antisocial.[23]

In both twin and adoption and fosterling research, theorists have noted the importance of environment as well as genetics in criminal behavior.

The most current research on biologically-based deviant behavior has relied upon a multidisciplinary perspective in explaining crime. "Scientists in such fields as genetics, biochemistry, endocrinology, neuroscience, immunology, and psychophysiology have been intensely studying aspects of human behavior that are relevant to the criminologist and criminal justice practitioner."[24] Among the areas being explored with respect to biology and crime is the relationship between violent criminal behavior and brain disorders such as brain tumors and epilepsy.[25]

PSYCHOLOGICAL THEORIES ON CRIME AND VIOLENCE

The psychological or psychogenic school of thought on criminality is largely attributed to the work of Sigmund Freud and his *psychoanalytic theory*.[26] The Austrian physician saw criminal behavior as the conflict between the personality's id, ego, and superego drives and unresolved instincts. Supporters of psychoanalytic theory believe that the answer to understanding and treating antisocial behavior is psychoanalysis, an "individualistic therapy program which concentrates on delving deep into the individual's past experiences to uncover the unconscious conflicts."[27]

The major criticism against the psychoanalytic theories to criminality is that they cannot be empirically validated. Because the personality parts are neither able to be observed nor measured, psychoanalytic findings are essentially just the "analyst's interpretation of a patient's interpretation of what is occurring in the subconscious."[28]

However, the psychological-positivistic approach to explaining crime has remained influential in criminological theory. R. R. Bootzin and J. R.

Acocella divided psychological theories on violent behavior into three categories:

- **Psychodynamic perspective**. Unconscious conflicts during childhood causes criminal behavior.

- **Behavioral perspective**. Improper conditioning leads to criminal behavior.

- **Humanistic-existential perspective**. Antisocial behavior is the result of failure on a personal level.[29]

Two key subtypes of psychological theories to receive their share of support in explaining criminal behavior are *personality-disorder theories* and *mental dysfunction theories*.

Personality-Disorder Theories

The psychopathic personality theory is perhaps the most visible personality-disorder theory today. The psychopath has been defined as "a person with an antisocial personality disorder, especially one manifested in aggressive, perverted, or criminal behavior."[30] Others view the psychopathic individual as one who is "mentally unstable, antisocial, amoral, hostile, egocentric, insensitive, callous, and fearless."[31] According to W. Wille, murderers can be classified as: depressives, psychotics, psychopaths, passive-aggressives, and hysterical personalities.[32]

Some of the most extensive study on the psychopath has been done by William McCord and Joan McCord, who postulated that the two traits that set the psychopath apart from others are guiltlessness and lovelessness.[33] They attribute the psychopathic personality to brain damage, physical trauma, and severe emotional deprivation during childhood.

Another type of personality-disorder theory is the *criminal personality theory*.[34] Developed by Samuel Yochelson and Stanton Samenow after years of studying violent criminal patients, the theory held that violent offenders sought out excitement through criminal activity, in response to the boredom of normal family life. The researchers rejected explanations for criminal behavior outside the individual.

Both psychopathic personality theory and criminal personality theory have been criticized for their lack of scientific validation. Furthermore, psychopathic adults are believed to account for less than one-quarter of all criminals, with the number of juvenile psychopaths proportionately much smaller.[35]

Mental Dysfunction Theories

Mental deficiency theories or *intelligence quotient (IQ) theories* have argued that criminal behavior is a reflection of low intelligence. While there was empirical support for early IQ research that found low intelligence to be a major cause of antisocial conduct,[36] more recent studies have, for the most part, found little difference between offenders and nonoffenders with respect to IQ.[37] However, research by Travis Hirschi and Michael Hindelang does suggest that a relationship exists between juvenile delinquency and intelligence.[38] IQ was shown to affect school performance, causing failure and incompetency, leading to antisocial behavior.

Mental illness theories have long purported criminal behavior, particularly violent criminality, to be caused by mental illness of some type. M. Guttmacher identified a number of types of killers including: schizophrenics acting in response to delusions and hallucinations, sociopaths, sadists, and persons with no major psychopathology.[39] However, most mental health experts contend that mental illness accounts for only a relatively small proportion of serious and violent criminals.[40] Environmental and situational variables are seen as more causal of criminal behavior.

SOCIOLOGICAL-CULTURAL THEORIES ON CRIME AND VIOLENCE

The sociological-cultural determinism approach to criminality tends to explain criminal behavior as a normal response to the social structure, social life, and cultural factors. Such prominent criminologists as Marvin Wolfgang and Franco Ferracuti have taken a sociological-cultural approach in their study of criminal homicides and a subculture of violence in society.[41] There are three primary perspectives within this thought: *social control theories, strain theories,* and *cultural transmission theories.*

Social Control Theories

Social control theories assume that all persons have the potential to commit criminal acts, but fear and social constraints prevents such. Criminality is explained as the result of external social control and internalized social values for some, creating the freedom to commit crimes. Control theorists are less concerned with what motivates one to violate the law than the social institutions that produce conditions favorable to committing crimes or refraining from such.

Prominent social control theories include *social disorganization theory, social bonding theory*, and *containment theory*. The concept of social disorganization was developed by the University of Chicago's sociology department, which became known as the Chicago School. This was used to describe "the breakdown in social conventional structure within a community...and the incapability of organizations, groups, and individuals [in] that community to effectively solve its problems."[42] Social disorganization theorists such as Clifford Shaw and Henry McKay contended that these ineffective social controls in certain areas directly correlated with the high crime rate.[43]

Social bonding theory was established by Travis Hirschi.[44] He advanced that a social bond consisting of attachment, commitment, involvement, and belief, tied youths to the social order. The weaker these bonds, the more likely one was to become involved in criminal activity.

A similar theory of containment was put forth by Walter Reckless, who believed that youths are restrained from becoming involved in antisocial behavior by a combination of inner and outer containments that act as buffers against the influences of criminal behavior.[45]

Social control theories have generally received empirical support for their basic principles. However, they have been criticized for failure to account for the role of internalized norms and values or the social-structural causes of criminality.

Strain Theories

Strain theories also evolved from the Chicago School, explaining crime as a response to a lack of socially approved opportunities. Two of the more influential strain theories are *theory of anomie* and *subcultural theory*.

The concept of anomie was developed by Emile Durkheim at the turn of the Twentieth century, in reference to a condition of relative normlessness within a group or society, whereby the social structure was unable to control deviance.[46] It was Robert Merton who applied anomie theory to society and cultural values in the United States.[47] He postulated that criminality was caused by the anomie interaction of culturally defined goals and the socially structured means of achieving them. Unequal access to approved means by some leads them to deviate from the norm, or commit crimes to achieve goals.

Although Merton's theory has been attacked for various shortcomings such as doubt that all Americans share the same goals and expectations for success, the sophistication of his work contributed to subsequent theories on the correlation between criminal behavior and differential economic opportunity.

Subcultural theories were established in the 1950s and 1960s, primarily to study lower class youth criminality and gang violence. Major contributors include Albert Cohen,[48] Walter Miller,[49] and James Short.[50] However, it was Richard Cloward and Lloyd Ohlin's opportunity theory that has been most influential in this school of thought.[51] The theory argued that the social structure largely influences one's access to legitimate and illegitimate means for achieving socially approved goals. It is the differential opportunity among the lower class, particularly youths and gangs, that the researchers believe results in deep frustration and involvement in criminal activities in order to achieve these goals. Critics have long argued that opportunity theory is flawed because of its concentration mainly on lower class criminality. Most agree that the theory does succeed in recognizing the existence of differential opportunity structures.

Cultural Transmission Theories

Cultural transmission theories view crime as learned behavior, or reflecting of the norms, values, beliefs, and behavior characteristics acquired from others. As such, cultural transmission theorists believe that criminal behavior is caused mainly "by conforming to the behavioral norms of a culture or subculture that are contrary to conventional norms and values with respect to behavior and the law."[52] Two of the more recognized cultural transmission theories are *differential association theory* and *social learning theory*.

Differential association theory was first introduced by Edwin Sutherland in his 1939 text *Principles of Criminology.*[53] The theory postulated that criminality is learned through interaction with those who frequently violate the law and express beliefs to justify their behavior. As such, crime is seen as a social rather than antisocial behavior, with the degree of involvement dependent upon the priority, frequency, intensity, and duration of one's criminal contacts and, inversely, noncrimnal contacts.

The major fault with differential association theory is that it cannot be validated through empirical testing. It has also been criticized for failing to explain how crime originated as a learned process. However, Sutherland's theory continues to receive overall support as a sociological explanation for criminal behavior.

Social learning theory is a modification of differential association theory. Developed by Robert Burgess and Ronald Akers, the theory posited that deviant behavior is learned through social interaction with persons who represent one's primary source of reinforcement.[54] These social reinforcements are seen as symbolic and verbal rewards for supporting group norms and expectations. Nonsocial reinforcements are noted, but believed to be less significant in the learning process and criminal behavior.

Critics of social learning theory contend that nonsocial reinforcers may actually be more influential than social reinforcers in antisocial behavior. Questions have also been raised about the scientific reliability of the theory. However, the basic belief of social learning theory has been empirically supported.[55] Furthermore, its principles have been incorporated within such later theoretical perspectives as deterrence theories and control theories.[56]

CRITICAL THEORIES OF CRIMINALITY AND CRIMINAL LAW

Critical or radical criminology is the most recent school of thought in theorizing on crime and violence. Its focus is more on the relationship between crime and social responses rather than an explanation for criminal behavior. In a study of homicide theories, Christine Rasche observed the critical school of thoughts' perspective on homicide:

> What causes [human] behaviors to be designated as crimes. . . . Why are some homicides designated as criminal while others are viewed as justified, or excused, or even mandatory (as in time of war)? The homicidal act remains the same, the outcome (a death) remains the same, but our interpretation of it and social responses to it varies considerably depending on how we label it.[57]

The critical criminological approach can be broken down into two inter-related yet different perspectives: *conflict theory* and *Marxist theory*. Conflict theory was introduced in the early Twentieth century by Thorsten Sellin.[58] The theory basically contends that crime is in effect the product of the powers that be in terms of the labeling mechanism. "When one nation conquers another and imposes its law over the conquered land, behaviors that might not have been acceptable yesterday may become criminalized today . . . . [As such], it is [more] important to understand the actions of norm creators, norm interpreters and norm enforcers than it is to understand norm breakers."[59]

Marxist theory, also known as radical theory on criminology, holds that the criminal laws themselves primarily serve the greater interests of the ruling class, who "use these laws to exploit, dominate and victimize the working and lower classes in order to perpetuate the economic and political system of capitalism."[60] As these laws are a function of the wealthy or capitalists, their socially harmful "crimes," including demoralization and exploitation, are generally not defined as crimes, unlike offenses that are labeled as such.[61]

Radical criminologists blame the high rate of street or lower class criminality on the economic functioning of the capitalist system, which creates unemployment and underemployment, leading to conditions that promote criminal behavior.

Critical criminology theories have been routinely criticized for their predictability, disregard for objective reality, failure to account for intragroup and racial and ethnic disparities in crime rates, and overstatement of principles.

NOTES

1. Christine E. Rasche, "Theorizing About Homicide: A Presentation on Theories Explaining Homicide and Other Crimes," in U.S. Department of Justice, *The Nature of Homicide: Trends and Changes - Proceedings of the 1996 Meeting of the Homicide Research Working Group* (Washington: National Institute of Justice, 1998), pp. 27-28.
2. *Ibid.*, p. 27.
3. *Ibid.* See also Cesare Beccaria, *On Crimes and Punishment*, trans. H. Paolucci (Indianapolis: Bobbs-Merrill, 1963). Originally published in 1764.
4. Rasche, "Theorizing About Homicide," p. 28.
5. *Ibid.* See also G. Vold and T. Bernard, *Theoretical Criminology*, 3rd ed. (Oxford: Oxford University Press, 1986).
6. See, for example, J. R. Harris, "On The Economics of Law and Order," *Journal of Political Economy 78* (1970): 165-74; R. F. Sullivan, "The Economics of Crime: An Introduction to the Literature," *Crime and Delinquency 19*, 2 (1973): 138-49.
7. F. E. Zimring and G. J. Hawkins, *Deterrence* (Chicago: University of Chicago Press, 1973).
8. See, for example, D. B. Cornish and R. V. Clark, eds., *The Reasoning Criminal: Rational Choice Perspectives on Offending* (New York: Springer, 1986).
9. Rasche, "Theorizing About Homicide," p. 28.
10. *Ibid.*, p. 29.
11. *Ibid.*
12. *Ibid.*
13. Cesare Lombroso and William Ferrero, *Criminal Man* (Montclair: Patterson Smith, 1972). Originally titled *L'Uomo Delinquente* in its 1876 publication. See also Charles Darwin, *Origin of Species* (New York: Bantam, 1999).
14. Ernest A. Hooten, *Crime and the Man* (Cambridge, Harvard University Press, 1939).
15. William A. Sheldon, *Varieties of Temperament* (New York: Harper & Row, 1942).
16. Sheldon Glueck and Eleanor T. Glueck, *Physique and Delinquency* (New York: Harper & Row, 1956).
17. Richard L. Dugdale, *The Jukes: A Study in Crime, Pauperism, and Heredity* (New York: Putnam, 1877).
18. Henry H. Goddard, *Feeblemindedness, Its Causes and Consequences* (New York: Macmillan, 1914).

19. Johannes Lange, *Crime as Destiny* (London: George Allen & Unwin, 1931). Originally published as *Vebrecken als Sochicksal* in 1928.

20. Karl O. Christiansen, "Seriousness of Criminality and Concordance Among Danish Twins," in R. Hood, ed., *Crime, Criminology and Public Policy* (London: Heinemann, 1977); Karl O. Christiansen, "A Preliminary Study of Criminality Among Twins," in Sarnoff A. Mednick and Karl O. Christiansen, eds., *Biosocial Bases of Criminal Behavior* (New York: Gardner Press, 1977).

21. Hans J. Eysenck, *The Inequality of Man* (San Diego: Edits Publishers, 1973), p. 167.

22. Bernard Hutchings and Sarnoff A. Mednick, "Registered Criminality in the Adoptive and Biological Parents of Registered Male Criminal Adoptees," in R. R. Fiene, D. Rosenthal, and H. Brill, eds., *Genetic Research in Psychiatry* (Baltimore: John Hopkins University Press, 1975).

23. S. A. Mednick, W. F. Gabrielli, and B. Hutchings, "Genetic Influences in Criminal Convictions: Evidence From an Adoption Cohort," *Science 234* (1984): 891-94.

24. Diana H. Fishbein, "Biological Perspectives in Criminology," in Dean G. Rojek and Gary F. Jensen, eds., *Exploring Delinquency: Causes and Control* (Los Angeles: Roxbury, 1996), p. 102.

25. See, for example, Vicki Pollock, Sarnoff A. Mednick, and William F. Gabrielli, Jr., "Crime Causation: Biological Theories," in Sanford H. Kadish, ed., *Encyclopedia of Crime and Justice*, Vol. 1 (New York: Free Press, 1983); H. D. Kletschka, "Violent Behavior Associated with Brain Tumors," *Minnesota Medicine 49* (1966): 1835-55.

26. Sigmund Freud, *New Introductory Lectures on Psychoanalysis* (New York: W. W. Norton, 1933).

27. R. Barri Flowers, *The Adolescent Criminal: An Examination of Today's Juvenile Offender* (Jefferson: McFarland, 1990), p. 119.

28. Joseph F. Sheley, *America's "Crime Problem": An Introduction to Criminology* (Belmont: Wadsworth, 1985), p. 202.

29. R. R. Bootzin and J. R. Acocella, *Abnormal Psychology: Current Perspectives*, 3rd ed. (New York: Random House, 1980). See also Robert K. Ressler, Ann W. Burgess, and John E. Douglas, *Sexual Homicide: Patterns and Motives* (New York: Lexington Books, 1988), pp. 4-7.

30. *The American Heritage Dictionary* (New York: Dell, 1994), p. 667.

31. Flowers, *The Adolescent Criminal*, p. 120.

32. W. Wille, *Citizens Who Commit Murder* (St. Louis: Warren Greene, 1974).

33. William McCord and Joan McCord, *The Psychopath* (Princeton: Van Nostrand, 1964). See also Lee N. Robins, *Deviant Children Grown Up* (Baltimore: Williams & Wilkins, 1966); F. Schulsinger, "Psychopathy: Heredity and Environment," *International Journal of Mental Health 1* (1972): 190-206.

34. Samuel Yochelson and Stanton E. Samenow, *The Criminal Personality*, Vol. 1 (New York: Jason Arsonson, 1976); Stanton E. Samenow, *Inside the Criminal Mind* (New York: Time Books, 1984).

35. Herbert C. Quay, "Crime Causation: Psychological Theories," in S. H. Kadish, ed., *Encyclopedia of Crime and Justice*, Vol. 1 (New York: Free Press, 1983), p. 340;

Herbert C. Quay, "Patterns of Delinquent Behavior," in Herbert C. Quay, ed., *Handbook of Juvenile Delinquency* (New York: Wiley-Interscience, 1987), pp. 118-38.

36. See, for example, Goddard, *Feeblemindedness, Its Causes and Consequences*; William Healy and Augusta Bronner, *Delinquency and Criminals: Their Making and Unmaking* (New York: Macmillan, 1926).

37. See, for example, S. H. Tulchin, *Intelligence and Crime* (Chicago: University of Chicago Press, 1972).

38. Travis Hirschi and Michael J. Hindelang, "Intelligence and Delinquency: A Revisionist Review," *American Sociological Review 42* (1977): 571-86.

39. M. Guttmacher, *The Mind of the Murderer* (New York: Arno Press, 1973).

40. Flowers, *The Adolescent Criminal*, p. 123; *President's Commission on Mental Health, Report to the President*, Vol. 1 (Washington: Government Printing Office, 1978).

41. Marvin Wolfgang, *Patterns in Criminal Homicide* (Philadelphia: University of Pennsylvania Press, 1958); Marvin Wolfgang and Franco Ferracuti, *The Subculture of Violence: Toward an Integrated Theory in Criminology* (London: Tavistock, 1967); Franco Ferracuti and Marvin Wolfgang, *Violence in Sardinia* (Rome: Bulzoni, 1970).

42. Flowers, *The Adolescent Criminal*, pp. 124-25. See also Robert E. Park and Ernest W. Burgess, *The City* (Chicago: University of Chicago Press, 1925).

43. Clifford R. Shaw and Henry D. McKay, *Juvenile Delinquency and Urban Areas* (Chicago: University of Chicago Press, 1969). See also Frederic M. Thrasher, *The Gang* (Chicago: University of Chicago Press, 1927).

44. Travis Hirschi, *Causes of Delinquency* (Berkeley: University of California Press, 1969).

45. Walter C. Reckless, *The Crime Problem*, 5th ed. (Santa Monica: Goodyear, 1973); Walter C. Reckless, Simon Dinitz, and Ellen Murray, "Self-Concept as an Insulator Against Delinquency," in James E. Teele, ed., *Juvenile Delinquency: A Reader* (Itasca: Peacock, 1970).

46. Emile Durkheim, *The Division of Labor in Society*, George Simpson, trans. (New York: Free Press, 1933).

47. Robert K. Merton, "Social Structure and Anomie," *American Sociological Review 8* (1938): 672-82; Robert K. Merton, *Social Theory and Social Structure* (New York: Free Press, 1957).

48. Albert K. Cohen, *Delinquent Boys* (New York: Free Press, 1955); Albert K. Cohen and James F. Short, Jr., "Research on Delinquent Subcultures," *Journal of Social Issues 14*, 3 (1958): 20-37.

49. Walter B. Miller, *Violence by Youth Gangs and Youth Groups as a Crime Problem in Major American Cities* (Washington: Law Enforcement Administration, 1975); Walter B. Miller, "Lower-Class Culture as a Generating Milieu of Gang Delinquency," *Journal of Social Issues 14* (1958): 5-19.

50. James F. Short, Jr., "Gang Delinquency and Anomie," in Marshall B. Clinard, ed., *Anomie and Deviant Behavior* (New York: Free Press, 1964), pp. 98-127.

51. Richard A. Cloward and Lloyd F. Ohlin, *Delinquency and Opportunity: A Theory of Delinquent Gangs* (New York: Free Press, 1960).

52. Flowers, *The Adolescent Criminal*, p. 129.

53. Edwin H. Sutherland, *Principles of Criminology* (Philadelphia: Lippincott, 1939); Edwin H. Sutherland and Donald R. Cressey, *Criminology*, 9th ed. (Philadelphia: Lippincott, 1974).

54. Robert L. Burgess and Ronald L. Akers, "A Differential Association-Reinforcement Theory of Criminal Behavior," *Social Problems 14* (1966): 128-47; Ronald L. Akers, *Deviant Behavior: A Social Learning Approach*, 3rd ed. (Belmont: Wadsworth, 1985).

55. See, for example, Barry McLaughlin, *Learning and Social Behavior* (New York: Free Press, 1971); Arthur Staats, *Social Behaviorism* (Homewood: Dorsey Press, 1975); Werner Honig, *Operant Behavior: Areas of Research and Application* (New York: Appleton-Century-Crofts, 1966).

56. See, for example, Hirschi, *Causes of Delinquency*; Akers, Deviant Behavior; M. P. Feldman, *Criminal Behavior: A Psychological Analysis* (London: Wiley, 1977).

57. Rasche, "Theorizing About Homicide," p. 31.

58. Thorsten Sellin, *Culture Conflict and Crime* (New York: Social Science Research Council, 1938).

59. Rasche, "Theorizing About Homicide," p. 31. See also Thomas Bernard, "The Distinction Between Conflict and Radical Criminology," *Journal of Criminal Law and Criminology 72* (1981): 366-70.

60. Flowers, *The Adolescent Criminal*, p. 132; R. Barri Flowers, *Minorities and Criminality* (Westport: Greenwood, 1988), pp. 71-72.

61. Gresham M. Sykes, "The Rise and Fall of Critical Criminology," *Journal of Criminal Law and Criminology 65* (1974): 206-13.

REFERENCES

Akers, Ronald L. (1985) *Deviant Behavior: A Social Learning Approach*, 3rd ed. Belmont: Wadsworth.

Alba, R. D., J. R. Logan, and P. Bellair. (1994) "Living With Crime: The Implications of Racial/Ethnic Differences in Suburban Location." *Social Forces 73*: 395-434.

Alexander, Yonah, and Michael S. Swetman. (2001) *Usama bin Laden's al-Quada: Profile of a Terrorist Network.* Ardsley: Transnational Publishers.

American Psychiatric Association. (1987) *Diagnostic and Statistical Manual of Mental Disorders*, 3rd ed. Washington: American Psychiatric Association.

_____. (1994) *Diagnostic and Statistical Manual of Mental Disorders*, 4th ed. Washington: American Psychiatric Association.

Arbetter, Sandra. (1995) "Family Violence; When We Hurt the Ones We Love." *Current Health 22*, 3: 6.

Auerhahn, Kathleen, and Robert N. Parker. (1999) "Drugs, Alcohol, and Homicide." In M. Dwayne Smith and Margaret A. Zahn, eds. *Studying and Preventing Homicide: Issues and Challenges.* Thousand Oaks: Sage, 1999.

Bachman, R. (1992) *Death and Violence on the Reservation: Homicide, Family Violence, and Suicide in American Indian Populations.* Westport: Auburn House.

Bailey, G. W., and N. P. Unnithan. (1994) "Gang Homicides in California: A Discriminate Analysis." *Journal of Criminal Justice 22*, 3: 267-75.

Barnard, G. W., M. Vera, and G. Newman. (1982) "'Till Death Do Us Part?' A Study of Spouse Murder." *Bulletin of the American Academy of Psychiatry and Law 10*: 271-80.

Battin, S. R., K. G. Hill, R. D. Abbott, R. F. Catalano, and J. D. Hawkins. (1998) "The Contribution of Gang Membership to Delinquency Beyond Delinquent Friends." *Criminology 36*: 93-115.

Beaman, V., J. L. Annest, J. A. Mercy, M. Kresnow, and D. A. Pollock. (2000) "Lethality of Firearm-Related Injuries in the United States Population." *Annals of Emergency Medicine 35*: 258-66.

Bean, F., and M. Tienda. (1987) *The Hispanic Population of the United States.* New York: Russell Sage.

Beasley, R. W., and G. Antunes. (1974) "The Etiology of Urban Crime: An Ecological Analysis." *Criminology 22*: 531-50.

Beccaria, Cesare. (1963) *On Crimes and Punishment.* Indianapolis: Bobbs-Merrill.

Bell, C. A. (1991) "Female Homicides in United States Workplaces, 1980-1985." *American Journal of Public Health 81*: 729-32.

Bender, L., and F. J. Curran. (1940) "Children and Adolescents Who Kill." *Journal of Criminal Psychopathology 1*, 4: 297.

Benedek, Elissa P. (1982) "Women and Homicide." In Bruce L. Danto, John Bruhns, and Austin H. Kutscher, eds. *The Human Side of Homicide*. New York: Columbia University Press.

Bergen, Peter L. (2001) *Holy War, Inc.: Inside the Secret World of Osama Bin Laden*. New York: Free Press.

Berkowitz, Leonard. (1986) "Some Varieties of Human Aggression: Criminal Violence as Coercion, Rule-Following, Impression Management and Impulsive Behavior." In Anne Campbell and John J. Gibbs, eds. *Violent Transaction s: The Limits of Personality*. Oxford: Basil Blackwell.

Berman, A. L. (1979) "Dyadic Death: Murder-Suicide." *Suicidal and Life Threatening Behavior 9*: 15.

Bernard, Thomas. (1981) "The Distinction Between Conflict and Radical Criminology." *Journal of Criminal Law and Criminology 72*: 366-70.

Bettin, Rebecca. Young Women's Resource Center. Testimony at Iowa House of Representatives Public Hearing on Dating Violence. March 31, 1992.

Bjerregaard, B., and A. J. Lizotte. (1995) "Gun Ownership and Gang Membership." *Journal of Criminal Law and Criminology 86:* 37-58.

Block, Carolyn R. (1985) "Race/Ethnicity and Patterns of Chicago Homicide, 1965-1981." *Crime and Delinquency 31:* 104-16.

_____, and Antigone Christakos. (1995) "Chicago Homicide From the Sixties to the Nineties: Major Trends in Lethal Violence." In U.S. Department of Justice. *Trends, Risks, and Interventions in Lethal Violence: Proceedings of the Third Annual Spring Symposium of the Homicide Research Working Group*. Washington: National Institute of Justice.

_____, A. Christakos, A. Jacob, and R. Przybylski. (1996) *Street Gangs and Crime: Patterns and Trends in Chicago*. Chicago: Illinois Criminal Justice Information Authority.

_____, and R. Block. (1995) "Street Gang Crime in Chicago." In M. W. Klein, C. L. Maxson, and J. Miller, eds. *The Modern Gang Reader*. Los Angeles: Roxbury.

Block, Herbert A., and Gilbert Geis. (1962) *Man, Crime, and Society*. New York: Random House.

Block, R., and C. R. Block. (1993) *Street Gang Crime in Chicago*. Washington: National Institute of Justice.

Blount, W. R., I. J. Silverman, C. S. Sellers, and R. A. Seese. (1994) "Alcohol and Drug Use Among Abused Women Who Kill, Abused Women Who Don't, and Their Abusers." *Journal of Drug Issues 24:* 165-77.

Blumstein, A. (1995) "Youth Violence, Guns, and the Illicit-Drug Industry." *Journal of Criminal Law and Criminology 86:* 10-36.

Bonger, W. (1943) *Race and Crime*. New York: Columbia University Press.

Bootzin, R. R., and J. R. Acocella. (1980) *Abnormal Psychology: Current Perspectives*, 3rd ed. New York: Random House.

Brown, J. S. (1991) "The Historical Similarity of 20th Century Serial Sexual Homicide to Pre 20th Century Occurrences of Vampirism." *American Journal of Forensic Psychiatry 12*, 2: 11-24.

Browne, Angela. (1987) *When Battered Women Kill*. New York: Free Press.

_____, and Kirk R. Williams. (1989) "Exploring the Effect of Resource Availability and the Likelihood of Female-Perpetrated Homicides." *Law and Society Review 23:* 75-94.

_____, Kirk R. Williams, and Donald G. Dutton. (1999) "Homicide Between Intimate Partners." In M. Dwayne Smith and Margaret A. Zahn, eds. *Studying and Preventing Homicide: Issues and Challenges*. Thousand Oaks, Sage.

Browning, F., and J. Gerassi. (1980) *The American Way of Crime*. New York: Putnam.

Brownstein, H. H., H. Baxi, P. Goldstein, and P. Ryan. (1992) "The Relationship of Drugs, Drug Trafficking, and Drug Traffickers to Homicide." *Journal of Crime and Justice 15:* 25-44.

Brumm, H. J., and D. O. Cloninger. (1995) "The Drug War and the Homicide Rate: A Direct Correlation?" *Cato Journal 14:* 509-17.

Burgess, A. W., C. R. Hartman, R. K. Ressler, J. E. Douglas, and A. McCormack. (1986) "Sexual Homicide." *Journal of Interpersonal Violence 1:* 251-72.

Burgess, Robert L., and Ronald L. Akers. (1966) "A Differential Association-Reinforcement Theory of Criminal Behavior." *Social Problems 14:* 128-47.

Buteau, Jacques, Alain Lesage, and Margaret Kiely. (1993) "Homicide Followed by Suicide: A Quebec Case series, 1988-1990." *Canadian Journal of Psychiatry 38:* 552-56.

Campbell, Anne. (1981) *Girl Delinquents.* New York: St. Martin's Press.

Campbell, Jacquelyn. (1992) "'If I Can't Have You, No One Can': Power and Control in Homicide of Female Partners." In J. Radford and D. E. Russell, eds. *Femicide: The Politics of Woman Killing.* New York: Twayne.

_____. (1995) *Assessing Dangerousness: Violence by Sexual Offenders, Batterers, and Child Abusers.* Thousand Oaks: Sage.

_____. (1995) "Prediction of Homicide of and by Battered Women." In J. Campbell and J. Milner, eds. *Assessing Dangerousness: Potential for Further Violence of Sexual Offenders, Batterers, and Child Abusers.* Thousand Oaks: Sage.

Campion, J. F., J. M. Cravens, and F. Covan. (1988) "A Study of Filicidal Men." *American Journal of Psychiatry 145:* 1141.

Caputi, J. (1987) *The Age of Sex Crime.* Bowling Green: Bowling Green State University Press.

Carlson, Bonnie E. (1977) "Battered Women and Their Assailants." *Social Work 22,* 6: 456.

Castillo, Dawn N. (1995) "Nonfatal Violence in the Work Place: Directions for Future Research." In U.S. Department of Justice. *Trends Risks; and Interventions in Lethal Violence: Proceedings of the Third Annual Spring Symposium of the Homicide Research Working Group.* Washington: National Institute of Justice.

_____, and E. L. Jenkins. (1994) "Industries and Occupations at High Risk for Work-Related Homicide." *Journal of Occupational Medicine 36:* 125-32.

Chaimberlain, T. (1986) "The Dynamics of Parricide." *American Journal of Forensic Psychiatry 7:* 11-23.

Chapman, S. G. (1986) *Cops, Killers and Staying Alive: The Murder of Police Officers in America.* Springfield: Charles C Thomas.

Christiansen, Karl O. (1977) "A Preliminary Study of Criminality Among Twins." In Sarnoff A. Mednick and Karl O. Christiansen, eds. *Biosocial Bases of Criminal Behavior.* New York: Gardner Press.

_____. (1977) "Seriousness of Criminality and Concordance Among Danish Twins." In R. Hood, ed. *Crime, Criminology and Public Policy.* London: Heinemann.

Cloward, Richard A., and Lloyd E. Ohlin. (1960) *Delinquency and Opportunity: A Theory of Delinquent Gangs.* New York: Free Press.

Cohen, Albert K. (1951) *Delinquent Boys: The Culture of the Gang.* New York: Free Press.

_____, and James F. Short, Jr. (1958) "Research on Delinquent Subcultures." *Journal of Social Issues 14,* 3: 20-37.

Cohen, Daniel A. (1995) "Homicidal Compulsion and the Conditions of Freedom: The Social and Psychological Origins of Familicide in America's Early Republic." *Journal of Social History.* Summer: 725-64.

Commonwealth Fund, The. "First Comprehensive National Health Survey of American Women Finds Them at Significant Risk." News release. New York. July 14, 1993.

Cook, Philip J. (1981) "The Effect of Gun Availability on Violent Crime Patterns." *Annals of the American Academy of Political and Social Sciences 455:* 63-79.

_____, and J. Ludwig. (1996) *Guns in America: Results of a Comprehensive National Survey on Firearms Ownership and Use.* Washington: Police Foundation.

_____, and Mark H. Moore. (1999) "Guns, Gun Control, and Homicide." In M. Dwayne Smith and Margaret A. Zahn, eds. *Studying and Preventing Homicide: Issues and Challenges.* Thousand Oaks: Sage.

Cooper, H. A. (1982) "Terroristic Fads and Fashions." In B. L. Danto and A. H. Kutscher, eds. *The Human Side of Homicide.* New York: Columbia University Press.

Cormier, B. S., and S. P. Simmons. (1969) "The Problem of the Dangerous Sexual Offender." *Canadian Psychiatric Association 14:* 329-34.

Cornish, D. B., and R. V. Clark, eds. (1986) *The Reasoning Criminal: Rational Choice Perspectives on Offending.* New York: Springer.

Crow, W. J., and R. Erickson. (1989) *The Store Safety Issue: Facts for the Future.* Alexandria: National Association of Convenience Stores.

Curry, G. D., and S. H. Decker. (1998) *Confronting Gangs: Crime and Community.* Los Angeles: Roxbury.

Daly, Martin, and Margo Wilson. (1982) "Homicide and Kinship." *American Anthropologist 84:* 372-78.

Damphousse, Kelly, Victoria E. Brewer, and Cary D. Atkinson. (1999) "Gangs, Race/Ethnicity and Houston Homicide in the 1990s." In U.S. Department of Justice. *Proceedings of the Homicide Research Working Group Meetings, 1997 and 1998.* Washington: National Institute of Justice.

Darwin, Charles. (1999) *Origin of Species.* New York: Bantam.

Davis, H. P., A. Honchar, and L. Suarez. (1987) "Fatal Occupational Injuries of Women, Texas 1975-1984." *American Journal of Public Health 77:* 1524-27.

Decker, S. H., and B. Van Winkle. (1996) *Life in the Gang: Family, Friends, and Violence.* New York: Cambridge University Press.

_____, S. Pennell, and A. Caldwell. (1997) *Illegal Firearms: Access and Use by Arrestees.* Washington: National Institute of Justice.

Dietz, P .E. (1986) "Mass, Serial and Sensational Homicides." *Bulletin of the New York Academy of Medicine 62:* 477-91.

Dobash, R. E., R. Dobash, M. Wilson, and M. Daly. (1992) "The Myth of Sexual Symmetry in Marital Violence." *Social Problems 39,* 1: 71-91.

Dugdale, Richard L. (1877) *The Jukes: A Study in Crime, Pauperism, and Heredity.* New York: Putnam.

Durkheim, Emile. (1897) *Le Suicide.* Paris: Alcain.

_____. (1933) *The Division of Labor in Society.* New York: Free Press.

Easteal, Patricia W. (1993) *Killing the Beloved: Homicide Between Adult Sexual Intimates.* Canberra: Australian Institute of Criminology.

Egger, S. A. (1984) "A Working Definition of Serial Murder and the Reduction of Linkage Blindness." *Journal of Police Science and Administration 12:* 348-57.

Egger, S. S. (1990) "Serial Murder." In S. A. Egger, ed. *Serial Murder.* New York: Praeger.

Elliot, D. S., D. Huizinga, and S. Menard. (1989) *Multiple Problem Youth: Delinquency, Substance Abuse, and Mental Health Problems.* New York: Springer-Verlag.

Erickson, R. (1991) "Convenience Store Homicide and Rape." In U.S. Department of Justice. *Convenience Store Security: Report and Recommendations.* Alexandria: U.S. Department of Justice.

Esbensen, F., and D. W. Osgood. (1997) *National Evaluation of G.R.E.A.T.* Research in Brief. Washington: National Institute of Justice.

Ewing, Charles P. (1997) *Fatal Families: The Dynamics of Intrafamilial Homicide.* Thousand Oaks: Sage.

Eysench, Hans J. (1973) *The Inequality of Man.* San Diego: Edits Publishers.

Fagan, J. (1989) "The Social Organization of Drug Use and Drug Dealing Among Urban Gangs." *Criminology 27:* 633-69.

_____. (1990) "Intoxication and Aggression." In M. Tonry and J. Q. Wilson, eds. *Drugs and Crime.* Chicago: University of Chicago Press.

_____. (1993) *Set and Setting Revisited: Influences of Alcohol and Illicit Drugs on the Social Context of Violent Events.* Rockville: National Institution on Alcohol Abuse and Alcoholism Research.

_____, D. Stewart, and K. Hanson. (1983) "Violent Men or Violent Husbands: Background Factors and Situational Correlates of Domestic and Extra-Domestic Violence." In D. Finkelhor, R. Gelles, G. Hotaling, and M. Straus, eds. *The Dark Side of Families.* Thousand Oaks: Sage.

Feldman, M. P. (1977) *Criminal Behavior: A Psychological Analysis.* London: Wiley.

Fendrich, M., M. E. Mackesy-Amiti, P. Goldstein, B. Spunt, and H. Brownstein. (1995) "Substance Involvement Among Juvenile Murderers: Comparisons with Older Offenders Based on Interviews with Prison Inmates." *International Journal of the Addictions 30:* 1363-82.

Ferracuti, Franco, and Marvin Wolfgang. (1970) *Violence in Sardinia.* Rome: Bulzoni.

Fingerhut, L. A., and J. C. Kleinman. (1990) "International and Interstate Comparisons of Homicide Among Young Males." *Journal of the American Medical Association 263:* 292-95.

Fishbein, Diana H. (1996) "Biological Perspectives in Criminology." In Dean G. Rojek and Gary F. Jensen, eds. *Exploring Delinquency: Causes and Control.* Los Angeles: Roxbury.

Fisher, Dawn. (1994) "Adult Sex Offenders: Who Are They? Why and How Do They Do It?" In Tony Morrison, Marcus Erooga, and Richard C. Beckett, eds. *Sexual Offending Against Children: Assessment and Treatment of Male Abusers.* New York: Routledge.

Flowers, R. Barri. (1986) *Children and Criminality: The Child as Victim and Perpetrator.* Westport: Greenwood.

_____. (1988) *Minorities and Criminality.* Westport: Greenwood.

_____. (1989) *Demographics and Criminality: The Characteristics of Crime in America.* Westport: Greenwood.

_____. (1990) *The Adolescent Criminal: An Examination of Today's Juvenile Offender.* Jefferson: McFarland.

_____. (1994) *The Victimization and Exploitation of Women and Children: A Study of Physical, Mental and Sexual Maltreatment in the United States.* Jefferson: McFarland.

_____. (1995) *Female Crime, Criminals and Cellmates: An Exploration of Female Criminality and Delinquency.* Jefferson: McFarland.

_____. (1996) *The Sex Slave Murders.* New York: St. Martin's Press.

_____. (1998) *The Prostitution of Women and Girls.* Jefferson: McFarland.

_____. (1999) *Drugs, Alcohol and Criminality in American Society.* Jefferson: McFarland.

_____. (2000) *Domestic Crimes, Family Violence and Child Abuse: A Study of Contemporary American Society.* Jefferson: McFarland.

_____. (2001) *Sex Crimes, Predators, Perpetrators, Prostitutes, and Victims: An Examination of Sexual Criminality and Victimization.* Springfield: Charles C Thomas.

_____. (2002) *Kids Who Commit Adult Crimes: A Study of Serious Juvenile Criminality and Delinquency.* Binghampton: Haworth.

_____. (2003) *Male Crime and Deviance: Exploring its Dynamics, Nature, and Causes.* Springfield: Charles C Thomas.

_____, and H. Loraine Flowers. (2001) *Murders in the United States: Crimes, Killers and Victims of the Twentieth Century.* Jefferson: McFarland.

Fontana, Vincent J. (1973) *Somewhere A Child is Crying.* New York: Macmillan.

Fox, James A., and Jack Levin. (1999) "Serial Murder: Myths and Realities." In M. Dwayne Smith and Margaret A. Zahn, eds. *Studying and Preventing Homicide: Issues and Challenges.* Thousand Oaks: Sage.

Freeman, M. A. (1979) *Violence in the Home.* Farnborough: Saxon House.

Freud, Sigmund. (1933) *New Introductory Lectures on Psychoanalysis.* New York: W. W. Norton.

Gallup, George, Jr., and Alec Gallup. (1999) *The Gallup Poll Monthly*, No. 401. Princeton: The Gallup Poll.

Gayford, J. J. (1975) "Wife Battering: A Preliminary Survey of 100 Cases." *British Medical Journal 1:* 194-97.

Gee, D. J. (1988) "A Pathologist's View of Multiple Murder." *Forensic Science International 38:* 53-65.

Gelles, Richard J. (1972) T*he Violent Home: A Study of Physical Aggression Between Husbands and Wives*. Thousand Oaks: Sage.

_____. "The Myth of Battered Husbands." *Ms* (October 1979): 65-66, 71-72.

_____, and Murray A. Straus. (1979) "Violence in the American Family." *Journal of Social Issues 35*, 2: 15-39.

Glueck, Sheldon, and Eleanor T. Glueck. (1956) *Physique and Delinquency*. New York: Harper & Row.

Goddard, Henry H. (1914) *Feeblemindedness, Its Causes and Consequences*. New York: Macmillan.

Goldney, R. D. (1989) "Suicidal Ideation in a Young Adult Population." *Acta Psychiatrica Scandinavica 79:* 481-9.

Goldstein, P. J., H. H. Brownstein, P. J. Ryan, and P. A. Bellucci. (1989) "Crack and Homicide in New York City, 1988: A Conceptually Based Event Analysis." *Contemporary Drug Problems 16:* 651-87.

_____, P. A. Bellucci, B. J. Spunt, and T. Miller. (1989) *Frequency of Cocaine Use and Violence: A Comparison Between Women and Men*. New York: Narcotic and Drug Research.

Graves, R. (1962) *Greek Myths*. New York: Penguin.

Green, Edward. (1970) "Race, Social Status, and Criminal Arrest." *American Sociological Review 35:* 476-90.

Guttmacher, M. (1973) *The Mind of the Murderer*. New York: Arno Press.

Hagedorn, J. J. (1988) *People and Folks: Gangs, Crime and the Underclass in a Rustbelt City*. Chicago: Lakeview Press.

Hales, T., P. Seligman, C. Newman, and C. L. Timbrook. (1988) "Occupational Injuries Due to Violence." *Journal of Occupational Medicine 30:* 483-87.

Harries, K. (1990) *Serious Violence: Patterns of Homicide and Assault in America*. Springfield: Charles C Thomas.

Harris, J. R. (1970) "On The Economics of Law and Order." *Journal of Political Economy 78:* 165-74.

Harris, M. B. (1996) "Aggression, Gender, and Ethnicity." *Aggression and Violent Behavior 1*, 2: 123-46.

Harrison, Maureen, and Steve Gilbert. (1996) *The Murder Reference: Everything You Never Wanted to Know About Murder in America*. San Diego: Excellent Books.

Harry, J. (1989) "Sexual Identity Issues." In *Report of the Secretary's Task Force Report on Youth Suicide*, Vol. 2. Washington: Department of Health and Human Services.

Hawkins, Darnell F. (1990) "Explaining the Black Homicide Rate." *Journal of Interpersonal Violence 5:* 151-63.

_____. (1999) "African Americans and Homicide." In M. Dwayne Smith and Margaret A. Zahn, eds. *Studying and Preventing Homicide: Issues and Challenges*. Thousand Oaks: Sage.

Hazelwood, R. R., and J. Douglas. (1980) "The Last Murder." *FBI Law Enforcement Bulletin 49:* 1-8.

_____, P. E. Dietz, and J. Warren. (1992) "The Criminal Sexual Sadist." *FBI Law Enforcement Bulletin 61:* 12-20.

Healy, William, and Augusta Bronner (1926) *Delinquency and Criminals: Their Making and Unmaking*. New York: Macmillan.

Heide, Kathleen M. (1993) "Parents Who Get Killed and the Children Who Kill Them." *Journal of Interpersonal Violence 8*, 4: 531-44.

_____. (1995) *Why Kids Kill Parents: Child Abuse and Adolescent Homicide*. Thousand Oaks: Sage.

_____. (1996) "Why Kids Keep Killing: The Correlates, Causes, and Challenges of Juvenile Homicide." *Stanford Law and Policy Review 71*: 43-49.

_____. (1997) "1998 Keynote Address: School Shootings and School Violence: What's Going on and Why?" In U.S. Department of Justice. *Proceedings of the Homicide Research Working Group Meetings, 1997 and 1998*. Washington: National Institute of Justice.

_____. (1997) "Dangerously Antisocial Kids Who Kill Their Parents: Toward a Better Understanding of the Phenomenon." In U.S. Department of Justice. *The Nature of Homicide: Trends and Changes–Proceedings of the 1996 Meeting of the Homicide Research Working Group*. Washington: National Institute of Justice.

_____. (1999) "Youth Homicide." In M. Dwayne Smith and Margaret A. Zahn, eds. *Studying and Preventing Homicide: Issues and Challenges*. Thousand Oaks: Sage.

_____. (1999) *Young Killers: The Challenge of Juvenile Homicide*. Thousand Oaks: Sage.

Hickey, E. (1991) *Serial Killers and Their Victims*. Pacific Grove: Brooks/Cole.

_____. (1997) *Serial Murderers and Their Victims*. 2nd ed. Belmont: Wadsworth.

Hirschi, Travis. (1969) *Causes of Delinquency*. Berkeley: University of California Press.

_____, and Michael J. Hindelang. (1977) "Intelligence and Delinquency: A Revisionist Review." *American Sociological Review 42*: 571-86.

Holmes, Ronald M. (1990) "Human Hunters." *Knightbeat 9*, 1: 43-47.

_____, and J. E. DeBurger. (1985) "Profiles in Terror." *Federal Probation 49*, 3: 53-61.

_____, and J. E. DeBurger. (1988) *Serial Murder*. Thousand Oaks: Sage.

_____, and S. T. Holmes. (1992) "Understanding Mass Murder." *Federal Probation 56*, 1: 53-61.

_____, and Stephen T. Holmes. (1994) *Murder in America*. Thousand Oaks: Sage.

Honig, Werner. (1966) *Operant Behavior: Areas of Research and Application*. New York: Appleton-Century-Crofts.

Hooten, Ernest A. (1939) *Crime and the Man*. Cambridge, Harvard University Press.

Horney, Julie. (1978) "Menstrual Cycles and Criminal Responsibility." *Law and Human Behavior 2*, 1: 25-36.

Houts, M. (1970) *They Asked for Death*. New York: Cowles.

Howell, J. C. (1995) "Gangs and Youth Violence." In J. C. Howell, B. Krisberg, J. D. Hawkins, and J. J. Wilson, eds. *A Sourcebook: Serious, Violent and Chronic Juvenile Offenders*. Thousand Oaks: Sage.

Huizinga, D. R. (1997) "The Volume of Crime by Gang and Nongang Members," paper presented at the Annual Meeting of the American Society of Criminology. San Diego.

_____, R. Loeber, and T. P. Thornberry. (1994) *Urban Delinquency and Substance Abuse*. Washington: Office of Justice Programs.

Hutchings, Bernard, and Sarnoff A. Mednick. (1975) "Registered Criminality in the Adoptive and Biological Parents of Registered Male Criminal Adoptees." In R. R. Fiene, D. Rosenthal, and H. Brill, eds. *Genetic Research in Psychiatry*. Baltimore: John Hopkins University Press.

Hutson, H. R., D. Anglin, and M. Eckstein. (1996) "Drive-by Shootings by Violent Street Gangs in Los Angeles: A Five-Year Review From 1989 to 1993." *Academic Emergency Medicine 3*: 300-3.

Inciardi, J. A., and A. E. Pottieger. (1991) "Kids, Crack, and Crime." *Journal of Drug Issues 21*: 257-70.

Jamison, Kay R. (1999) *Night Falls Fast: Understanding Suicide*. New York: Vintage.

Jenkins, P. (1988) "Serial Murder in England, 1940-1985." *Journal of Criminal Justice 16*: 1-15.

_____. (1990) "Sharing Murder." *Journal of Crime and Justice 12*: 125-48.

_____. (1992) "A Murder 'Wave'?" *Criminal Justice Review 17*, 1: 1-19.

Jung, R. S., and L. A. Jason. (1988) "Firearm Violence and the Effects of Gun Control Legislation." *American Journal of Community Psychology 16*: 515-24.

Jurik, N. C., and R. Winn. (1990) "Gender and Homicide: A Comparison of Men and Women Who Kill." *Violence and Victims 5*, 4: 227-42.

Kalmuss, D. S. (1984) "The Intergenerational Transmission of Marital Aggression." *Journal of Marriage and the Family 46:* 16-19.

Kantor, Glenda K., and Jana L. Jasinski. (1998) "Dynamics and Risk Factors in Partner Violence." In Jana L. Jasinski and Linda M. Williams, eds. *Partner Violence: A Comprehensive Review of 20 Years of Research.* Thousand Oaks: Sage.

_____, and Murray A. Straus. (1989) "Substance Abuse as a Precipitant of Wife Abuse Victimization." *American Journal of Drug and Alcohol Abuse 15:* 173-89.

Kasarda, J. (1993) "Inner-City Concentrated Poverty and Neighborhood Distress: 1970-1990." *Housing Policy Debate 4*, 3: 253-302.

Kellermann, A. L., and J. A. Mercy. (1992) "Men, Women, and Murder: Gender-Specific Differences in Rates of Fatal Violence and Victimization." *Journal of Trauma 33:* 1-5.

_____, F. P. Rivara, N. B. Rushforth, J. G. Banton, D. T. Reay, J. T. Francisco, A. B. Locci, J. P. Prodzinski, B. B. Hackman, and G. Somes. (1993) "Gun Ownership as a Risk Factor for Homicide in the Home." *New England Journal of Medicine 329:* 1084-91.

Kennedy, D. M., A. A. Braga, and A. M. Piehl. (1997) "The (Un)Known Universe: Mapping Gangs and Gang Violence in Boston." In D. Weisburd and T. McEwen, eds. *Crime Mapping and Crime Prevention.* New York: Criminal Justice Press.

Keppel, Robert D., and William J. Birnes. (1997) *Signature Killers: Interpreting the Calling Cards of the Sexual Murderer.* New York: Pocket Books.

Kleck, G. (1991) *Point Blank: Guns and Violence in America.* New York: Aldine de Gruyter.

Kleiman, D. (1988) *A Deadly Silence.* New York: Atlantic Monthly Press.

Klein, M. W. (1995) *The American Street Gang: Its Nature, Prevalence, and Control.* New York: Oxford.

_____, C. L. Maxson, and L. C. Cunningham. (1991) "'Crack,' Street Gangs, and Violence." *Criminology 29:* 623-50.

Kletschka, H. D. (1966) "Violent Behavior Associated with Brain Tumors." *Minnesota Medicine 49:* 1835-55.

Kraus, J. F. (1987) "Homicides While at Work: Persons, Industries, and Occupations at High Risk." *American Journal of Public Health 77*, 10: 1285-89.

Krugman, Richard D. (1983-1985) "Fatal Child Abuse: An Analysis of 20 Cases." *Pediatrics 12:* 68-72.

Kuehl, S. (1998) "Legal Remedies for Teen Dating Violence." In Barbara Levy, ed. *Dating Violence: Young Women in Danger.* Seattle: Seal Press.

LaFree, G. (1995) "Race and Crime Trends in the United States, 1946-1990." In D. F. Hawkins, ed. *Ethnicity, Race and Crime: Perspectives Across Time and Place.* Albany: State University of New York Press.

Lange, Johannes. (1931) *Crime as Destiny.* London: George Allen & Unwin.

Langevin, R., M. H. Ben-Aron, P. Wright, V. Marchese, and L. Handy. (1988) "The Sex Killer." *Annals of Sex Research 1:* 263-301.

Langley, Robert, and Richard C. Levy. (1977) *Wife Beating: The Silent Crisis.* New York: Dutton.

Laquer, Walter. (1987) *The Age of Terrorism.* New York: Little Brown.

Leibman, F. H. (1989) "Serial Murderers." *Federal Probation 53*, 4: 41-45.

Lerner, R. M. (1994) *America's Youth in Crisis.* Thousand Oaks: Sage.

Lester, David. (1995) *Serial Killers: The Insatiable Passion.* Philadelphia: Charles Press.

Leventhal, John M. (1999) "The Challenges of Recognizing Child Abuse: Seeing is Believing." *Journal of the American Medical Association 281*, 7: 657.

Levin, J., and J. A. Fox. (1985) *Mass Murder.* New York: Plenum.

Levine, Murray, Jennifer Freeman, and Cheryl Compaan. (1994) "Maltreatment-Related Fatalities: Issues of Policy and Prevention." *Law and Policy 16*, 449: 458.

Leyton, E. (1986) *Compulsive Killers.* New York: New York University Press.

———. (1989) *Hunting Humans.* London: Penguin.

Lichtblau, Eric. "A Long Road for Massip: Postpartum Psychosis: Recovery is Torturous." *Los Angeles Times* (February 3, 1989), p. 1-1.

Lin, William. (1997) "Perpetrators of Hate." *Yale Political Quarterly 19*, 2: 12.

Lindquist, P. (1991) "Homicides Committed by Abusers of Alcohol and Illicit Drugs." *British Journal of Addiction 86:* 321-26.

Liscomb, J. A., and C. C. Love. (1992) "Violence Toward Health Care Workers: An Emerging Occupational Hazard." *American Association of Occupational Health Nurses Journal 40:* 219-28.

Liss, G. M., and C. A. Craig. (1990) "Homicide in the Workplace in Ontario: Occupations at Risk and Limitations of Existing Data Sources." *Canadian Journal of Public Health 81:* 10-15.

Lizotte, A. J., J. M. Tesoriero, T. P. Thornberry, and M. D. Krohn. (1994) "Patterns of Adolescent Firearms Ownership and Use." *Justice Quarterly 11:* 51-73.

Lombroso, Cesare, and William Ferrero. (1972) *Criminal Man.* Montclair: Patterson Smith.

Lunde, D. T. (1975) "Hot Blood's Record Month: Our Murder Boom," *Psychology Today 9:* 35-42.

———. (1979) *Murder and Madness.* New York: Norton.

Maloney, Michael. (1994) "Children Who Kill Their Parents." *Prosecutor's Brief: California District Attorney's Association Journal 20:* 20-22.

Martinez, Ramiro. (1996) "Latinos and Lethal Violence: The Impact of Poverty and Inequality." *Social Problems 43:* 131-46.

———. (1997) "Homicide Among Miami's Ethnic Groups: Anglos, Blacks, and Latinos in the 1990s." *Homicide Studies 1:* 17-34.

———, and Matthew T. Lee. (1999) "Latinos and Homicide." In M. Dwayne Smith and Margaret A. Zahn, eds. *Studying and Preventing Homicide: Issues and Challenges.* Thousand Oaks: Sage.

Marzuk, Peter M., Kenneth Tardiff, and Charles S. Hirsh. (1992) "The Epidemiology of Murder-Suicide." *Journal of the American Medical Association 267*, 23: 3179-83.

Maxson, Cheryl. (1999) "Gang Homicide." In M. Dwayne Smith and Margaret A. Zahn, eds. *Studying and Preventing Homicide: Issues and Challenges.* Thousand Oaks: Sage.

———, and M. W. Klein. (1996) "Defining Gang Homicide: An Updated Look at Member and Motive Approaches." In C. R. Huff, ed. *Gangs in America,* 2nd ed. Thousand Oaks: Sage.

Mayhall, Pamela D., and Katherine Norgard. (1983) *Child Abuse and Neglect: Sharing Responsibility.* Toronto: John Wiley & Sons.

McCord, William, and Joan McCord. (1964) *The Psychopath.* Princeton: Van Nostrand.

McDowall, D., C. Loftin, and B. Wiersema. (1995) "Easing Concealed Firearms Laws: Effects on Homicide in Three States." *Journal of Criminal Law and Criminology 86:* 193-206.

McLaughlin, Barry. (1971) *Learning and Social Behavior.* New York: Free Press.

Mednick, S. A., W. F. Gabrielli, and B. Hutchings. (1984) "Genetic Influences in Criminal Convictions: Evidence From an Adoption Cohort." *Science 234:* 891-94.

Meehan, P. J., and P. W. O'Carroll. (1992) "Gangs, Drugs, and Homicide in Los Angeles." *American Journal of Disease Control 146:* 683-87.

Meloy, J. R. (1992) *Violent Attachments.* Northvale: Aronson.

Merton, Robert K. (1938) "Social Structure and Anomie." *American Sociological Review 8:* 672-82.

———. (1957) *Social Theory and Social Structure.* New York: Free Press.

Miller, Walter B. (1958) "Lower-Class Culture as a Generating Milieu of Gang Delinquency." *Journal of Social Issues 14:* 5-19.

———. (1970) "White Gangs." In James F. Short, Jr., ed. *Modern Criminals.* Chicago: Aldine.

———. (1974) "American Youth Gangs: Past and Present." In A. Blumberg, ed. *Current Perspectives in Criminal Behavior.* New York: Knopf.

_____. (1975) *Violence by Youth Gangs and Youth Groups as a Crime Problem in Major American Cities*. Washington: Government Printing Office.

_____. (1992) *Crime by Youth Gangs and Groups in the United States*. Washington: Office of Justice Programs.

Mones, P. A. (1991) *When A Child Kills: Abused Children Who Kill Their Parents*. New York: Pocket Books.

Money, J. (1990) "Forensic Sexology." *American Journal of Psychotherapy 44:* 26-36.

Moore, J. W. (1978) *Homeboys: Gangs, Drugs and Prison in the Barrios of Los Angeles*. Philadelphia: Temple University Press.

_____. (1990) "Gangs, Drugs, and Violence." In M. De La Rosa, E. Y. Lambert, and B. Gropper, eds. *Drugs and Violence: Causes, Correlates, and Consequences*. Rockville: National Institute on Drug Abuse.

Morales, Alex. (1998) "Seeking a Cure for Child Abuse," *USA Today 127*, 2640: 34.

Morris, C. (1967) *The Tudors*. London: Fontana.

National Youth Gang Center. (1997) *1995 National Youth Gang Survey*. Washington: Office of Juvenile Justice and Delinquency Prevention.

Newhill, C. E. (1991) "Parricide." *Journal of Family Violence 64:* 375-94.

Norris, Joel. (1989) *Serial Killers*. New York: Anchor.

Northwest National Life. (1993) *Fear and Violence in the Workplace: A Survey Documenting the Experience of American Workers*. Minneapolis: Northwest National Life.

O'Brien, Shirley. (1980) *Child Abuse: Commission and Omission*. Provo: Brigham Young University Press.

Oliver, J. E. (1978) "The Epidemiology of Child Abuse." In Selwyn M. Smith, ed. *The Maltreatment of Children*. Baltimore: University Park Press.

Osgood, D. W. (1995) *Drugs, Alcohol, and Violence*. Boulder: University of Colorado, Institute of Behavioral Science.

Pagelow, M. D. (1984) *Family Violence*. New York: Praeger.

Palmer, Stuart, and John A. Humphrey. (1980) "Offender-Victim Relationships in Criminal Homicide Followed by Offender's Suicide, North Carolina, 1972-1977." *Suicide and Life-Threatening Behavior 10*, 2: 106-18.

Park, Robert E., and Ernest W. Burgess. (1925) *The City*. Chicago: University of Chicago Press.

Parker, R. N. (1989) "Poverty, Subculture of Violence, and Type of Homicide." *Social Forces 67:* 983-1007.

_____, and L. Rebhun. (1995) *Alcohol and Homicide: A Deadly Combination of Two American Traditions*. Albany: State University of New York Press.

Petee, Thomas A. (1999) "Situational Factors Related to Public Mass Murder Incidents: 1965-1998." In U.S. Department of Justice. *Proceedings of the Homicide Research Working Group Meetings, 1997 and 1998*. Washington: National Institute of Justice.

_____, K. G. Padgett, and T. S. York. (1997) "Debunking the Stereotype: An Examination of Mass Murder in Public Places." *Homicide Studies 1*, 4: 317-37.

Piers, Maria W. (1978) *Infanticide*. New York: W. W. Norton.

Pitt, Steven E., and Erin M. Bale. (1995) "Neonaticide, Infanticide, and Filicide: A Review of the Literature." *Bulletin of the American Academy of Psychiatry and Law 23:* 379.

Polk, Kenneth, and David Ransom. (1991) "The Role of Gender in Intimate Homicide." *Australian and New Zealand Journal of Criminology 24:* 20.

Pollock, Vicki, Sarnoff A. Mednick, and William F. Gabrielli, Jr. (1983) "Crime Causation: Biological Theories." In Sanford H. Kadish, ed. *Encyclopedia of Crime and Justice*, Vol. 1. New York: Free Press.

Prentky, R. A., A. W. Burgess, F. Rokous, A. Lee, C. Hartman, R. Ressler, and J. Douglas. (1989) "The Presumptive Role of Fantasy in Serial Sexual Homicide." *American Journal of Psychiatry 146:* 887-91.

President's Commission on Mental Health. (1978) *Report to the President,* Vol. 1. Washington: Government Printing Office.

Quay, Herbert C. (1983) "Crime Causation: Psychological Theories." In S. H. Kadish, ed. *Encyclopedia of Crime and Justice,* Vol. 1. New York: Free Press.

_____. (1987)"Patterns of Delinquent Behavior." In Herbert C. Quay, ed. *Handbook of Juvenile Delinquency.* New York: Wiley-Interscience.

Rappaport, R. G. (1988) "The Serial and Mass Murderer." *American Journal of Forensic Psychiatry 9,* 1: 39-48.

Rasche, Christine E. (1998) "Theorizing About Homicide: A Presentation on Theories Explaining Homicide and Other Crimes." In U.S. Department of Justice. *The Nature of Homicide: Trends and Changes - Proceedings of the 1996 Meeting of the Homicide Research Working Group.* Washington: National Institute of Justice.

Reckless, Walter C. (1973) *The Crime Problem,* 5th ed. Santa Monica: Goodyear.

_____, Simon Dinitz, and Ellen Murray. (1970) "Self-Concept as an Insulator Against Delinquency." In James E. Teele, ed. *Juvenile Delinquency: A Reader.* Itasca: Peacock.

Resnick, P. (1969) "Child Murder by Parents: A Psychiatric Review of Filicide." *American Journal of Psychiatry 126,* 3: 325-34.

Ressler, Robert K., Ann W. Burgess, and John E. Douglas. (1988) *Sexual Homicide: Patterns and Motives.* New York: Lexington Books.

_____, A. W. Burgess, C. R. Hartman, J. E. Douglas, and A. McCormack. (1986) "Murderers Who Rape and Mutilate." *Journal of Interpersonal Violence 1:* 273-87.

Robins, Lee N. (1966) *Deviant Children Grown Up.* Baltimore: Williams & Wilkins.

Rogers, C. (1993) "Gang-Related Homicides in Los Angeles County." *Journal of Forensic Sciences 38,* 4: 831-34.

Romero, Leo M., and Luis G. Stelzner. (1985) "Hispanics and the Criminal Justice System." In Pastora Cafferty and William C. McCready, eds. *Hispanics in the United States: A New Social Agenda.* New Brunswick: Transaction Books.

Rose, H. M., and P. D. McClain. (1990) *Race, Place, and Risk: Black Homicide in Urban America.* Albany: State University of New York Press.

Rosenbaum, Milton. (1990) "The Role of Depression in Couples Involved in Murder-Suicide and Homicide." *American Journal of Psychiatry 147,* 8: 1036-39.

Russell, Diana E. (1982) *Rape in Marriage.* New York: Macmillan.

_____. (1984) "A Study of Juvenile Murderers of Family Members." *International Journal of Offender Therapy and Comparative Criminology 28:* 177-92.

Saltzman, Linda, and James Mercy. (1993) "Assaults Between Intimates: The Range of Relationships Involved." In Anna Wilson, ed. *Homicide: The Victim/Offender Connection.* Cincinnati: Anderson.

Samenow, Stanton E. (1984) *Inside the Criminal Mind.* New York: Time Books.

Sargeant, D. (1971) "Children Who Kill–A Family Conspiracy?" In J. Howells, ed. *Theory and Practice of Family Psychiatry.* New York: Brunner-Mazel.

Schaefer, R. T. (1993) *Racial and Ethnic Groups.* 5th ed. New York: Harper Collins.

Schlesinger, L. B., and E. Revitch. (1983) "Sexual Dynamics in Homicide and Assault." In L. B. Schlesinger and E. Revitch, eds. *Sexual Dynamics of Anti-Social Behavior.* Springfield: Charles C Thomas.

Schloesser, Patricia, John Pierpont, and John Poertner. (1992) "Active Surveillance of Child Abuse Fatalities." *Child Abuse and Neglect 16:* 3-10.

Schulsinger, F. (1972) "Psychopathy: Heredity and Environment." *International Journal of Mental Health 1:* 190-206.

Schultz, L. (1968) "The Victim-Offender Relationship." *Crime and Delinquency 14,* 2: 135-41.

Sears, D. (1991) *To Kill Again.* Wilmington: Scholarly Resources.

Segrave, K. (1992) *Women Serial and Mass Murderers.* Jefferson: McFarland.

Sellin, Thorsten. (1938) *Culture Conflict and Crime.* New York: Social Science Research Council.

Shaefer, R. T. (1993) *Racial and Ethnic Groups.* 5th ed. New York: Harper Collins.

Shah, Saleem, and Loren Roth. (1974) "Biological and Psychological Factors in Criminality." In Daniel Glaser, ed. *Handbook of Criminology.* Chicago: Rand McNally.

Shaw, Clifford R., and Henry D. McKay. (1969) *Juvenile Delinquency and Urban Areas.* Chicago: University of Chicago Press.

Sheldon, William A. (1942) *Varieties of Temperament.* New York: Harper & Row.

Sheley, Joseph F. (1985) *America's "Crime Problem": An Introduction to Criminology.* Belmont: Wadsworth.

_____, and J. D. Wright. (1995) *In the Line of Fire: Youth, Guns, and Violence in America.* New York: Aldine de Gruyter, Inc.

Shin, Y., D. Jedlicka, and E. S. Lee. (1977) "Homicide Among Blacks." *Phylon 39:* 399-406.

Shireman, Charles H., and Frederic G. Reamer (1986) *Rehabilitating Juvenile Justice.* New York: Columbia University Press.

Short, James F., Jr. (1964) "Gang Delinquency and Anomie." In Marshall B. Clinard, ed. *Anomie and Deviant Behavior.* New York: Free Press.

_____, and F. L. Strodtbeck. (1965) *Group Process and Gang Delinquency.* Chicago: University of Chicago Press.

Smart, Carol. (1977) *Women, Crime and Criminology: A Feminist Critique.* Boston: Routledge and Kegan Paul.

Smith, M. D. (1996) "Sources of Firearm Acquisition Among a Sample of Inner city Youths: Research Results and Policy Implications." *Journal of Criminal Justice 24:* 361-67.

Solomon, Theo. (1973) "History and Demography of Child Abuse." *Pediatrics 51,* 4: 773-76.

Spergel, I. A. (1984) "Violent Gangs in Chicago: In Search of Social Policy." *Social Science Review 58:* 199-226.

_____. (1995) *The Youth Gang Problem: A Community Approach.* New York: Oxford.

Spunt, B., H. Brownstein, P. Goldstein, M. Fendrich, and H. J. Liberty. (1995) "Drug Use by Homicide Offenders." *Journal of Psychoactive Drugs 27:* 125-34.

Staats, Arthur. (1975) *Social Behaviorism.* Homewood: Dorsey Press.

Stack, Steven. (1997) "Homicide Followed by Suicide: An Analysis of Chicago Data." *Criminology 35,* 3: 435-53.

Stark, E., and A. Flitcraft. (1988) "Violence Among Intimates: An Epidemiological Review." In V. B. Van Hasselt, R. L. Morrison, A. S. Bellack, and M. Hersen, eds. *Handbook of Family Violence.* New York: Plenum.

Steinmetz, Suzanne K. (1978) "The Battered Husband Syndrome." *Victimology 2:* 507.

Straus, Murray A. (1976) "Domestic Violence and Homicide Antecedents." *Bulletin of the New York Academy of Medicine 62:* 446-65.

_____, Richard J. Gelles, and Suzanne K. Steinmetz. (1980) *Behind Closed Doors: Violence in the American Family.* Garden City: Doubleday/Anchor.

Sullivan, R. F. (1973) "The Economics of Crime: An Introduction to the Literature." *Crime and Delinquency 19,* 2: 138-49.

Sutherland, Edwin H. (1939) *Principles of Criminology.* Philadelphia: Lippincott.

_____, and Donald R. Cressey. (1974) *Criminology,* 9th ed. Philadelphia: Lippincott.

_____, and Donald R. Cressey. (1978) *Criminology,* 10th ed. Philadelphia: J. B. Lippincott.

Sykes, Gresham M. (1974) "The Rise and Fall of Critical Criminology." *Journal of Criminal Law and Criminology 65:* 206-13.

Tattersall, Clare. (1999) *Drugs, Runaways, and Teen Prostitution.* New York: Rosen.

Terrace, Temple. "A Gift Abandoned," *St. Petersburg Times* (April 14, 1991), p. 5.

Thomas, J. L. (1992) "Occupational Violent Crime: Research on an Emerging Issue." *Journal of Safety Research 23:* 55-62.

Thornberry, T. P. (1998) "Membership in Youth Gangs and Involvement in Serious and Violent Offending." In R. Loeber and D. P. Farrington, eds. *Serious and Violent Offenders: Risk Factors and Successful Interventions.* Thousand Oaks: Sage.

_____, and J. H. Birch. (1997) *Gang Members and Delinquent Behavior.* Washington: Office of Justice Programs.

Thrasher, Frederic M. (1927) *The Gang.* Chicago: University of Chicago Press.

Totman, J. (1978) *The Murderesses: A Psychosocial Study of Criminal Homicide.* San Francisco: R & E Associates.

Toufexis, Anastasia. "Why Mothers Kill Their Babies." *Time* (June 20, 1998), p. 81.

Tucker L. S., and T. P. Cornwall. (1977) "Mother-Son Folie a Duex: A Case of Attempted Parricide." *American Journal of Psychiatry 134,* 10: 1146-47.

Tulchin, S. H. (1972) *Intelligence and Crime.* Chicago: University of Chicago Press.

U.S. Department of Education and Justice. (2000) *Indicators of School Crime and Safety.* Washington: Offices of Educational Research and Imprisonment and Justice Programs.

U.S. Department of Health and Human Services. (1999) *Child Maltreatment 1997: Reports from the States to the National Child Abuse and Neglect Data System.* Washington: Government Printing Office.

U.S. Department of Justice. (1994) *Murder in Families.* Washington: Bureau of Justice Statistics.

_____. (1998) *Youth Gangs: An Overview.* Washington: Office of Juvenile Justice and Delinquency Prevention.

_____. (1999) *Juvenile Offenders and Victims: 1999 National Report.* Washington: Office of Juvenile Justice and Delinquency Prevention.

_____. (2001) *Youth Gang Homicides in the 1990s.* Washington: Office of Juvenile Justice and Delinquency Prevention.

_____. Bureau of Justice Statistics. (1991) *Female Victims of Violent Crime.* Washington: Office of Justice Programs.

_____. Bureau of Justice Statistics. (1992) *Drugs, Crime, and the Justice System.* Washington: Government Printing Office.

_____. Bureau of Justice Statistics. (1993) *Murder in Large Urban Counties, 1988.* Washington: Government Printing Office.

_____. Bureau of Justice Statistics. (1993) *Survey of State Prison Inmates, 1991.* Washington: Government Printing Office.

_____. Bureau of Justice Statistics. (1994) *Criminal Victimization in the United States 1992: A National Crime Victimization Survey Report.* Washington: Government Printing Office.

_____. Bureau of Justice Statistics. (1997) *Criminal Victimization in the United States 1994: A National Crime Victimization Survey.* Washington: Government Printing Office.

_____. Bureau of Justice Statistics. (1997) *Sex Offenses and Offenders: An Analysis of Data on Rape and Sexual Assault.* Washington: Government Printing Office.

_____. Bureau of Justice Statistics. (1999) *Prior Abuse Reported by Inmates and Probationers.* Washington: Office of Justice Programs.

_____. Bureau of Justice Statistics Bulletin. (2000) *Capital Punishment 1999.* Washington: Office of Justice Programs.

_____. Bureau of Justice Statistics. (2000) *Correctional Populations in the United States, 1997.* Washington: Department of Justice.

_____. Bureau of Justice Statistics Bulletin. (2000) *Prisoners in 1999.* Washington: Office of Justice Programs.

_____. Bureau of Justice Statistics Crime Data Brief. (2000) *Homicide Trends in the United States: 1998 Update.* Washington: Office of Justice Programs.

_____. Bureau of Justice Statistics Factbook. (1998) *Violence by Intimates: Analysis of Data of Crimes by Current or Former Spouses, Boyfriends, and Girlfriends.* Washington: Government Printing Office.

_____. Bureau of Justice Statistics Selected Findings. (2000) *Firearm Injury and Death From Crime, 1993-97.* Washington: Office of Justice Programs.

_____. Bureau of Justice Statistics Special Report. (1998) *Workplace Violence, 1992-96.* Washington: Office of Justice Programs.

_____. Bureau of Justice Statistics Special Report. (2000) *Effects of NIBRS on Crime Statistics.* Washington: Office of Justice Programs.

_____. Bureau of Justice Statistics Special Report. (2000) *Intimate Partner Violence.* Washington: Office of Justice Programs.

_____. Federal Bureau of Investigation. (1985) "The Men Who Murdered." *FBI Law Enforcement Bulletin 54,* 8: 2-6.

_____. Federal Bureau of Investigation. (2000) *Crime in the United States: Uniform Crime Reports 1999.* Washington: Government Printing Office.

Valdez, A. (1993) "Persistent Poverty, Crime, and Drugs: U.S.-Mexican Border Region." In J. Moore and R. Pinderhughes, eds. *In the Barrios: Latinos and the Underclass Debate.* New York: Russell Sage.

Vold, G., and T. Bernard. (1986) *Theoretical Criminology,* 3rd ed. Oxford: Oxford University Press.

Voss, Harwin L., and John R. Hepburn. (1968) "Patterns in Criminal Homicide in Chicago." *Journal of Criminal Law, Criminology, and Political Science 59:* 499-508.

Walker, Lenore E. (1984) *The Battered Woman Syndrome.* New York: Springer.

_____. (1989) *Sudden Fury.* New York: St. Martin's Press.

Websdale, Neil. (1999) *Understanding Domestic Homicide.* Boston: Northeastern University Press.

Weimann, Gabriel, and Conrad Winn. (1994) *The Theater of Terror: Mass Media and International Terrorists.* New York: Longman.

Weisman, Adam M., and Kanshal K. Skarma. (1997) "Parricide and Attempted Parricide." In U.S. Department of Justice. *The Nature of Homicide: Trends and Changes–Proceedings of the 1996 Meeting of the Homicide Research Working Group.* Washington: National Institute of Justice.

Welte, J. W., and E. L. Abel. (1989) "Homicide: Drinking by the Victim." *Journal of Studies on Alcohol 50:* 197-201.

Wertham, F. (1937) "The Catathymic Crisis." *Archives of Neurology and Psychiatry 37:* 974-78.

Wieczorek, W., J. Welte, and E. Abel. (1990) "Alcohol, Drugs, and Murder: A Study of Convicted Homicide Offenders." *Journal of Criminal Justice 18:* 217-27.

Wille, W. (1974) *Citizens Who Commit Murder.* St. Louis: Warren Greene.

Williams, Mark. (1997) *Cry of Pain: Understanding Suicide and Self-Harm.* New York: Penguin.

Wilson, Margo I., and Martin Daly. (1993) "Spousal Homicide Risk and Estrangement." *Violence and Victims 8,* 1: 3-16.

Wissow, Lawrence S. (1998) "Infanticide." *New England Journal of Medicine 339,* 17: 1239.

Wolfgang, Marvin E. (1958) "An Analysis of Homicide-Suicide." *Journal of Clinical and Experimental Psychopathology and Quarterly Review of Psychiatry and Neurology 19,* 3: 208-18.

_____. (1958) *Patterns in Criminal Homicide.* Philadelphia: University of Pennsylvania Press.

_____. (1969) "Who Kills Whom." *Psychology Today 3,* 5: 54-56.

_____, and Franco Ferracuti. (1967) *The Subculture of Violence: Toward an Integrated Theory in Criminology.* London: Tavistock.

_____, and R. B. Strohm. (1956) "The Relationship Between Alcohol and Criminal Homicide." *Quarterly Journal of Studies on Alcoholism 17:* 411-26.

Wolman, Benjamin B. (1999) *Antisocial Behavior: Personality Disorders From Hostility to Homicide.* Amherst: Prometheus Books.

Wright, J. D., J. F. Sheley, and M. D. Smith (1992) "Kids, Guns, and Killing Fields." *Society 30,* 1: 84-89.

Yablonsky, Lewis. (1962) *The Violent Gang.* Baltimore: Penguin.

Yen, Marianne. "High-Risk Mothers; Postpartum Depression, in Rare Cases, May Cause an Infant's Death." *Washington Post* (August 23, 1988), p. 18.

Yllo, Kersti, and Murray A. Straus. (1978) "Interpersonal Violence Among Married and Cohabitating Couples." Paper presented at the annual meeting of the National Council on Family Relationships. Philadelphia.

Yochelson, Samuel, and Stanton E. Samenow. (1976) *The Criminal Personality,* Vol. 1. New York: Jason Arsonson.

Young, T. J. (1993) "Parricide Rates and Criminal Street Violence in the United States: Is There a Correlation?" *Adolescence 28,* 109: 171-72.

Zahn, M. A. (1989) "Homicide in the Twentieth Century Trends, Types and Causes." In T. R. Gurr, ed. *Violence in America; Vol. 1. The History of Violence.* Thousand Oaks: Sage.

Zimring, F. E., and G. J. Hawkins. (1973) *Deterrence.* Chicago: University of Chicago Press.

_____, and G. Hawkins. (1997) *Crime is Not the Problem: Lethal Violence in America.* New York: Oxford University Press.

INDEX